W9-BUH-864

WITHDRAWN

Frontier House

SIMON SHAW

WITH LINDA PEAVY
& URSULA SMITH

PHOTOGRAPHY BY AUDREY HALL

ATRIA BOOKS
New York   London   Toronto   Sydney   Singapore

thirteen
WNET NEW YORK

wall to wall

ISBN: 0-7434-4270-9

First Atria Books hardcover printing May 2002

10 9 8 7 6 5 4 3 2 1

ATRIA BOOKS is a trademark of Simon & Schuster, Inc.

For information regarding special discounts for bulk purchases, please contact Simon & Schuster Special Sales at 1-800-456-6798 or business@simonandschuster.com

Book design by Lindgren/Fuller Design

Printed in the U. S. A.

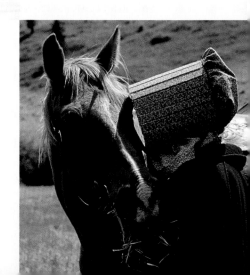

CONTENTS

Foreword • vi

1 The American Dream • 1

*A "Most Beneficent" Piece of Legislation—
The Homestead Act of 1862* • 4

*"There Is No Country Like…Crow Country"—
The Story of the Boulder Valley* • 9

2 Time Travelers • 15

*"We Will All Be Poor Here Together"—
Homesteader Dreams and Realities* • 17

3 Countdown • 29

*"To Start Anew in the Race of Life"—
Historical Parallels for the Families of* Frontier
House • 42

*"Buy Two of the Largest Trunks You Can Find"—
Preparations for the Journey West* • 49

4 The Promised Land • 53

*"This Is the Awfles Mess I Ever Was In"—
The Darker Side of Wagon Journeys West* • 62

*"This Was Not the West as I Had Dreamed
of It"—The Homesteader Faces Reality* • 68

5 Home Sweet Home • 71

*"Some Kind of Home of Our Own"—Big
Dreams and Humble Beginnings* • 76

6 Meltdown • 91

*"People Are Ill-Natured and Look Only to
Their Own Advantage"—Community Spirit Is
Tested on the Frontier* • 96

7 A Bride Comes West • 105

*"I Don't Know How She Did It but She Did"—
The Lives of Women on the Homestead* • 110

*"Absolutely Indescribable"—Weddings on the Far
Frontier* • 122

8 Do or Die • 129

*"The Big Outside World"—The General Store and
the U.S. Mail* • 133

*"The Man Became a Landowner, and…the
Landowner Became a Man"—Men's Work on the
Homestead* • 140

9 All Work and No Play • 153

*"Just Like…[a] Tumbleweed"—The Magical,
Tragical World of Childhood on the Frontier* • 158

*"A Teacher Must Expect Hardship"—Winifred
Shipman and Her Chicken-House School* • 167

10 Downhill to Winter • 177

"A Helluva Big Gamble"—Montana Moonshine • 180

*"Just What Is Needed in This Country"—The
Completion of the Northern Pacific Rail Route* • 189

11 The Final Reckoning • 193

*"Step Right Up, Folks!"—Frontier Fairs and
Festivals* • 200

*"Regardless of What I Did the Cold Crept In"—
Life in the Crucible of Winter* • 204

12 New Frontiers • 215

Producers' Acknowledgments 226 • *Resource List* 227 • *Photography Credits* 227
Source Notes 228 • *Bibliography* 230

FOREWORD

Let's start with a confession. Ever since I can remember, I have suffered from a serious addiction to the "Wild West." Beyond childhood romps playing cowboys and Indians I was spellbound by the lure of a life where men and women pitched themselves against a world full of rugged challenges. For years, every movie, television show, comic, and book detailing heroic endeavors in cow towns and across prairies was a favorite escape from my real life, growing up in a small village in the middle of England. Even today I harbor a collection of Western ephemera, my "cowboy corner" of treasured kitsch. Imagine then how I felt when I first heard of the idea to re-create 1880s Western living. My dream was about to become reality.

Confession number two. I was wrong. Call me plain naive, but the encounter bore little relation to the fantasy. Maybe I should have seen this coming, but when your historian on all matters Western is John Wayne, you are indeed in for a rude shock. I wasn't alone. Sharing this experience were advocates of other Hollywood depictions of American history, fans of shows like *Little House on the Prairie.* There mom, dad, and the kids live poor but happy amidst glades of ripening corn. How's that saying go? "The past is another country." This was indeed a journey to an alien land.

My first recognition of this happened appropriately out in the West, on my first visit to Montana. Growing up around gentle valleys and on city streets doesn't prepare you for such country. Once the newness of magnificent, seemingly endless vistas had worn off, my next feeling was one of extreme humbling. As a speck in a vast ocean of land and sky you experience a new and frighteningly real sense of vulnerability in such country. Even though you view it from an air-conditioned vehicle, you understand how at risk such places make you to a change in the weather or running short on fuel. (During that first visit we witnessed a June day when the temperature dropped by fifty degrees in a few hours.) It wasn't as though my books and movies hadn't told me this, but until I put my foot on the land, I never really understood the jeopardy and awe such territory commands. What I should have recognized at that moment was this was the first piece in a giant jigsaw of rude realities that make up the real "Wild West."

As I write this, I wonder what those original pioneers of the American West would have made of our experiment in attempting to re-create their lives. I suspect if they could take a glimpse at the world we inhabit, they would be mystified at our purpose. Why would we, having come so far, even wish to spend a day in their shoes? For me at least this has been a sobering experience. Gone is the romance those movies and television shows once promised. Instead I see a world of daily challenge, danger, and near impossible odds. The facts speak for themselves: barely 40 percent of homesteaders ever succeeded on their homestead in the West. For the remainder, the encounter was simply too harsh. Mother Nature, sickness, hunger, and poverty so often won the day. Evidence of their frustrations still dot the landscape: ruined shacks stand testament to their endeavors. In some, ragged curtains still flap in the wind, small evidence of men's and women's hopes to civilize wilderness. A rusting plow often accompanies the scene, perhaps the final purchase that brought a family to bankruptcy.

By witnessing firsthand just how hard those struggles were, one cannot fail to recognize the formidable spirit that built America. For me it's proved a graphic way to understand better what it is that really unites such a vast country. Bonding every nation is its people, and what I now see is a heritage of Americans who took huge risks to make new beginnings. If our venture has proved anything, it's that every one of those pioneers deserves our admiration for daring to dream of a better life.

Simon Shaw
Series Producer, *Frontier House*

1

The American Dream

If you were told that an artist had devised this place, you'd believe it. Tucked in a perfect valley that nestles at the feet of a mesmerizing mountain range lies the place we call Frontier Valley. Even Montanans, who've grown accustomed to living among majestic settings, pause to take in its beauty. Sit quietly here and nature will come to you. Deer and elk graze nearby, eagles will watch you from on high. Time your visit right and hundreds of species of wildflowers and butterflies will accompany you. Last spring we brought a dozen strangers here. Men, women, and children from across America who imagined we had delivered them to a heaven on earth. But beauty and serenity comes with a price. This valley, a lush carpet of green for much of the year, can be deep in snow for up to six months. (Minus forty degrees isn't uncommon where the plains meet the mountains.) The real residents here are hungry predators such as coyotes, bears, and mountain lions. In high summer the sun chars every blade of grass to a crisp brown. Raging forest fires are an annual hazard. In truth, you and I probably wouldn't find it such an enticing place once Mother Nature had shown us the full picture of life here. But this place really was home for a small community who volunteered to take part in a unique experiment. For six months they put their real lives on hold to forsake the modern world and stepped into the shoes of their ancestors to taste life when being on the frontier promised no safety nets. Isolation, danger, unpredictable weather, and punishing workloads became their everyday expectations. Their experience affected them in ways no one expected. From the youngest (nine years old) through to the most senior member of the community (sixty-eight), this was a life-changing encounter.

It all began at 9 A.M. on Tuesday, November 21, 2000, when PBS television affiliate KPTS broadcast an appeal to its Kansas audience: "It's time to make American history.... Could you live as a pioneer out in the American West? ... We're looking for volunteers." In making the twenty-second broadcast the station was, unknowingly, starting the first current in a wave that was about to envelop the nation. Seventeen minutes later the first response landed via e-mail at frontier@pbs.org. By the end of that day thirty-eight other applications had arrived. By the end of the month upward of one hundred and fifty responses were received daily as the message flashed from Hawaii to New York City. Christmas saw over two thousand hopeful families join the rush. By our deadline of January 15, 2001, more than fifty-five hundred applications had been received. As we started to wade through the piles of eager entrants it became clear that the dream of carving a new life out in the untamed land of the West was still a potent force in modern America.

Life in this day and age is way too fast. I just want the opportunity to slow down and take advantage of the more important things like the smell of pure,

Frontier Valley.

clean air and to know that I have a part in giving something to my children that was not bought or ordered.—Family, Florida

The Promised Land.

My son is a dotcomer and making lots of money at twenty-three but has decided that wealth isn't everything.—Mom, New York

I always feel that we are spoiled by our technological developments and want to develop a proper amount of respect for those who gave their lives so that future generations could live on.—Father, San Francisco

Like most girls growing up in the 1970s I was addicted to Little House on the Prairie *and often wondered what it was really like to live during such exciting, yet uncertain times. I realize that life in the* Frontier House *would hardly be* Little House *but I'm certain it would be a fantastic bit of hard yet inspiring reality.*—Family, Washington, D.C.

We offered no prizes. No big money rewards. And the experience promised the very opposite of glamour. Yet that first response spoke for many: "Can it be that we are alone in seeking a better life by wanting to downscale and decelerate from our frenzied daily pattern?" The Wyness family anticipated a groundswell of opinion in their swiftly dispatched submission. Soon National Public Radio was fanning the flames with a broadcast feature asking, "What can we learn from living in the past?" Newspaper columnists took the baton forward, from the *New York Times* to the *San Francisco Chronicle.* It seems our offer, setting up a homestead on 160 acres of land with only 1880s know-how, food, and equipment, was an unmissable opportunity to a hard core of people in the world's most technologically advanced nation.

Shortly after launching our quest to find modern families for the encounter, a package arrived from the Montana Historical Society. Along with scores of other authorities on the era, they were helping us put together a picture of the lifestyle we aimed to re-create. Among the contents was a postcard of a railroad poster that powerfully illustrates why frontier fever infected the minds of so many. Its symbolism captures the promise by which many thousands of families were lured out West in the nineteenth and early twentieth centuries. Gold coins spill from the plow as it cuts a swath through Montana. Little did those seduced by its declaration of an affluent future know that much of the territory the railroad promoted in its poster was "badlands," often unworkable acres that would eventually prove the ruin of many. Many of those excited by the apparent offer of a place in the New World came with little knowledge of working land in such a harsh environment; clearly they were unsuited in every way for the encounter. Looking at the growing numbers of twenty-first-century applicants prompted the question: Were any of these better prepared?

A "Most Beneficent" Piece of Legislation
The Homestead Act of 1862

The concept of homesteading had been at the heart of public debate for decades before that morning in late May of 1862 when Abraham Lincoln signed the bill that made the Homestead Act the law of the land. The legislation was based on the populist ideal that the public lands of the United States belong to the people, are to be "held in sacred trust for the benefit of the people, and should be granted in limited quantities, free of cost, to landless settlers."

Though the original act was amended several times over the next two decades, by the early 1880s, the period of particular interest to *Frontier House* families, it still contained all the essential elements: "[A]ny person who is the head of a family, or who has arrived at the age of twenty-one years, and is a citizen of the United States, or who shall have filed his declaration of intention to become such" could claim up to 160 acres—that is, one-quarter of a one-mile-square section of land—by filing a claim with the local land office, living on that quarter section for at least six months each year over the next five years, and making improvements on the land. A small filing fee, usually between $10 and $20, was required. At the end of five years, if the basic requirements had been met, the homesteader received a patent, a deed free and clear, to the land. Under hardship conditions, a homesteader who needed more time to "prove up" could request—and was often granted—an extension of time in which to do so. Conversely, a homesteader who did not wish to wait the full five years—and who had the cash in hand—could obtain early title through "preemption," buying the 160 acres for $1.25 an acre.

The wording of the original Homestead Act was, at best, vague as to the nature and extent of the "improvements" that had to be made before a homesteader was granted title to the land. Indeed, the law set forth no specifics as to the size or type of building that had to be built or the amount of land that had to be cultivated. Over time, however, prevailing wisdom said that the house had to have at least one door and one window and that a minimum of ten acres had to be put into production. The standards varied, however, when it came time for the land agent to determine the eligibility of the homesteader to be given title.

Available under the Homestead Act were millions of unappropriated public acres, most of them lying west of the Mississippi River. In general, the climate of the times in the post–Civil War years was favorable for a mass migration. The West was portrayed as an exciting place with a bright future. The railroads, eager to increase business along newly constructed routes, published a variety of ads and pamphlets designed to entice prospective homesteaders to settle in this region or that. "You will only have to tickle [the land] with a plow," one such ad proclaimed, "and it will laugh a harvest that will gladden your hearts." The railroads were not alone in using the lure of free land as part of a carefully orchestrated redistribution of the country's growing population. During the years that followed the panic of 1873, Eastern industrialists saw in the act an opportunity to entice the unemployed and indigent away from the populous centers of the East Coast. Horace Greeley, editor of the *New York Tribune,* described the Homestead Act as a "most beneficent" piece of legislation, one intended "to diminish...the number of paupers and idlers and increase the proportion of working, independent, self-subsisting farmers."

But city folks weren't farmers, and even those who might have wanted to take part in this noble agricultural experiment could hardly have afforded to do so. The thought of free land was enticing enough, but financing the move across the country, getting started, and surviving for those first five years cost money the urban poor did not have. Thus the vast majority of the homesteaders came not from the crowded population centers in the Northeast but from rural areas in the Midwest. And the distance traveled in miles mattered less than the difference free land could make in the lives of homesteading families. For example, one of the first to file a claim under the new legislation was Daniel Freeman, a Union scout from Iowa, who transported his wife, Agnes, and their children to the tall-grass country of southeastern Nebraska, a move that assured their prosperity on land that is, today, the site of the Homestead National Monument.

The Freemans came early, but in their wake came a wave of homesteaders pouring out of the Ohio and Mississippi river valleys in search of homesteads on the fertile plains of Kansas and Nebraska. That first wave soon gave way to an influx of immigrants from Scandinavia, Germany, and the British Isles, most of whom brought with them to the Western frontier not only their dreams of free land but also their farming experience.

As this promotional brochure indicates, railroads had a vested interest in luring homesteaders to settle near their lines and ship their grain and other products via rail. The idea that wealth followed the plow was little different from—and no more valid than—the adage that rain followed the plow.

For this proud homesteader, proving up and receiving her deed warranted a visit from the itinerant photographer.

Those who were destined to succeed also generally brought a modicum of material resources, for the costs of proving up could be considerable. In addition to putting up a house of some kind and a few outbuildings, the homesteader had to invest in work animals, a milk cow and chickens, a wagon, a plow, fencing, and a well or some other source of drinking water. It was estimated that breaking the first 40 acres of a 160-acre homestead and putting it into production could cost up to $1,000.

Of course, not every homesteader started out with that kind of capital. When 22-year-old Howard Ruede decided to leave his Pennsylvania home in 1877 to look for a homestead in Kansas, he withdrew his savings—$75—from the bank, bought a train ticket for $23.05, and set out. Though high hopes rode on short capital, Ruede counted on his determination and his strength to carve out his dream.

For Ruede the dream came true. For others, the dream proved more elusive, especially as the prime agricultural lands of Kansas and Nebraska filled up. By 1883, the year in which the would-be pioneers of *Frontier House* were ostensibly living out their own version of the homestead dream, families were being drawn farther and farther west to the more arid lands of the Great Plains and the Interior Basin—to the Dakotas, Colorado, Wyoming, and Montana. They were drawn by local promoters like Matt Alderson, who published a widely circulated pamphlet touting the attractions of Montana Territory, particularly of the Yellowstone Valley. Montana, Alderson boasted, was entering "upon a growth that will be as much greater than her sister Territories as her resources are superior." Here, he said, was where "immigrants [should]...go to farming."

And indeed they did. Ultimately, Montana was far in the vanguard of the homestead states. Between 1868 and 1961, 32 million of the 270 million acres claimed under the law were claimed in Montana. The state that held second place—Nebraska—trailed with only some 22 million acres claimed. It should be noted, however, that the vast majority of those Montana homesteaders staked their claims in the early years of the twentieth century, after the areas more naturally endowed for farming had been claimed.

By the third decade of the twentieth century, the homestead phenomenon had largely played itself out, though the venerable act upon which the movement was based was not repealed until 1976. And even then, in recognition of the spirit that had for more than a century moved Americans to look to the frontier for free land and a new life, Congress extended the law for another ten years in Alaska.

It is all history now. But it was a formative part of our history. The Homestead Act of 1862 opened the American West to settlement, thereby fostering that most American of traits—the spirit of independence.

Everyone was after good land. Even though it came free, "proving" your section took more than inexhaustible reserves of energy and a little know-how. Diaries from those on overland trails record similar ambitions—to find a pocket of fertile land, with nearby good water and timber to furnish shelter. Not surprisingly, at the end of many journeys travelers often found the best land had already been snapped up. Neat houses straddled the creekside, fields were already plowed, wells dug. Newcomers would require diligence and not a little good fortune in finding the next best plot. By the 1880s, even out in remote corners of the West, this was often the first discovery at the end of a difficult trek.

Finding the land where we would film our endeavor brought us face-to-face with this reality. To give our participants a real sense of "the frontier" we had unique requirements. Settling on Montana wasn't the hard part—it offered remoteness, beauty, and historical precedent as the state where the most homestead claims were filed. Even today its very name conjures up distant dreams in the minds of many urban Americans. Our research led us to districts rich in homesteading history, places like the Gallatin Valley, a fertile swath that's wrapped around Bozeman. There, and in many other locations diligently scouted, we discovered that these areas of productive soils still promised potential abundance to farmers today. Perhaps not surprisingly though, the only patches we found that remained undeveloped in such heavily farmed regions were lying fallow for good reason. A promising meadow soon revealed its true nature as walking boots sank into a deep mush of bog land. Another site that boded well was struck off the list when taking a spade to the ground hit bedrock just inches from the surface. A concrete lookout, complete with what appeared to be gun turrets, belonging to a nervous religious organization that overlooked another encouraging site had us hastening on. Our search found us having to look more and more remotely. In July of 2000 we made our first foray into the unknown, a journey that took us off the beaten track, where we found ourselves clinging to precipices in our 4x4s and examining the bleakest lands, occupied only by grizzlies and lonely coyotes. On occasion we found what, at first glance, offered good opportunities, but so very often, modern houses on neighboring land, power cables, or the roar of a passing jet engine would sober our enthusiasm.

Some weeks into the search we got lucky. North of Missoula we found an ideal opportunity. Up in the Nine-Mile region, an area of great beauty, we found a forested area set way back on the edge of a cinematically perfect mountain. It was a homesteader's dream with three enticing meadows offering both water and timber aplenty. An existing cabin deep in the woods beguilingly showed firsthand evidence of just what sort of life had been played out here. Written in pencil on the door was the still discernible boast: "Caught My First Bear. October 1889." Local landowners looked set to welcome the project, and for a brief moment we began making plans for how we might reutilize existing structures. A local diviner was ready to dowse for wells. Our construction expert staked the site. Then nature intervened. Fierce fires took hold as another devastating drought year hit Montana. Daily we called landowners Betty and Ralph each time a ring of flames moved closer. In late August 2000 the location was completely consumed by fire, yet another victim of one of the driest summers on record. We were back to the drawing board.

You don't have to look far in Montana to find homesteading history. Many of its residents are of pioneer stock, their names revealing family roots. Gary Wunderwald, one of the state's many German descendants, came to our rescue. As former director of the Montana Film Commission he knows the state better than most, having staked out locations for many of the movies and commercials shot there. After a careful trawl of his files he unearthed a new site. This time we turned our backs on western Montana and headed south to an area rich in pioneer history. Passing the Crazy Mountains (legend has it named after a desperate settler who had been separated from her children), we entered Sweet Grass County. Lush pastures edge the mountains in a district renowned for its fine ranches. This is now cattle country but once saw one of the biggest concentrations of sheep farming in all of America. Road names passed en route such as Froze to Death Creek give clues to its difficult terrain. We knew it was remote as we completed the journey. Twenty-five miles out of the small community of Big Timber, the radio fell silent. Not a station on the dial. Occasional ranches dotted the road; otherwise we were in pristine land. Chasing the Boulder River, we drove past fields deep in hay toward the mountains that ring the magnificent Gallatin National Forest. A look at the map confirmed we were in the right territory, as dozens of abandoned homesteads dotted the page.

With our deadline tightening it would have been easy to accept a location that made a good second best. But here we lucked out. Not only a filmmaker's dream (both *The Horse Whisperer* and *A River Runs Through It* were shot here), this territory also provided the perfect history. Ceded by the Crow Indians in 1882, the area was then opened to white settlers and promoted as a "homeseeker's paradise." Ranch owner Ken and his partner, Connie, guided us to a near secret valley at the end of a rough drive over five miles of dirt road. Here a generously flowing creek fed twelve hundred acres of rich pastures and deep forest. "Everything a homesteader dreamed of," said Ken, himself of pioneer stock. "Ten families tried it here...like so many, few of them made it." As we gazed out over the land that day, it appeared to hold only great promise and supreme beauty; in short, a wonderful place to live. Meadows deep in grass, berry bushes heavy with blossom, even in late summer the creek was flowing well...yes, we'd found homeseeker's paradise.

"There Is No Country Like…Crow Country"
The Story of the Boulder Valley

When William Clark and the members of the Corps of Discovery passed through the Yellowstone Valley on their return trek from the Pacific Coast in the summer of 1806, that broad expanse of lush grasses, sparkling waters, and abundant game was the home and primary hunting grounds of the Apsaalooke, or the Crow, Indians. Before the century was out, however, much of that scenic and productive landscape had been claimed by white settlers.

In actuality, for centuries before the Crow became the area's dominant settlers, the land had been home to the Sheepeater Indians, a branch of the Shoshone. Over time the Blackfeet, Gros Ventre, Cheyenne, Assiniboin, Flathead, Nez Percé, Bannock, Mandan, and Sioux—as well as the Crow—all occupied the region, at times coexisting on the plains and in the foothills and at times viciously contesting territorial rights.

By the mid-nineteenth century, with westward migration rapidly increasing, the U.S. government moved to bring peace among the warring tribes and to secure safe passage across Indian lands for miners bound for California and settlers bound for Oregon. In September of 1851 at Fort Laramie, the government convened a gathering of some ten thousand Indians, representing all of the Western tribes, and there negotiated a treaty that assigned specific boundaries to the territory held by each tribe. Using a crude map sketched by Jim Bridger, the famed mountain man and guide, the chief negotiator for the United States pointed in turn to each of the "reserves" assigned to the respective tribes. In return for their pledge to stay within their own territories, the tribes were to receive annuities from the federal government to compensate for the loss of game and other damages that resulted from white settlement.

The land reserved to the Crow included some 38 million acres that lay south and east of the Yellowstone River. It was land they had already come to dominate through an informal alliance with the whites forged many years earlier, land that had become sacred to the tribe. "Crow country is a good country," one of their chiefs, Arrapoosh, had said. "The Great Spirit has put it exactly in the right place…. It has snowy mountains and sunny plains, all kinds of climates and good things for every season…. Everything good is to be found there. There is no country like…Crow country."

But that "good country" was about to be wrested from the Crow. The discovery of gold and other minerals in what was now Montana Territory brought a rapid increase in migration and settlement—and resulted in a new treaty in 1868, one that reduced the Crow lands to a mere fraction

Crow warriors, 1890. Prime hunting grounds for many tribes over the centuries, the Boulder Valley was increasingly dominated by the Crow.

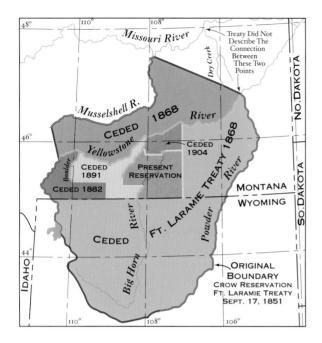

Originally granted reservation lands amounting to some 38 million acres, the Crow Indians were persuaded to cede some two-thirds of those acres to the federal government in 1868. Still more acres were given up in 1882, 1891, and 1904, reducing the Crow reservation to a mere faction of its original size.

of their original "reserve" and marked the beginning of the end of the Crow presence in the Boulder Valley. Then, in 1882, another treaty opened up even more land in the valley to white settlement, land already being squatted on by miners drawn there by deposits of gold and other minerals in the upper Boulder River.

Frustrated by the relative lack of gold in the streams that drained the valley, most of the prospectors moved on to new discoveries at Maiden and Gilt Edge to the north. Others, tired of mining and not willing to rush to one more gold strike, took up homestead claims in the Boulder Valley in hopes of providing meat and produce to nearby mining camps such as Independence and to newly established settlements such as Melville and Dornix, which were giddy with anticipation over the coming of the railroad. In fact, the entire Yellowstone Valley was about to experience an explosion in town building and homesteading as the Northern Pacific Railroad edged westward from Billings. In advance of the track layers came the publicists. Posters and newspapers proclaimed the Boulder Valley a "homeseeker's paradise." Land-hungry claimants were lured by such propaganda—and by the beauty and richness of the country. The valley was ringed by the Crazy Mountains to the north, the Absarokas to the west. Game and wildlife roamed the foothills and the lush meadows. The Boulder and its many tributaries offered a plentiful supply of water. The very qualities that had made the valley a sacred place to the Crow were the qualities that drew the homesteader.

The settlers who came to the Boulder Valley were primarily American-born, and they came, by and large, from rural roots. Most of them (47 percent) came from the Midwest, with fewer numbers from the East (16 percent), the West (7 percent), and the South (4 percent). Among the earliest of the valley's pioneers was one William McLeod, whose life story mirrors much of the "hopscotch" history of the American frontier. Born in 1833 in Palmyra, Missouri, to parents who were natives of the Carolinas, McLeod was barely twenty years old when he followed in the wake of the forty-niners, crossing the plains to California. However, the young man finally dedicated himself not to prospecting, but to stock raising. A dozen years after his arrival, he married Martha Sowell, a fellow Californian, and the couple had two children. In 1873, when wanderlust again overcame him, William moved his family north to Burns, Oregon, trailing a herd of cattle.

Eight years later, McLeod made one final move. Now in his late forties, he brought his wife and his daughters—along with 200 horses and 125 cattle—to the Boulder Valley of Montana Territory, selecting a homestead on the upper Boulder River. Because the land he chose that summer of 1881 had not yet been ceded to the government by the Crow, he sought permission from the Indian agent to take his livestock onto the acreage—in effect, to "squat"—in anticipation of what everyone knew was the inevitable, the tribe's final relinquishment of the rich Boulder Valley. A year later, in 1882, with the Indians' cession of all their land west of the East Boulder River, McLeod filed his claim. Having finally satisfied his wanderlust, he remained on that homestead until his death in 1914. By that time, this homesteader had placed his mark so firmly on the valley that the small settlement that sprang up at its heart still bears his name.

In 1883, two years after McLeod's arrival in the Boulder Valley, the tracks of the Northern Pacific reached Big Timber, the hub of the valley's commerce. That long-anticipated event—plus the removal of the Crow to lands farther east—brought new growth to the Boulder Valley. By the fall of 1884, some nine other homesteaders had filed claims on land near the main Boulder River or on one of its tributaries. But despite its natural beauties and resources, the Boulder Valley was not kind to the homesteader. Its mountainous elevation meant short growing seasons that made it especially ill-suited to small-scale farming, which became increasingly clear to settlers.

So the homesteaders who succeeded in the valley did so by following the example of William McLeod—turning to ranching and consolidating their 160 acres into larger holdings through preemption and purchase of nearby holdings. They built their herds as they built their land base, and by the turn of the twentieth century, the Boulder Valley was home to some eighteen thousand head of cattle, an equal number of sheep, and two thousand head of horses. The hunting ground of the Crow, the supposed "homeseeker's paradise" had become the rancher's bonanza.

From the comfort of the twenty-first century it's easy to ask why so many staked their family's lives on such a perilous venture as homesteading, especially as many had little knowledge of the life they were about to encounter. Add to that the perils faced en route, and the daring spirit is to be more greatly admired. Imagine yourself, however, as a penniless emigrant, newly arrived in a land full of promise. Or as a veteran emerging from the turmoil of the Civil War looking for a new start for your family. Imagine further the prospect of "free land," yours for the asking.

"Climb to the top of any of the surrounding mountains and view the landscape o'er. You will see tracts of land in many places seemingly almost level and not a stick of fencing thereon, not a furrow turned. No one can gaze upon the scene without being struck with the fact that the valley has not yet been called upon to contribute even a tithe of its resources. With an ambition and determination to work, but little capital is needed to give a man a good home and a valuable farm."

With such claims, small wonder that frontier fever took hold. Another twenty pages of bold promises accompany these in a booklet published by Montana booster Matt Alderson in the early 1880s. Send twenty-five cents and it would be mailed to any of your friends as an incentive to join the rush. Even today, reading such tantalizing invitations, you can almost sense the flurry of excitement settlers must have felt in their anticipation of a better life. With railroad companies laying tracks ever deeper into the West, the campaign to woo newcomers was fought with vigor, and many "homeseeker's paradises" were promised in this promotion. With such palpable expectation in the air, the arrival of the iron road seemed the ideal period in which to freeze the clock and set our time-travel experiment. Having fixed on our location, we fixed our date when iron rails finally marched through the land bringing floods of eager newcomers: 1883.

The frenzy of e-mail applications from would-be modern pioneers was just the beginning. Back in our New York office, sacks of mail continued to arrive even weeks after the application deadline. We finally shut the door on applicants in late January 2001, prompting protests from those left behind. Inducements followed, in the form of promises of financial donations to PBS, candy bars, candid photos, homemade corsetry—even a gory video from a Dakota farmer showing his seven-year-old son and nine-year-old daughter expertly butchering a pig. Everyone, it seemed, wanted to ensure his or her application really caught our eye. From the final total of fifty-eight hundred, we now needed to find just three families and had only three months to make all the arrangements.

Paring down the thousands of *Frontier House* applications was a thorny process. Not only did we have to meet the needs of the television audience by finding articulate and interesting individuals, they would also need to be able to endure what would at times doubtless be a harsh encounter. It would have been easy to choose people who brought survival skills or those who were already adept at working land in testing conditions. Instead we wanted to find people who typified life in modern America. So out went the forest rangers from Colorado, a family who ranched at high elevation in New Mexico, the professional hunter from Maine along with his frightening arsenal of black-powder firearms, and reluctantly, the brave couple from Maryland who were keen to experience childbirth on the frontier.

Having narrowed the field, we called in an expert to advise on family dynamics under pressure. Undoubtedly the experience would prove punishing physically, but the mental pressures could be equally intense, especially when mom and dad were volunteering their children. Laurie Kaplan of the Ackerman Institute in New York is a great listener. As a family therapist, she has acted as a go-between in hundreds of cases of family breakdown. After she briefed the selection team on where she felt the pressure points would occur, the search proper began. Our "short list" had over five hundred possible families. Each had to be interviewed, first by phone; those who made it to the next level were visited. In four months, our quest to find just three families took us to twenty states and forty-two families in over a quarter of a million miles in air travel. As everyone else stopped to enjoy Christmas, the selection team mined Web applications and hit the phones. While New Year's rolled by, another interview was taking place. Having stared fixedly at computer screens and been umbilically attached to their phones for close to three months, in the early weeks of 2001 associate producer Mark Saben and researcher Emily Ann were set loose to find our ideal participants. They had just six weeks to deliver the ideal lineup.

For three of those families, those initial calls would be the first step toward a life-altering experience. "Oh, my God. I didn't expect you to call. Are you sure you mean us?" asked Karen Glenn of Pleasant View, Tennessee. "My mom and dad think this is a great idea…hang on, I'll put you on with them," said fourteen-year-old Aíne Clune from their home just outside Los Angeles. Nate Brooks of Boston responded with one word: "Wow." At that point, everyone on our then long short list was asked to send a home video of themselves or to keep a written diary of their thoughts about the potential project.

So why do I want to go to the frontier? There are many reasons why I really want to do this. From the moment I first learned of the project I knew in my heart that I truly wanted to do this. I want to do this with a passion that is almost inexplicable. Only once before in my life have I felt the same about an adventure. That was twenty-one years ago when I met my husband Gordon and I knew, in an instant, that I wanted to marry him and was prepared to follow him halfway across the world.… I think I can endure a lot. I've camped in snow and ice, twenty degrees below and stuck it out. I worked very hard as a child growing up on a farm. It will be interesting to see if I have the mettle to survive on the frontier.—Adrienne Clune

Guess what?! My mom [Karen Glenn] entered us in this thing where if you get chosen you go to Montana…not for six days but for six months! *We get to live like they did in the 1880s and we get to ride horses and own a farm.… I can't wait to ride horses wherever I go and go to the bathroom in an outhouse!…I can't believe we will get to go. We are just a regular old family. I will need to learn to milk a cow. My nana has showed me how to skim butter because when she was young she used to use a churn.*—Erinn Patton

Some point on December third, Nate wanted to show me something on the Internet, the Frontier House *Web site, and asked me what I thought. I knew immediately that this was good and that both of us really wanted to do it.…Wednesday night and I was cooking. I was thinking about potatoes for some reason and how something like preparing to make a potato dish on the frontier when you are really hungry and then finding a rotten potato— something like that could wreck your whole day. Then the phone rang and Nate got it. (Thank God, I would have freaked out.) Nate went into capable, deep-thinking mode. I could tell by the way he was talking it was* Frontier House, *but I still gave him that "Are you serious? It's them?" face. He nodded in astonishment—it was very cool.*—Kristen McLeod

2

Time Travelers

In *Time and Again,* Jack Finney's classic novel, young illustrator Si Morley is enticed into taking a journey as part of a U.S. government experiment in time travel. On the brink of acceptance Morley is asked by one of the scientists in charge, "Has it occurred to you that we may all be nuts?"

"That's why I joined up," replies Morley.

"Good; obviously you're the type we need."

As we began making journeys to visit our short-listed families, we couldn't help wondering, "Do they think we are mad?"

So how would you manage without toilet paper? Are you happy about sleeping within a few inches of your dad? Have you a problem with smelling? Lice? Nits? Would lack of contraception be an issue? What would you do if a bear tried to get into your cabin? How long have you gone without makeup…television… the phone? What's the most difficult thing your family has had to face? These and dozens more questions were on the agenda in our grilling of potential participants. For some, the barrage came as a shock. The probing was simply too personal, or too difficult to contemplate. The people from the television show who had been so polite on the phone were in their homes and asking very private questions. If they couldn't deal with the ordeal in the comfort of their own home though, what chance would they have of conveying their experience while facing an unforgiving television camera on the frontier?

Our criteria in making the selections were fairly straightforward. Do these people want to do this just to be on television? Are they as excited about making this journey as we are? Do they feel like it will be a long summer camp? Can they convey their feelings in a vivid way? Are they quitters? For those who survived elimination, one question remained: Do you know what you are getting into? Reading diaries of the era, listening to the consultants who were helping us surmount the complex challenges of re-creating the era, revisiting the land and talking to Montanans about what we proposed, always prompted that difficult question...indeed, did *we* know what we were getting into?

Taking on this experience demanded a lot. Not only were we asking for lives to be put on hold for six months. This would involve hardship, stamina, and virtual isolation from all but your immediate family. It required a special relationship between all participants and with the core of the production crew with whom irregular contact would be maintained. It would above all undoubtedly find people exposed to testing conditions under the scrutiny of a camera crew. This was going to be a collaboration with people who were going to become a surrogate family. To know whether that bond could be made required time to get to know one another, so our favored half dozen remaining families began spending time with members of the production team. We needed to know what made these people tick. What did they like to do while relaxing? What did they eat? Do they spend much time together? If so, doing what? How did everyone in the family really feel about this mad idea? It was during these off-camera moments that the most telling conversations would be had. One question was most revealing in pointing the way to our final selection: "Just how hard should we make this experience?" The query opened a door to make the participants conjure their own fate. Should we go hungry? Cold? Could I cope if my children became depressed by the experience? What would I do if my wife wanted to go home?

Those eventually selected would have to agree to live by a set of rules to ensure that everyone would share goals and understand the boundaries of the experiment. These were our expectations:

THE RULES

All participants agree to live as closely to the pioneer lifestyle of the 1880s as possible. This includes the wearing of clothing and the preparation and consumption of foods typical of the era, use of period equipment and work routines. Wherever possible this lifestyle will be directed by the participants themselves. If persistent difficulties occur, participants may seek advice from *Frontier House* consultants, normally via the postal service or, in urgent cases, via telegraph.

Communications with the outside world. To maintain authenticity we will make outside communications consistent with life on a remote homestead in the 1880s. This means use of the postal service, which will operate from a remote store. Any modern communication devices, such as mobile phones, must be surrendered at the exchange of clothing. Mail arriving for participants will be held at the store until a participant makes collection. Incoming packages may be opened to ensure the contents are consistent with the period.

Visitors from the modern world. Like all other aspects, visits from family and friends should be consistent with the era. Visits to the frontier were rare as transport was complex and time-consuming. Therefore we do not anticipate participants receiving numerous visitors. Visitors who do come will be accommodated, entertained, and fed at the participant's property and expense. We ask that visitors respect the project and surrender all modern devices such as cell phones, radios, contemporary media, and modern foodstuffs. They will be asked to wear clothing similar to the period dress worn by participants.

Finance. Each family will be given a budget at the start of the project. This will be worked out by our historians based upon research of families moving out West in the 1880s. From this you must manage what to buy and when. A barter system will operate in our store whereby goods may be traded rather than bought. (For example the store may offer credit for fresh eggs, bread, dairy products, fish, and vegetables. You may also trade homemade produce such as jams, craft objects, and newly made clothing.)

The store may also offer an advance, particularly if you wish to purchase an expensive commodity, such as a plow or sewing machine. To take advantage of this, security on the loan will be required; for instance, the rights to a valued possession such as a horse. The storekeeper may demand payment on an outstanding loan at any time.

Period medicines/cures. For minor medical needs you may use the various supplies in the medicine box provided. These have been researched and sanctioned by our medical adviser and are mostly herbal remedies of the day, usable at the recommended dosages. In severe medical cases all rules are suspended and immediate assistance should be sought by alerting a member of the production team, who will arrange a visit from our doctor.

Leaving the project. Anyone is welcome to leave at any time. We sincerely hope this will not occur, but we will not prevent anyone's departure. Our only request is that, should the circumstances arise, a decision be made rationally and in consultation with the production team. A decision to leave should be communicated with the video diary camera. We will assist with all departure arrangements.

"We Will All Be Poor Here Together"
Homesteader Dreams and Realities

Who were these itchy-footed dreamers who pulled up stakes and headed West in the last half of the nineteenth century and the first half of the twentieth? Their stories are as varied as the landscape upon which they settled, their motives as diverse as their ethnic backgrounds and their economic circumstances. There were, of course, commonalities. Most were pushed by dissatisfaction with their current circumstances and pulled by hope of a better life in the West. But dissatisfaction and hope were only a part of the mix. Almost always some other factor was involved—perhaps the urging of a friend or a relative who had already made the move, or perhaps simply the irresistible lure of adventure.

Uriah and Mattie Oblinger with their daughter,
Ella — circa 1873.

Inevitably, several factors were at work as the prospective homesteader came to what was, after all, a momentous decision.

But these pioneers could not always articulate exactly what lay behind their decision. One Oregon homesteader admitted that he had left behind in Iowa a "fine farm" with "much improvements" just because he was "not satisfied with the country." An Illinois farmer picked up his family and moved to Nebraska because he had a vague notion he could do "better" farther west. Why would men who were already "west" choose to keep on moving? What was the restlessness that urged them onward?

For some it seemed almost to be in the genes. Samuel Bostwick — a descendant of people whose dreams had brought them across the Atlantic — was nine years old in 1843 when his parents decided to leave their native Vermont and try their luck in Illinois. Four years later, the Bostwicks gave up on Illinois and moved to Council Bluffs, Iowa. In 1860, Sam, now twenty-six years old, newly married, and discouraged with farming prospects in the Midwest, transported his bride, Mary, to the goldfields of Colorado, where their first child, Chester, was born. Leaving his wife to care for little Chester — and birth a second child — Bostwick set out in the fall of 1863 for Alder Gulch, a new strike in what was about to be designated Montana Territory. By the time Mary, Chester, and the baby joined him early in 1864, Alder Gulch had become Virginia City — a boomtown of some five thousand men. By midsummer, with the influx of wives and children of some of those men, Mary began to feel at home — at which point, Sam sold his mining claim and moved her and the children to the Gallatin Valley, some ninety miles to the northeast. There, having rightly discerned that he could do better at farming than he could at mining, he filed on a homestead and traded his pick for a plow. Having land of his own seemed to cure Sam Bostwick of his wanderlust, as Mary and he settled into life on Bostwick Creek, raising their eight children in the shadow of the Bridger Mountains near Bozeman.

There are echoes of the Bostwicks' story in the stories of many other homesteaders. In Baltimore, Maryland, in the mid-1880s, Bartley Curtis, an Irish immigrant, met and married Mary Dunn, also Irish-born. The couple moved first to Dakota Territory, where they had four children before Curtis's itching feet carried them north to Calgary. A year later the family recrossed the border and settled in Choteau, Montana. But, as his daughter recalled years later, the lack of instant success there and rumors of better land in the eastern part of the state stirred Bartley Curtis's "gypsy blood," and in 1894, the family headed off toward Billings "in a covered wagon — father, mother, kids, and seventy-five cents."

It was not always "gypsy blood" or "itching feet" that drew the homesteader West. For some it was the irresistible lure of owning their own land. Thirty-year-old Uriah Oblinger of Onward, Indiana, left his wife, Mattie, and his two-year-old daughter, Ella, behind in 1872 when he set out in the company of his brother and two brothers-in-law in a wagon train bound for Nebraska. Tired of farming rented land, Oblinger had had enough of some-one else's "bossing." For him, as for countless others, the frontier was, as historian Freder-ick Jackson Turner would later observe, "a gate of escape from the bondage of the past."

In Nebraska, Oblinger met initial disappointment, finding "all the good…[homesteading sites] taken up." Finally he settled on a parcel that had been abandoned by a previous claimant who had returned to the East without even turning up the sod. Delighted by the prospects in a land where there were "mostly young families, just starting in life the same as we are," he predicted a life of hard work surrounded by neighbors who shared their hopes and dreams and weren't ashamed of poverty. "We will all be poor here together," he proclaimed.

Whether or not she found such predictions as reassuring as her husband intended them, Mattie responded without hesitation to his invitation to join him in Nebraska, ready enough for reunion after nine lonely months back home in Indiana. In May of 1873 she boarded the westbound train in the company of little Ella and two wooden crates—one filled with all the family's worldly goods and the other with live chickens.

Uriah's long-awaited letter inviting her to join him on their new land in Nebraska had hardly prepared her for the situation that awaited her there. There was no well—and no money to pay for having one dug. Water had to be hauled from a sluggish stream, and not a drop was wasted. Cooking pots and tin dishes were "washed" with sand. Rainfall was spotty, and twice grasshoppers devoured their entire crop. A prairie fire destroyed the schoolhouse and would have burned their home as well had Uriah not plowed a fire break to keep the flames from reaching the roof. Despite such trials, his spirit remained undimmed. "What a pleasure it is to work one's own farm," he wrote home to Indiana, "for you can feel that it is yours and not…someone [else's]. I would rather live as we do [here] than have to rent and have someone bossing us as we used to."

His wife was far less enthusiastic about the advantages of homesteading. "Mother," she wrote home after several years on the Nebraska homestead, "you said…for us to keep a stiff upper lip. Well, that is no trouble for us…for we have had to keep a stiff upper lip so much…that they have about grown stiff."

That homestead was to be Mattie Oblinger's final resting place, for she died birthing her fourth child in February of 1880 and was buried with the newborn. As his brother-in-law reported to those back home, Uriah and his three little girls were left "in a sad condi-tion." Yet Uriah tried his best to hold on to his hard-won land. He rented out his acreage and hired himself out to plow his neighbors' lands, but to no avail. Ultimately he abandoned the homestead—as had the man who had first claimed it—and moved himself and his daughters back East.

Variations on the Oblinger story abound in frontier history. Even in a prime agricul-tural state like Kansas, only 41 percent of settlers filing between 1863 and 1873 proved up on their claims. Another 10 percent commuted their entries to cash purchase and bought the land, while the remaining 49 percent failed to last the required five years and thus never secured title. Across the West as a whole—and through the lifetime of the Homestead

Act—only one-third to one-half of those who filed a claim under its terms actually proved up and obtained title. And 70 percent of those successful entries were made by latter-day homesteaders, most of whom enjoyed the advantage of the improved farming implements of the twentieth century and the expanded opportunities offered by the Enlarged Homestead Act of 1909.

Invariably, the successful claimants were those who found work away from the homestead to provide the cash flow that farming did not. Men hired out to drive cattle, build fences, freight goods, deliver mail, cut and sell timber. Women grew vegetables, raised hens, milked cows, churned butter, made cheese, then periodically loaded all they could spare of their produce, eggs, and dairy products onto wagons bound for the nearest store, where the work of their hands was bartered for flour and sugar, dried fruits and canned tomatoes, and yard goods from which the children's clothes could be made. Single women and teenaged daughters—sometimes married women, too—taught school for extra cash.

Even today abandoned homesteads dot the landscape of the West. Located primarily in areas where only grass could be counted on to grow, these structures give mute testimony to the fact that rain did not always "follow the plow," despite many a homesteader's belief in that adage. The sad truth was that, as the Oblingers' story illustrates, hard work and resourcefulness alone did not ensure success. Indeed, Lady Luck seems often to have played a major part in the outcome of the homesteading venture.

Our first sense of certainty in locating our modern pioneers came early in the process. An interview on NPR's Scott Simon program prompted a flurry of e-mails. As we returned to work Monday morning, some two hundred new applications had landed. Among them was an intriguing bid from a young couple in Boston who wrote with passion about why this experience would be so right for them. For years they had been planning to move West, away from the twenty-first-century grind of a big city. Adventure was a key element in their, thus far, unplanned move. What had long since been planned though was a summer marriage. As Mark Saben scoured the e-mail that morning, the prospect made him jump: a wedding on the frontier?

An early visit to see Nate Brooks, a student activities coordinator, and Kristen McLeod, a social worker, confirmed our excitement. A day spent touring some of their favorite haunts in Boston revealed a fascinating and vibrant couple. In the African-American Meeting House we learned of their excitement for building a new life in which they could take charge. In Harvard Square, they told us of their year spent as volunteer teachers in Namibia, and back home in their small apartment in Malden, they talked of their excitement at being able to connect, in such a unique way, with the past.

NATE AND KRISTEN'S APPLICATION

FAMILY NAME	FIRST NAME	AGE	OCCUPATION/INTERESTS
Brooks	Nathan (Nate)	27	College student
McLeod	Kristen	27	Social worker

What attracted you to this project?

The chance to reconnect to the land and to human history through a challenging experiential endeavor. Timing: Our backgrounds, current life choices, and future plans fit this project perfectly. Hands-on exploration of how gender roles have changed and impacted families. Possibility of using our upcoming wedding as part of the project.

What hobbies and interests do you have?

NATE: Culinary arts, backpacking, fishing, reading, sports, and environmental education. KRISTEN: letter writing, travel and exploring, hiking, spirituality, midwifery, social and community-building activities.

What image do you have of pioneer living?

Connecting with the natural cycles of life. Adventurous. Overcoming great challenges. Long days of physical labor. Community support. Isolated, gritty, and cold. Faithful.

What's the most challenging thing you and your family (or group) have experienced?

We spent a year in Namibia, Africa, volunteering as English resource teachers. The ease and convenience of modern living was replaced with labor-intensive undertakings: boiling drinking water, washing clothes by hand, sleeping under mosquito nets, and adjusting to oppressive weather. In addition to being without the support of family and friends, the physical demands of our new environment were soon rivaled by the powerful self-realizations of our fears, biases, and shortcomings.

If you were chosen, what do you think you would miss most about modern life?

Convenience, convenience, and having the world at your fingertips. The ability to buy or call your way out of hardships and undesirable circumstances...and who could imagine life without Goretex, National Public Radio, and the myriad of international spices and wines that enhance our meals?

What qualities do you and your family have that make you suited to this experience?

1. Strong communication skills that we have developed over our seven years together—by being open, honest, and flexible we are able to support each other and compromise on tough issues. 2. Our faith gives us strength, the courage to take risks, and draws us together as a team. 3. Resourcefulness in our own ways— Nate's ingenuity and ability to creatively problem-solve under pressure. Kristen's patient way of finding information and resources and then applying what she finds in creative and practical ways.

What would you hope to get out of the experience?

A greater appreciation for the history of our ancestors and a sense of connection with humankind. Opportunities to share and reflect on the experience through a

Kristen McLeod and Nate Brooks.

variety of different mediums. Confidence that comes from doing, overcoming, and achieving.

What do you think will be the most difficult challenges of pioneer life?
Staying true to the script with twenty-first-century knowledge and sensibilities. The repetitive nature of frontier living. Unexpected hardships that can't be resolved with a credit card.

What skills would you like to learn from the experience?
NATE: House building, blacksmithing, astronomy, hunting, frontier cooking. KRISTEN: Soapmaking, candlemaking, organic gardening, cleaning a fish, and playing guitar (or other time-appropriate instrument).

What interests you about this project? Do you have any concerns about your participation? How much do you know about your family history— do you have pioneer roots?
NATE: The lessons I learned growing up on a self-sufficient farm became the building blocks of my education. So much of my work ethic, self-confidence, creativity, and values can be traced back to the simple tasks of churning butter, planting corn, spinning wool, and mending fences. *Frontier House* would give me the rare gift of revisiting the experiences of my youth. KRISTEN: Considering our goals in relation to the project, I sense that we are a unique match. Our plan is to move out West after our 2001 wedding, and the thought of changing the century and then proceeding with the plan is thrilling. As a newly married couple in 1880, I will be given the once-in-a-lifetime opportunity to experience the traditional role of a "homemaker wife"—a role that I am reluctant to fully embrace in our modern day.

In a rare meteorological moment it snowed in Los Angeles in February 2000. A home video of a family screaming with delight at that moment was our cue to book flights to go visit them. The Clunes, from just north of La Canada Flintridge, welcomed us into their home with the first historical nugget: "This was the summer home of the Hersheys, the chocolate barons." Adrienne and Gordon are passionate about history, as is evident from the remarkable collection of artifacts that decorates their comfortable home. "It's in our blood. If you're looking for a good reason to take us, just look at our family history...homesteaders from Manitoba," Gordon explained while handing out his collection of period guns. In the kitchen Adrienne was putting the finishing touches to a magnificent beef Wellington and uncorking a bottle of vintage wine. "Don't worry," she said. "We don't always eat like this. I grew up on a farm in Ireland so I know what it is like to live simply." Their boys—Justin, twelve, and Conor, eight—were eagerly perfecting their aim as pellets from their air guns flew from a first-floor window toward targets on their home firing range. "Hi," exclaimed fourteen-year-old Aíne midway through a phone call to her boyfriend.

If two words can sum up a family, *vigor* and *passion* would encapsulate the Clunes. Their enjoyment of life and the possibilities it affords is conspicuous. (Plans for a new home overlooking the Malibu coast was their latest excitement on our visit.) The combination of Gordon and Adrienne's thirst for knowledge about the past and their children's excitement about their possible participation made them an ideal choice for the project. The only sticking point (apart from finding someone to take over the daily management of Gordon's family business) was whether Aíne would feel too isolated. Teenagers from Los Angeles would endure a massive culture shock out on the frontier. "It's okay," said Aíne. "I've just got off the phone with my cousin Tracey. She wants to come, too."

APPLICATION OF GORDON CLUNE

The Clunes: Aíne, Tracey, Adrienne, Justin, Gordon, and Conor.

FAMILY NAME	FIRST NAME	AGE	OCCUPATION/INTERESTS
Clune	Gordon	40	President of company
	Adrienne	39	Homemaker/Home economist
	Aíne	14	Piano/Artistic
	Justin	12	Hunter/Hiker
	Conor	8	Hunter/Hiker
	Tracey	15	Cousin of family

What attracted you to this project?

Living in LA for many years has, to a degree, desensitized me to the reality of our dependence on Mother Nature. Time races by. In a moment my children will be grown and moved out of our house. I can remember a time when time was irrelevant. When I was born, my folks, who lived and worked in the city of Winnipeg, out of necessity had me go live with my Polish immigrant grandparents on a homestead until I was five years old. I have vivid memories of the prairies of Melrose, Manitoba. I can remember helping my grandmother gather eggs, plant vegetables, and milk the cow. The solitary life of growing up on a very remote farm helped shape, for better or worse, who I am today. I was raised on a farm without running water, equipped with an outhouse. Although I remember much, I admit I have a romanticized notion of a simpler life, a life that existed for me that I would like to share with my family.

What hobbies and interests do you have?

History, art, camping, hunting, hiking, fishing, reading, golf, tennis, cars.

What image do you have of pioneer living?

Hard work. Family survival through togetherness and teamwork. Preparation for the bumps and blows that Mother Nature deals out. Preparation in growing, harvesting, canning, pickling, and preserving food. Taking care of farm animals necessary for our survival. Hauling water from a well to the house. Chopping wood to heat the house. Supplementing our diet with game and fish. Home schooling.

What's the most challenging thing you or your family have experienced?
Aside from my daughter dating this year at fourteen, my family and I got lost four-wheel-driving up in the mountains of Carson, Nevada. We drove over passes and came across a herd of wild mustangs before night fell and the snow and the ice made the conditions very difficult for us. My family worked well together and knew to be quiet, and only when we saw lights in the distance did they know to be excited and thankful for our deliverance.

If you were chosen, what do you think you would miss most about modern life?
I know we are hooked on electricity. Even the farm I was raised on had electricity with a TV. I would miss lights at the turn of a switch. Warmth is taken for granted. But most of all I would miss taking hot showers every day.

What qualities do you and your family have that make you suited to this experience?
We eat dinner together every day and have great conversations. My wife cooks and bakes everything from scratch. She was raised on a farm in County Wicklow, Republic of Ireland. Myself and my boys are great hikers and great shots with various rifles. We are a very enthusiastic group and travel well together.

What do you think will be the most difficult challenges of pioneer life?
Providing food for the family. Dependence on animals. Basic hygiene.

What skills would you like to learn from the experience?
I would like to know if me or my family would actually prefer to live a simpler life than the fast-pace life that we lead now. It would be interesting to compare the contentment of the simpler life to the contentment of the fast life.

Pleasant View sounds like the name of a fictitious town in a Spielberg movie. It's real enough, sitting some twenty-five miles outside Nashville. A weekend in Tennessee to visit the Glenn family found us caught up in a whirl of family activities. In a mad rush between two baseball games (in which twelve-year-old Erinn and eight-year-old Logan were representing family honor), mom Karen and stepdad Mark were eager to demonstrate the ethos of their unique family. "We see life as a game: you play hard and you play to win." Mark is bellowing advice from the coach's bench as a last-minute score sees Logan's team bring the Glenns a close-call victory. It's the last game of the season. "But we start volleyball next weekend," says Karen. Friendly competition is a key quality for the Glenns. It was driven home as Karen pounded another strike at the bowling center. "I'm the pawn. She is the queen," explained Mark as Karen decided where we'd take dinner. Over a bowl of pasta they relaxed and infected us with their other persona: fun and friendliness that could warm a Montana winter.

Karen had prompted their application. Spotting the ad in their local newspaper while taking a lunch break from her job as a school nurse, she knew it was for them.

"I grew up a total tomboy with my dad as my mentor. We hunted, fished, just loved spending so much time together in the wild. I know he'd have wanted me to do this." Mark announced their application to his college teaching colleagues and was met with blank stares. "They don't understand just how exciting this could be. I told them I am going to get so much satisfaction out of doing this. Imagine plowing a field, that would be cool." For Karen's children, Erinn and Logan, the only anxiety was leaving their constant comfort, miniature dachshund Pork Chop, behind. "Our other dog, Chester, could come though, couldn't he? He wouldn't get eaten by the bears."

KAREN GLENN'S APPLICATION

FAMILY NAME	FIRST NAME	AGE	OCCUPATION/INTERESTS
Glenn	Karen	35	Mother/Registered nurse
Glenn	Mark	44	Stepfather/College instructor
Patton	Erinn	12	Sports
Patton	Logan	8	Sports
	Chester	3	Family dog

The Glenns: Erinn Patton, Karen and Mark, and Logan Patton.

What attracted you to this project?

The opportunity to separate from what we perceive as a "normal" all-American life and be given the chance to live as a family. We are a blended family of four years and have come to recognize and appreciate our innate differences and similarities, working together to get things done, depending on one another to compromise and pitch in, to identify the common good in our day-to-day tasks. This unique experience would not only bond us but also develop a deeper understanding of alone but together. This challenge would not only build character and trust but offer the education that I yearn for myself and my children. My father was born in a log cabin in the heart of the Catoctin Mountains, Maryland, in 1917. He taught me about woods, about guns, about the animals, and about the respect for all of these. I want to do this in his honor.

What hobbies and interests do you have?

My interests are diverse. I love gardening, hunting, fishing, sports (playing and coaching). I love the outdoors—hiking, teaching my kids about the various trees, birds, and bugs we find. Teaching archery during the summer, loading worms on a hook, and seeing my plants thrive and produce. I can load a gun, shoot a bow, skin or scale anything, cook it, and enjoy eating it. I can build a fire better than most and don't hesitate to swing an ax to cut down a tree or split it up. I'm my daddy's girl. The little bit I did get from my mom is the ability to make a meal out of just about anything.

What image do you have of pioneer living?

Hard hard work. Rough hands, granola smell (all right we stink!), never enough time to get all the chores done, always something that needs fixing…basically heaven on earth! No worry about how my hair looks, are my clothes on the fashion edge, is my makeup okay, does this make my butt look big! First couple of weeks sore, tired, disenchanted. Next couple of weeks starting to make sense, next couple of weeks getting the hang of it all, and the last couple dreading the return home.

If you were chosen, what do you think you would miss most about modern life?

I would miss *Newsweek.* I like keeping current on what's going on about the world. Second I would miss cinnamon-hazelnut coffee creamer.

What qualities do you and your family have that make you suited to this experience?

We get along! We work well together; my family members are extremely intelligent and skilled problem-solvers. We travel a lot together and enjoy adrenaline situations. I am surrounded by achievers, not quitters, and my family would not back out once it got rough; they would just dig in much deeper to prove whatever could be done.

What skills do you have that may help you?

I can sew with a needle and thread. I can cook on an open fire, and I can hunt game like the big boys. I am organized, detail-oriented and demand 100 percent of my team. I love my family, respect their inabilities (and my own), and recognize their special talents. I tend to be the leader of the pack, am very comfortable with limited means, don't mind dirt, and I'm not afraid.

What would you hope to get out of the experience?

Memories. Lots of memories. Lots of remember-whens. Satisfaction that if the computers did all shut down and the world as we knew it changed, we would still survive and thrive. Proving that not having is not being poor. It may even be better than having. Pick us!

After they had given such confident accounts of themselves, it was intriguing to read the same response in both the Clunes' and the Glenns' diaries shortly after we dropped the bombshell that they had indeed been selected. "Why us?" asked members of both families in a sudden uncertainty about their participation. For Nate and Kristen, though, a bigger concern took hold. With such inevitably high demands on each member of the project, a full medical checkup became necessary. Close questioning about their health revealed a fundamental problem: Kristen was severely allergic to horses. A weekend in rural Maine confirmed the diagnosis after wheezing and a tightening of the chest took hold shortly after contact. With sinking hearts we asked Nate and Kristen to lunch on a weekend they were visiting friends in New York. With such an apparently insuperable problem it looked inevitable we would have to end their participation. As we moved nervously toward the admission, an idea occurred. As the main exposure to horses would be during the initial phase of the project (during the training and on the wagon train journey), why couldn't Kristen join us at a later point? But why? As we remembered a diary of an 1880s Montana homesteader, inspiration suddenly dropped from the heavens. "Didn't husbands-to-be go ahead and build the cabin before his bride arrived?" A rescue plan was hatched that would allow us to tell a fascinating historical story. With the expertise of Dr. Franklin Adkinson, an allergy specialist at the Johns Hopkins Hospital in Baltimore, who would help manage any reactions Kristen may have, Nate and Kristen's participation was finally sealed. But could Nate hope to build a cabin solo? "I have an idea. Leave it with me," he said as we parted company. Twenty-four hours later we were talking to Nate's dad, Rudy, a retired corrections officer who'd returned home from the golf course to a phone call from his son. "Fancy a trip to Montana, Dad? Have I got an idea for you!"

"I wouldn't choose to do this," Rudy guardedly admitted when we first called him about the idea. At sixty-eight he was right to be cautious; inevitably the project would test everyone physically and mentally. Being Nate's assistant in building a cabin would mean a tough time for Rudy—the exertions of such a challenge and the rough living until the shelter was completed. "But it sounds fascinating and I'd love to be there to help Nate and Kristen," said Rudy. "Some friends will think I'm mad, but count me in."

Our suspicion that the chosen participants might suspect our sanity had some truth behind it. Karen Glenn's diary of April 27, 2001, summed up the mood:

Nate and Rudy Brooks.

*Last night I got my first panic attack. It hit me—**Am I nuts?** What am I getting my family into? How could I ever conceive that this would be beneficial, exciting, normal, or **fun?** My life, however hectic and crazed, is at least fairly predictably unpredictable. I manage, we manage. Limitations are fairly obvious and boundaries apparent. This project is limitless and boundaries undefined. What was I thinking again?—somebody please tell me. Who are these people we are entrusting our lives to? We know their names and where they are from, but other than a few meetings and phone calls, I really don't know them at all. Did they come from solid families or Dysfunctional with a capital D. Are they happy in their lives, their jobs, their responsibilities? Are they going to lose it on us about some item of behavior when they end the day in a comfortable bed, with clean linen, running water, and **toilet paper?***

Background checks, interviews, pictures, taking video of our lives to find out who we are, who our support network is, what we do, how we cope— and none of these things do we know about them.

I have to trust. I have no option but to trust. I have to relinquish total control into the hands of the unknown and trust.

This project in many ways is quite a bit more challenging to us than it may have been to a family back in the 1880s. With one exception. I am guaranteed a return ticket home to normality. I trust.

3

Countdown

Re-creating an accurate picture of the past was our primary goal in the challenge to make *Frontier House* reality. The West and its development is a subject that has fascinated millions from the earliest days of its settlement. Yet so often the story is seen through a distorted lens. Our images are drawn from film and television accounts that began life as dime novels, often written by authors who had never traveled west of the Mississippi. Hence the first lesson learned in attempting to reconstruct the era was to question everything, trust nothing until we could find it corroborated elsewhere. And that's where the headaches began! Read a dozen diaries of homesteading life and rarely do you find the same story. Ask clothing historians a simple question like "Did women wear corsets out on the frontier?" and stand back to watch an argument develop. As our inquiries into the past gathered momentum, a series of ever more complex debates took shape. Historical accounts often read as the definitive source, until you read the next. In research for the project, scholarly debates bounced around the states on issues ranging from the likelihood and types of contraception practiced by settlers in the 1880s to the right recipe for sourdough. What became clear was that how people dressed, ate, washed, cooked, etc., was subject to interpretation dependent upon a hundred varying issues. There was no "normality" or stereotypical experience. To get closer to the truth we would have to create models based upon real people, real places.

Finding historians who understand the practices of the past was the next challenge. A dozen academics can quickly be found to discuss the evolution of the cookstove, but finding one who knows both the history and how to bake a loaf of bread in one is a harder task. From afar, it's easy to get the impression that re-creating a "simple lifestyle" should be a straightforward task. But, as the deadline to filming

grew ever nearer, our list of challenges where practical expertise was required grew ever longer. For starters, we needed to find appropriate livestock of the era, re-create the types of foods that sustained settlers, stock a home medicine cabinet without poisoning the user, make clothes from period materials, completely furnish a general store of the era, build authentic cabins (complete with holes for vermin to visit), and hopefully, ensure no one would get hurt in re-creating a lifestyle renowned for accidents and tragedies. Each field needed its own champion, and in addition to being assured practitioners in their craft, ideally these experts also needed to have lived as closely as they could to the period they would help re-create. The approach of filming led to a flurry of activity by scores of historians and experts in almost forgotten skills. At the center of the whirlwind were a handful of rare individuals, men and women who not only knew the history of their craft but could pass on the skills, too. If history had an "A-Team," we'd found them!

The first of our specialists was our historic preservation consultant, Bernie Weisgerber. Meet him and you'd imagine he'd stepped straight off a Western movie set, but Bernie's the real thing. With more than thirty years' experience working on the reconstruction and preservation of log cabins, there isn't a notch or wood joint that Bernie doesn't know. To watch him wield an ax is a truly terrifying sight, yet beneath that distinctive Western growl, he's one of the most supportive and kindly men you could hope to work with. From the first conversation Bernie was enthusiastic: "You're mad to try it. But count me in!" Like many of our specialist advisers, Bernie brought a personal understanding of the challenges faced by back-to-the-basics living. Earlier in his life, he spent two years tucked away in the mountains of Virginia making do without electricity, phone, running water, and modern sanitary facilities. "By the end of the first year my wife had left me," he admitted. "At the end of year two, even my dog was mad at me!" With a lifetime of practical skills in log cabin construction and historic restoration, Bernie Weisgerber was a natural for overseeing the planning and training that would be necessary for our homesteaders to construct their cabins. And having lived in the Rockies for the past twenty-five years, he knew the incredible task that lay ahead.

Finding a livestock specialist with an understanding of the region and a knowledge of historic breeds was a challenge. Our search finally ended in Wyoming with the gloriously named Rawhide Johnson. (Shortly after his birth, his father commented that the skin of his jaundiced son was as yellow as rawhide. The name stuck.) Growing up on a ranch in a part of the Rockies nicknamed "Little Siberia," Rawhide knew firsthand how hard being a mountain homesteader could be: "We had no electricity, no hot water on tap, and lived many miles from town. Winters often lasted the best part of a year. I hope these people you chose are going to like isolation."

Women on the frontier were a precious commodity. In some parts of the West fewer than one in ten were women. Hence the birth of the mail-order bride. Once in their new territory, these women had to adapt to new ways of working; gone were the gentle ways of towns where refinement and gentility were considered a woman's way. Cows needed to be milked, meals prepared by campfire, soap had to be made. Rest and pleasure were things of the past. A unique individual was needed to teach the skills our women would require. After a lengthy and diligent search, Associate Producer Micah Fink tracked down Vermonter Susan Cain. Susan was a champion of the woodstove, and her Dutch-oven baking was legendary. Raised on a dairy, she was an expert at milking, churning butter, and making cheese. She understood and had experience with the basic hygiene practices of

LEFT: Susan Cain.

RIGHT: Ursula Smith and Linda Peavy.

the past, and she taught all these skills in living-history classes around the country. What really caught Micah's attention was that Susan had recently single-handedly broken in a team of oxen. Such qualities made Susan a natural to impart the women's roles on the project. "From childhood I've always wondered if I could survive in the old ways," she said. "Being involved in living history has allowed me to get as close as I could to finding the answer to that question, but these people are really going to find out. I wish I could have traded roles."

Historians Linda Peavy and Ursula Smith are mold breakers who began working together back in 1978 in Bozeman, Montana. From the first, they were researching and writing women's lives, but their focus soon narrowed. "After a 1983 Women's West conference," Linda explained, "we became so intrigued by the idea of 'the extraordinariness of ordinary lives' and by all that can be learned by studying the day-to-day experiences of women on the frontier that we set out to 'write' a wrong by filling in some historical gaps in the old John Wayne version of life in the West." Twenty years and nine books later the two are still working together. Their bank of knowledge concerning Western family history proved an amazing resource in re-creating the homesteading experience. "I knew if we didn't get selected as consultants I'd want to volunteer as a participant," Linda admitted. "Not so fast," Ursula said. "Remember, I tried that life on our own one hundred and sixty acres in South Dakota—while bringing up six children." They took on the unenviable task of checking the authenticity of many aspects of the encounter we planned for our families. "We wanted to be a part of what we saw as a bold sociological experiment that would give us the opportunity to see families attempting to live and farm within the limitations of the 1883 frontier," Ursula explained. Linda's rationale was more personal: "How could we pass up a chance to return to Montana?"

You'd imagine that running a ten-thousand-acre cattle ranch and being a mother of six, grandmother of ten, and foster mom to twelve would be more than enough. Christine Schuman is one of those terrifying Montanans who seem to have the energy of a dozen people. Aside from her family and ranching duties, she's an accomplished costume designer, having made the clothes many of us have admired in many movies, especially Westerns. Her fit for this project was uncanny; she'd grown up on a homestead in eastern Montana. "My mother came from the East and almost had a nervous breakdown the first two years here, as we did not have electricity until I was in grade school and running water until I was in high school," she told us. "I know how difficult this is going to be on the women. I want the clothing to be absolutely authentic." With seventeen antique sewing machines on which to create our costumes, Christine set to it like a dervish possessed. Vintage fabrics were fashioned into elegant Sunday-best suits, yards of red flannel were transformed into a dozen crotchless undies, and twenty-two bones were sewn, remorselessly, into each corset. "Sewing for eighteen kids gives you good practice."

Finding thousands of rare and workable period artifacts in a matter of weeks might sound like a mission from hell, but for Dave Kinsey the assignment he was handed turned out to be a joy. "I appreciate things like nice old saws. They turn my crank," said Dave. A manager of the living-history farm at Bozeman's Museum of

Christine Schuman.

the Rockies, he's used to eccentric challenges as creaky artifacts are pressed back into action. Realizing our need to track down a multitude of antiques and faithful reproductions, we observed Dave with particular interest during a visit to the museum. We witnessed his excitement at showing us working versions of long-neglected objects, and visiting his museum storage quarters—a room piled high with washtubs, scythes, butter churns, woodstoves, and antique saws—was like entering an Aladdin's cave of frontier treasures. The job of settlers' outfitter fit him like a glove and he steamed away with gusto when assigned the task of finding everything from period ladders to authentic tooth powder.

With our experts working away to make this experience as authentic as possible, we had to find someone well qualified to make the experience as safe as possible, given the inherent dangers of 1883 frontier living. Once again we lucked out, finding in Seattle a safety expert whose interests and expertise matched our needs perfectly. Clarence Atchison was as accustomed to donning his reenactment buckskins and spending a weekend as a mountain man as he was to making sure engineering and construction companies met current OSHA safety standards, and he welcomed the challenge of helping us minimize the risks our families took without compromising the authenticity of their experience. With our experts in place, the countdown to 1883 began in earnest.

Saturday, May 5. Bozeman airport. At 12:51 P.M. Flight 388 from Denver touched down with a unique cargo. The first of our time travelers, the Glenns, had arrived. We spotted twelve-year-old Erinn first, a striking vision in shocking-pink T-shirt and precarious raised platforms racing into the arrivals lounge. Logan, Karen, and Mark followed two minutes behind, waylaid by the view of the Bridger Mountains, brilliant in late-spring snow cover. Months of anticipation were behind us, yet for everyone the recognition that the enterprise was truly beginning was hard to accept. Chester, their black Labrador, brought us to our senses, barking excitedly from the luggage zone. Six hours in transit from Nashville in a four-foot-square pet cage had been long enough. Three further flights that day completed the lineup of participants. Barring two lost suitcases and a missing dog leash, our crew was all intact and ready for the adventure.

As part of the "bachelor team," Rudy took cooking lessons.

Eighty miles and a century and a half away from modern Bozeman lie Virginia City and Nevada City, two jewels in the rich heritage of Montana. Rescued from the grips of developers in the 1990s, these tiny towns bear witness to a unique past and curious present life. It's hard to believe it today, but these small settlements were once the biggest news in the West. You can't buy a gallon of gas there today, yet 150 years ago all roads in Montana Territory found visitors en route to the burgeoning communities set high up in the hills. A gold strike in Alder Gulch on May 26, 1863, quickly lured thousands upon thousands of hopefuls out to the mining frontier. At the height of its production an ounce of the extra-pure gold mined here was worth $18, a relative fortune in its day. Today these towns are a quiet home to hundreds of historic buildings, many still full of their original artifacts, which continue to call strangers from afar. Rarely do you find such well-preserved collections of antiques in situ. Scouring one store, we found hundred-year-old boxes of underwear, unopened and still in immaculate condition. Alongside lay a grim reminder of the times, a child's coffin. At every building it's possible to feel something of the past life when bills were settled by weighing gold dust. With little changed from its earlier days it made the perfect start to our journey back in time.

Preseason Virginia City and Nevada City are normally enviably quiet communities. Little disturbs the permanent community of 150, barring the occasional whistle of the steam train as it's fired up for the arrival of summer visitors. Last spring a whirlwind of activity descended just ahead of our families. Pipes in the towns' two hotels were unfrozen. The Madison restaurant quadrupled its food orders. Long-abandoned cabins were scrubbed out. Antique stoves were relit. Strange accents were overheard in the Pioneer bar. Rumor had it Hollywood was here. Instead, a dozen newcomers and a dog hit town. Accompanying them came our consultants, towing curious loads. Livestock specialist Rawhide Johnson brought a consignment of strange animals: cattle of curious breeds, a brace of rare hens, four dogs, and six horses. Cabin-construction expert Bernie Weisgerber came with his pickup bristling with an assortment of axes, saws, and alien hardware, familiar only to early settlers, while living-history adviser Susan Cain shipped in enough antique-recipe sourdough and salted hams to feed the neighborhood.

What followed was a "history boot camp." With the clock ticking toward the start of the experience, it was time to begin the immersion into a past life. The transition began simply enough. Without showers, televisions, or telephones in any of the hotel rooms, it was the first good-bye to modern conveniences. Unpacking their small selection of modern clothes brought for their first few days, our families were eager to start the adventure. Days began at 5 A.M. with milking duty. By nine in the evening most were crawling into their beds to rest muscles hitherto rarely exercised. But it wasn't just the body that took the impact. With an eye toward historical precedent, one of the first jobs was to revise current thinking on the role of the sexes. From our first meetings with many of the consultants, the feeling was unanimous: men and women played different roles back in the 1880s. So, too, should our participants. The afternoon of the second day began amicably enough, but within ten minutes the emotional temperatures were rising. It all began with Susan Cain reading a quotation from the Bible.

Ephesians 5:22–23: "Wives, submit yourselves unto your own husbands, as unto the Lord. For the husband is the head of the house, even as Christ is the head of the church."

A grim hush followed the passage, at last broken by Adrienne: "But women out West didn't play second fiddle to men surely?"

"Not always. That was the beauty of the frontier," answered Susan in her firmest tone. "But sure as heck they arrived with these preconceptions. That's why we're starting with them now."

For modern women, accepting a new landscape to a relationship would be an ordeal. "Not for nothing were all the fights made for equality," Adrienne continued.

Karen was stoical in her silence throughout the session as Susan laid out the way gender dictated the daily burdens out on the frontier: "So, from tomorrow the women will be with me here in the kitchen. The men will work learning carpentry skills with Bernie." Somehow the irony of Susan's being the one to frog-march our families back in time was lost on everyone as a new and indelicate matter was raised: "We're off to the outhouse," she said, "and no, there isn't any toilet paper out there either."

TOP: Karen Glenn gets her first taste of campfire cooking.

Long hours of hard work saw our families through a punishing learning curve over their two weeks at Virginia City. A curious acceptance of the role of the sexes crept over everyone with the recognition there was so much to learn and that, if they didn't listen attentively, they'd be in trouble with so many new skills required. As Bernie drilled the men in the lost art of axmanship, Susan nursed the women through a harder history lesson. To bake without a thermometer you plunge your hand into a red-hot oven to test how long you can stand it. "Count to twenty and it's hot enough for scones." Washing without rubber gloves means red, raw, and blistered hands. A long-anticipated chicken dinner took all day after the ordeal of wringing the wretched creature's neck. And every activity seemingly required gallons of hot water and mountains of kindling that had the children tearing back and forth from the cabin. Like many old towns in the West, Virginia City and Nevada City are awash with legends of ghosts and ghouls that inhabit many a bedroom. Strangely, no one had problems sleeping in our frenzied fortnight, none of our would-be homesteaders anyhow.

As the reality of the project began to kick in, it was the consultants and production team who grew most anxious. Razor-sharp axes, vats of boiling water, and children constantly running around the arsenal of dangerous implements were cranking up the tension. Re-creating the lifestyle of homesteaders was hard enough, but doing so without incurring severe injury or illness was harder. We couldn't wrap the families in cotton wool and create a totally unrealistic experience, nor could we ignore the very real hazards ahead. So, at this point, the families were introduced to the "emergency box," a bright orange container that would be placed in each cabin, containing medical supplies, powerful flashlights, and a two-way radio to reach the production center in a dire emergency. Each box was sealed, and breaking the seal would have to be declared to the other modern implement that would accompany the families—a video diary camera that could record their feelings twenty-four hours a day. Two other concessions were made in recognition of modern concerns. Sunscreen was provided to the families to counter the diminished atmospheric layers of protection from the sun, which would prove scorching up at the location's elevation of fifty-five hundred feet. Plus the adults were also allowed to make their own decisions on contraception. Although the first mass-produced vulcanized-rubber condoms appeared in 1844, often advertised as "French Preservatives," it was unlikely that such methods would be regularly available out in remote areas of the West. Their scarcity partly resulted from the ban on mailing contraceptives or information about their use under the Comstock Law of 1873, which meted out heavy penalties or imprisonment to offenders. Having been shown 1883 frontier alternatives, such as the pig-intestine condom, the families opted for modern methods, except for Gordon and Adrienne Clune, who had already taken care of such matters with a vasectomy some years earlier.

A smaller wooden box containing some grim reminders of the past was also distributed to each family. Inside sat bottles of castor oil, a tub of goose grease, and small vials of assorted remedies of the day. Although medicine back East was making considerable headway in the 1880s, out in the harsh environment of the frontier, folks simply couldn't afford a doctor, so most often the family health care was provided by mom. In many cases we could not provide the same remedies of the era, which included tonics containing significant quantities of narcotics such as cocaine and laudanum. Nor could we recommend many of the treatments outlined in home-doctor volumes of the day, such as pouring gunpowder on a snakebite wound and igniting it. Back then, many ailments were seen as internal problems that could be flushed out by taking a purgative. Everything from boils to coughs were fought off with regular spoonfuls of cure-alls, often a dose of castor oil. A generous application of goose grease was recommended to reduce swelling. Ongoing sicknesses were commonly treated with herbal remedies passed on from generation to generation. Each of our families received a small selection of herbs including feverfew for the relief of headaches and sage for tea for diarrhea. Except in the case of emergency, the medical box would be our families' only method of medical care. One final addition was accepted gladly, a crude but effective painkiller—a bottle of whiskey.

Justin Clune takes charge of Blanca.

Up at the corrals, the animals were mystified. Three Jersey milk cows (complete with young calves), half a dozen horses, a dwindling family of hens, four dogs, and four newly born puppies were taking turns initiating hardened city people into a new lifestyle. The day began at dawn when sleepy-eyed children arrived to hand-milk Blanca, Crystal, and Jessica, the three Jersey cows who, with their newly born calves, would accompany the families to Frontier Valley. Later our patient horses were put through their paces as the adults, mostly unaccustomed to riding, took turns at trying to master their only mode of transport. Rawhide Johnson watched throughout with a mixture of admiration and occasional abject horror as our urban warriors tried to bond with the animals. Eventually he felt comfortable enough to assign each family their new and vital team members. Each family was provided its own milk cow and calf, horses, and dogs. Encouragingly, the most vulnerable, the ten-day-old puppies, were embraced like fine china in the hands of the children as their new homes were assigned. "Looks like we'll be taking dogs home," observed Adrienne. For Karen, though, a different dilemma:

> *We got the weaker of the cows. Crystal is not producing much milk. It's real unusual for me to be worried about cows as I don't like cows, but I am now worried about her as she is not well. It's got me real worried. The first sign of trouble, they are coming to help my Crystal; I don't want to lose my cow out there.*

Karen surprised even herself at the concern she was feeling toward an animal she'd always viewed with dislike. Elsewhere, others were starting to revise lifelong opinions. Returning exhausted from a day in carpentry class, Gordon Clune addressed the video diary:

> *Something just occurred to me. I was working on the sawhorses and thought about how I have been asked to go work on a house on a day off, and I remember thinking I do not want to give my day off to that, we hire someone*

to do it. Now I realize that I have been missing the chance of doing something creative. Now I realize a game of golf is a waste of time.

Exhausted but encouraged by their progress, our dozen trainee pioneers grew daily more confident in their newfound skills. Before long, delicious stove-baked meals, accompanied by fresh bread and home-churned butter, graced the table. Milk stools were crafted by hand. Intricate notches for cabin building were rehearsed. Even the horses accommodated the saddle-shy with few losses of dignity. It all went well. Too well. Ten days in and Adrienne spotted the symptom first in a perceptive video diary report:

It looks like people are becoming more stressed as we get to know each other and people are letting their guard down. Everyone is getting tired. Every day at least one of the ladies is breaking down and crying. I think it's something to do with living in cramped conditions. Working in the kitchen in such a small space is hard. There are lots of conflicts building up, certainly with the women. It's interesting, but familiarity does breed contempt.

And it wasn't just the women who were feeling the stress. In the carpentry classes a friendly but conspicuous competition was taking place. Nicknames like the Timber Beast and Saw Warrior were handed out. Ax handles split with over-enthusiasm. Keen eyes were glued to others' efforts. Everyone was keyed up to prove himself. Nate conveyed his feelings to the video diary:

It's interesting to think about selfishness and how frontier folk in 1883 survived. Was it the ones that looked out for themselves or was it the people who let others borrow the cow or the horse? Competition is tied to wanting to succeed, and you think about doing that in an environment where there is a survival mentality. In a survival situation who are the people that will rise above and not resort to undercutting their neighbor? I am interested to see how that will play out.

An explosion was brewing and it was sparked by the introduction of the firearms. Short of the ax and the horse, the gun was probably the most important tool to the homesteader. But with hunting regulations firmly in place, our participants wouldn't be able to hunt for much of their stay. However, with predators such as coyotes hungrily sniffing around (our chickens at Virginia City met an untimely end on their second night), we recognized that a gun could be handy out on the frontier. To help our homesteaders decide about taking ownership, we held an introduction to the firearm at the town shooting range. The chosen weapon was a reproduction of an American double-barrel shotgun from the era, its place of manufacture today, Russia. To Gordon, a keen collector of vintage weapons, our choice was unsatisfactory. With gun in hand (which he had brought from his own collection), he faced the video diary:

This is a Winchester made in 1866.... We have a gun that's embarrassing. It's sad, I can't believe we are in America and have something like that. It's probably not important in the grand scheme of things but it is to me. I feel very very disappointed about this.

Making his unhappiness plain, Gordon openly criticized the choice of the weapon and mourned our inability to hunt out of season. Everyone noticed his absence that night at dinner, and his dark mood took some days to shake off. The limited hunting opportunities and the veto by our safety adviser on Gordon's using his rifle—because of the danger of stray bullets injuring participants—had greatly annoyed him. Disappointed by the restrictions, he tried to draw the others into the matter. The result was our first real tension among the participants. Karen, herself a keen hunter, declared Gordon's views "obsessive" and "offensive." This event was the first moment of real tension between our participants and marked the beginning of a fragile and often strained relationship between the two families.

The subject continued to be a bone of contention. Karen grew weary of it and off-loaded to the video diary:

If Gordon brings up one more issue about firearms, I will shoot him.... If you want a hunting experience with your boys in Montana, set it up with an outfitter who will be glad to take your money and you will be happy, we will be happy, but give it a break. If you want to go eat some of that rabid rabbit meat, do, but don't come to my cabin looking for toilet paper 'cause there ain't none. He is driving me crazy.

Watching the development of the family dynamics was fascinating. No one was more intrigued than our newcomer to the project, Nate's dad, Rudy Brooks. Unlike the rest of the participants he'd been brought into the project at the last moment and was spending the time at Virginia City absorbing the minutiae of the amazing endeavor. After retiring from a career in law enforcement working with juvenile delinquents, he'd been enjoying a quiet retirement in California. Now he was swinging axes, learning to ride horses, and preparing for a testing experience at age sixty-eight. Of all the family members he'd lived most closely to the circumstances they were heading for, having grown up out in the country in a two-room shack with no electricity and no running water. Observing the participants was intriguing him. "I've been a people watcher all of my life, and it's amazing and amusing to watch the families interact.... There is some personal discord between a couple here, and I think it will be interesting to see what happens when we get to the frontier. I think it may bring them closer together."

With only a few days before departure to the frontier, the families concentrated on mastering the limited tools that would be their only aids. Each had been outfitted with basic cooking utensils, tools, and household wares typically brought West by homesteaders. One vital piece of information was missing though: how

much money they would have at their disposal. After studying the records of settlers in the 1880s, and taking into consideration the personal and professional traits of the *Frontier House* families, our historians Linda Peavy and Ursula Smith had drawn up three individualized profiles of the circumstances and possessions of our would-be homesteaders. Now their fates would be individually disclosed as each family opened a chest containing their personal belongings and clothes. Resting on top was a small leather booklet that revealed their status. As they gathered by their family trunks, all were nervous as they knew that within moments they could be plunged into poverty or could inherit scant clothing unsuitable for the experience. With a modicum of kindness, our historians had drawn up backgrounds typical of many settlers arriving at the time. With knowledge of the hardships, few homesteaders arrived penniless. Many had saved for years. However, for our modern families the tight budgets they were about to inherit would prove a challenge.

The Clunes went first. Linda and Ursula had researched a background that placed Gordon as the son of an immigrant miner who'd made his fortune in the California Gold Rush. Now Gordon was relocating his family after a shift in fortunes following the collapse of the family business. Their total wealth, after paying for their outfitting for the frontier, $326.66. From that they would have to pay for everything that would sustain their lives, including hired labor to help in the construction of a log cabin. All of the Clunes were encouraged that their home would already be under construction when they arrived. Next, the Glenns learned how Mark had wanted to be a farmer, but as a teacher's wages in Tennessee would not support the purchase of agricultural land in the South, they had chosen to try homesteading on "free" land. They brought a total of $319.42 but would inherit an abandoned cabin on their land. (Screams of delight echoed around the Nevada City Hotel to that revelation.) Going last, Nate and Rudy gingerly opened their chest. With anxieties about the financial and social pressures surrounding his forthcoming marriage, Nate had elected to set up home out West in advance of his bride's arrival. Total wealth: $247. For him and Rudy, the short straw; Nate would have to build a cabin from scratch. Luckily the "Timber Beast" had proved himself handy with an ax and crosscut saw in the past two weeks.

Each background story had been carefully researched and modeled on records of the era. Our homesteaders were inheriting a real history including a few valued possessions. Treasured objects from the past were being admired: family Bibles, pocket watches, silk handkerchiefs, a single china cup. Mark was particularly

The Glenn family in their
Sunday best.

pleased with a simple telescope that would allow him to chart the stars. In exchange we removed their digital watches, cell phones, and jewelry. With vintage attire waiting, they were about to step into the past.

Now the transformation could begin. Alongside the few personal possessions provided to our modern homesteaders lay the layers of clothing handmade to match garments brought West by late nineteenth-century settlers. For costume designer Christine Schuman, the re-creation had been an intriguing process. Unlike the outfits she created for Western movies, this time there had been no concessions to comfort. From studying diaries of the era and scrutinizing photographs of Montana settlers, she'd created two outfits for each participant. The first were work clothes, simple garments made from popular fabrics of the day, and often, a single bolt of cloth would be used to make numerous pieces. The second were more elaborate—"Sunday best" outfits.

"To Start Anew in the Race of Life"
Historical Parallels for the Families of *Frontier House*

Homesteaders. The word itself conjures for most the image of a proud, though weary, couple standing with their children in front of a dugout, soddy log cabin, or tar-paper shack—a home of their own, built by their own hands on land they're struggling to "prove up on." Likely as not, the family imagined is white. Their voices, if imagined at all, sound a lot like those on *Little House on the Prairie.* There are no foreign or regional accents—not even an Irish brogue or a Southern drawl. If their English is slightly imperfect, their linguistic failings are quaint rather than bothersome, audible—and admirable—testimony to the deprivations they have endured.

The bias of this image is hardly surprising, since one of the most pervasive myths of homesteading history is the homogeneity, the *sameness,* of those who went West. In actuality, the promise of free land and a fresh start drew a population as varied as the landscape on which they settled. And given the rich, if largely unrecognized, diversity of the actual homesteading population, it is not difficult to find historical parallels for the three families chosen for the *Frontier House* experience.

Everything gleaned through the written applications and taped interviews of those three families would suggest they are thoughtful and deliberate people, the kind who, 120 years ago, would have weighed the benefits of setting out in search of free land against the risks and inconveniences of such a venture, the kind who would have sought out publications such as Henry Copp's *The American Settler's Guide: A Brief Exposition of the Public Land System of the United States of America.* Published in 1880, Copp's guide issued a three-part invitation that would have had uncanny appeal for the *Frontier House* families.

Copp's first invitation—to "all in the Atlantic states who are discouraged with the slow, tedious methods of reaching independence"—would no doubt have been of special interest to Nate Brooks and Kristen McLeod of Boston, had they been residents of that same city in the early 1880s. And this despite the fact that Boston would have offered more opportunities for this particular couple than most other cities in the Atlantic states. Boston—

indeed all of Massachusetts—had no bans against interracial marriage, and the 1806 African Meeting House, the site of many abolitionist gatherings, would have been a significant and supportive site for their wedding. But legal sanctions and a religious ceremony alone would not have guaranteed social acceptance of their life together. Thus, given their backgrounds and ambitions, Nate and Kristen would likely have been among those who listened to promoters like Henry Copp and decided to seek "the rich rewards awaiting [them] on public lands" in the West.

Waiting on a Mississippi River levee for a steamboat, these families are typical of the thousands of African-Americans who fled the South.

Contrary to prevailing notions of frontier demographics, African-Americans went West in fairly significant numbers during the last decades of the nineteenth century. Consider the McDonalds of Missouri. In 1864, Richard and Mary McDonald loaded all their belongings and their three children into a covered wagon and joined a train bound for newly designated Montana Territory. A free man, but not yet vested with the rights and privileges of full citizenship, Richard McDonald was hardly in a position to file claim to a homestead. He did, however, have sufficient funds to purchase a small tract of land on Sourdough Creek in present-day Bozeman. There he built a one-room cabin before leaving Mary to manage home and garden while he packed flour and other goods to Virginia City. Over the next decade, that boomtown's burgeoning population assured a steady and lucrative market that yielded sufficient profits to allow the McDonalds to expand their small cabin into a spacious two-story dwelling.

If the notion of black homesteaders still seems a bit surreal, consider that in the late 1870s, in a phenomenon known as the Exoduster Movement, some twenty thousand freed slaves, disillusioned by the realities of life in the postwar South, left their homes in Tennessee, Georgia, Alabama, Mississippi, and Louisiana and took up homesteads in the "promised land" of Kansas. No more inclined than their white counterparts to settle down permanently when there were farther horizons beckoning, some of these African-American settlers eventually pushed on to Colorado and Wyoming and up into the Dakotas, Idaho, and Montana.

The George Waite family farmed acreage on the lower Boulder in south-central Montana, not far from the site where Nate and Kristen Brooks would one day stake their *Frontier House* claim. Though the Waites left no written evidence as to how welcome they felt upon their arrival in the valley, former neighbors still recall their warm hospitality, the delicious foods Mrs. Waite prepared for the threshing crews who harvested their grain, and the musical talents of their children, William and Mattie, founding members of an orchestra that provided dance music for patrons of a local nightclub.

While the Waites went West together as a married couple, thousands of men left wives and sweethearts back home when they set out in search of a homestead. Indeed, such separations were the rule rather than the exception for couples like Nate Brooks and Kristen McLeod, couples for whom thoughts of spending the rest of their lives together were inextricably bound to dreams of new beginnings in the West. For one such couple, Ed Adams and his fiancée, Katherine Niles of Belleville, Illinois, the achievement of both goals began in 1882 with Ed's departure for Montana Territory. A year later, Katherine responded to Ed's long-awaited invitation to join him by setting out on a railroad journey to present-day Columbus, Montana, where she was met by her eager suitor and a circuit-riding minister who married the two on the spot. Immediately after the simple ceremony, the newlyweds climbed into a spring wagon and headed out across the plains toward their first home, the one-room cabin Ed had built for his bride-to-be. Within a year Katherine Adams made yet another move, this time to acreage not far from the homestead cabin Nate Brooks and his bride, Kristen, would occupy during their *Frontier House* experience.

There are equally compelling historical parallels for the other two *Frontier House* families. Consider the Clunes, he the son of Canadian Irish immigrants and she the lass Gordon met on a visit to Ireland. Their modern homesteading venture should resonate with many Americans whose parents and grandparents and great-grandparents were among the thousands of immigrants from Europe who poured into the American West during the last two decades of the nineteenth century. For those prospective homesteaders there was instant appeal in the rhetoric found in such publications as Copp's *American Settler's Guide,* which promised that "laborers in other countries who find it difficult to support their families can here acquire wealth, social privileges, and political honors by a few years of intelligent industry and patient frugality." Phil Philipson of Liverpool was looking for just such advancement when he arrived in Montana in 1892 and took up a homestead on the West Boulder before returning to England to marry Elizabeth Dickinson and bring her to the small frame house he had erected up Johnnie Bull Gulch.

More than a century later, Gordon and Adrienne Clune and their children would attempt to replicate the life the Philipsons had carved out for themselves in the Boulder Valley. If their interview tapes made it evident that they would do so with a distinctly Irish flair, those same tapes made it clear that the Clunes shared the same do-or-die spirit of the Philipsons—and of the Bruffeys. George Bruffey had started his life in Montana as proprietor of a successful store in the Madison Valley. He was, in fact, the very merchant whose 1882 account books were an invaluable aid to the *Frontier House* staff and consultants in establishing the kinds of goods and produce such a store would have offered contemporary customers—and in determining what prices to charge for those goods. Despite his early success, however, by the time Bruffey moved his wife, Matilda, and their ten children to a homesteading claim on Mission Creek up the West Boulder River, his fortunes had apparently suffered a change for the worse. "I was broke," he declared in a memoir written years later.

Ever the entrepreneur, George Bruffey immediately set to work to remedy that situation. The entire family joined in, spending that summer of 1891 clearing brush and picking rock. They planted potatoes, cabbages, and other vegetables. They cut wood and

Blacks weren't the only Southerners to seek a new life in the West, especially once restrictions against homesteading by Confederate veterans were lifted. Former rebel Andrew Jackson "Jack" Smith, shown here in front of his cabin near the West Fork of the Gallatin River in Montana.

hauled it ten miles to town, where they sold it for $4 a cord. They built a house large enough to shelter their sizable family, assembled a herd of twenty dairy cows, and made preparations for the winter ahead. Indeed, the Bruffey team had managed so well that each of the children received a new pair of boots for Christmas. A measure of success by any homesteading standard.

The potential for that kind of success would have appealed to Southern families whose fortunes had been drastically altered by the vicissitudes of the Civil War. Under such circumstances, Southerners looked with particular interest to Copp's *American Settler's Guide,* keying on the promise that "th[ose]...burdened with debt" would have an opportunity "to start anew in the race of life" on homesteads in the West. And by 1883, the year Karen and Mark Glenn of Tennessee would have been considering a move to Montana Territory, the restrictions of the original Homestead Act against anyone who had "borne arms against the United States Government or given aid and comfort to its enemies" would no longer have been in effect. Those restrictions had earlier been a stumbling block for Confederate veterans like Green Blakely, who headed to Montana Territory in the mid-1860s. Moving around among the various mining camps, Blakely and his wife, Matilda, worked toward saving enough money to buy a small farm. However, once the

Homestead Act was amended in the late 1860s to allow former rebels to claim their share of free public land, the Blakelys moved to the Boulder Valley, squatting on prime acreage there well before the 1882 agreement in which the Crow ceded that portion of the valley to the United States. They were soon caught up in building a home and working the soil, apparently viewing the dangers of squatting on Indian land as mild when compared with those they'd experienced while living in the midst of a Civil War. And, yes, in due time, the patient and persistent Blakelys were able to prove up on the homestead they had prematurely claimed as their own.

With no lack of historical parallels for Southerners settling in what one early resident termed "that Rebel Paradise, Montana Territory"—and given the personalities and philosophies evident in the *Frontier House* application and interview tapes of Mark and Karen Glenn—had that couple been living near Nashville back in 1883, they would likely have been every bit as eager to pull up stakes and head to Montana Territory as they were, given that opportunity, in the year 2001. And given the number of deserted mining cabins that dot the landscape of that area even today, the Glenns of 1883 might even have been as lucky as the Glenns of 2001 in finding a homesteading site with a deserted cabin (though that cabin would not likely have been as cozy or well constructed as the one Bernie Weisgerber and his crew built for their *Frontier House* experience). After all, now and again such bits of good fortune did indeed brighten the lives of those who dared "to start anew in the race of life" as homesteaders on the American frontier.

Nate's new wardrobe was typical. In contrast to his modern outdoor gear, which was lightweight, waterproof, and hard-wearing, he was inheriting a bulky pile of cumbersome and less forgiving garments, mostly made from heavy woolens. The stiff leather boots, although sturdy, were a harsh contrast to his aerodynamically designed trainers.

Nate's clothing provided for the frontier:

1 pair of good pants	2 pair of woolen socks
1 chambray shirt	1 dozen pair cotton socks
1 heavy, full-length coat	2 pair heavy work pants
1 pair of dress suspenders	3 heavy cotton work shirts
1 pair of dress boots	2 woolen work shirts
1 pair of work boots	2 pair flannel drawers
1 straw hat	6 pair cotton drawers
1 union suit	1 woolen nightshirt
1 pair heavy work gloves	1 cotton nightshirt

Amidst great hilarity, an exchange was made, modern T-shirts and sneakers cast aside for their formal clothing. With so many layers it probably shouldn't have been a surprise that it took so long for the women to ease themselves into their new, unforgiving outfits. A chemise, corset, corset cover, petticoat, double-lined skirt, and a lined bodice cocooned each in an ensemble that weighed in at

an extra ten to twelve pounds for every woman. Twenty metal stays sewn into the corsets constricted them in a taut body press. (Girls had been trained into corsets from tender ages in the nineteenth century.) Small wonder that the lower level were drawers that were open at the base, as the removal of each layer for a call of nature would have taken an eternity. A bulky bustle pad located just above their behinds completed the look, to howls of laughter. As they lined up in their finery, they made a short but important trip, as was traditional, to have a photograph taken. For many homesteaders this was the last moment to have a respectable image taken of one and all. A valued portrait to send home to show all was well in their new lives. As the Clunes lined up in front of the gunpowder flash, tears welled in Adrienne's eyes. Forbidden by Susan Cain to wear makeup (for only actresses and street girls did so in the 1880s), Adrienne was feeling vulnerable under the scrutiny of the video and photographic equipment. She bravely held on until returning to her hotel room, revealing her pain to the video camera:

> *I have been looking forward to this day for so long. Not being allowed to wear makeup today was such a shock. I am prepared not to on the frontier, but thought we would have had it today. I thought I looked like crap, I am sorry. Tried not to cry all day. Did not want to cry for camera and photos, so I had to bottle it all up. It ruined my day.*

The recognition that makeup should not have been so important dawned shortly after as Adrienne came to terms with the loss, but like everyone else about to depart to their new life, she was having to build up an acceptance that everything that sustains us in our daily lives was about to change.

Radically.

LEFT: Nate is fitted in his wedding suit.

RIGHT: The Brooks family.

RIGHT: Adrienne and Aíne are coaxed into their corsets.

BELOW: Reminiscent of period portraits, the Clunes look glumly into the camera.

"Buy Two of the Largest Trunks You Can Find"
Preparations for the Journey West

In September of 1885, having settled upon a homestead claim in the Bridger Mountains of Montana Territory, David Christie sent his wife, Emma—who was home in Blue Earth County, Minnesota—a series of letters explaining how she was to prepare herself, the children, and the household goods for the trip west and detailing plans for the proposed Northern Pacific rail journey from Mankato to Bozeman. They were to travel first-class, David insisted, since any other accommodations would mean she and the children—five little boys and an infant daughter—"would be put into a Smokeing carr with a lott of rough men.... If it does cost a little more it is the proper way." Emma's first-class ticket would cost $56.75; the three children under five would travel free, but the three older boys would be charged half the adult fare.

Beyond money for fares, Emma would need enough cash to "buy 2 of the largest trunks [she could] find." In those trunks she was to pack David's auger, handsaw, square, and ripsaw, as well as the family's clothes and bedding. She could bring her flatware but not her dishes, David said, since they were heavy and could be cheaply replaced in Bozeman. Weight was definitely a consideration, since each full-fare passenger was allowed only 150 pounds in personal belongings. Emma's sewing machine would therefore have to be left behind, perhaps to be shipped later.

All in all, David figured that Emma could ready the family and the household for the trip west for something under $150. By his reckoning she could raise at least that much by selling her milk cow and fattened hog and "everything else that she could." If she realized more than $150, David wrote, it would be best if she kept only a few dollars for herself and sent all the rest to him, as he had only $12 left after buying the materials needed to build their house. Somehow Emma managed to get together the money, pack her trunks, and close out family business in Minnesota. In October of 1885 she and the six little

Christies boarded the train at Mankato, carrying with them "plenty of lunch and Didies." Two days later they were in Bozeman.

In 1886, the Tintinger family of Iowa, lured by the oldest son's glowing reports of life in Big Timber, Montana Territory, sold "everything except the farm, which...sold two years later" and headed west. Two of the older boys rode in the cattle car with their father and the family's dairy cows, pigs, chickens, and household goods, while the four younger children and their mother boarded an emigrant car. Though considerably more comfortable than traveling with farm animals, the emigrant car offered few luxuries. Passengers endured "long hard seats with no cushions," and "beds" were improvised by turning down two facing seats and pulling a blanket over oneself.

The Tintingers' journey took somewhat longer than the Christies' had, largely due to train delays and missed connections. Even so, their migration was a streamlined version of the trek across the plains made a few years earlier by Ada Colvin, a young woman bound from Whitewater, Wisconsin, to southern Nebraska to claim a homestead for herself. Having arranged to go west with neighbors traveling in a six-wagon train, she set out in late April of 1879 in the company of 14 people, 142 head of cattle, 8 horses, and 2 hogs. Three months later, on July 29, the colorful caravan reached its destination. The journey behind her, Ada immediately filed her claim in the North Platte, Nebraska, land office. But barely a month after taking up her homestead, Ada Colvin, sick, lonely, "and money all [but] gone," bought a rail ticket home to Wisconsin. Boarding the train at Table Rock, Nebraska, on September 17, she was sitting in her mother's parlor two nights later, no doubt grateful for the improved transportation that made her speedy return possible.

If Ada Colvin and Emma Christie traveled west with little money to spare, there were others who started that journey with pockets full of discretionary funds. En route from Iowa to Oregon in 1878, Mary Riddle bought herself "a watch and a revolver" in a trail town in Nebraska, while her husband, Moses, bought himself a fiddle. By her own account, Pamelia Fergus of Little Falls, Minnesota, had $750 with her when she started west in 1864, $100 of which she spent on a shopping spree in Omaha.

Most homesteading families were obliged to count on little beyond the goods they packed from home: chairs, beds, and bedding; cooking pots and kettles; medicine chests and recipe books; sewing kits and knitting needles; under- and outerwear for all; school books, slates, and pencils; journals, pens, and paper; the family Bible; and, if space permitted, favorite dolls, books of essays or poetry, playing cards, dominoes, and chess sets. For those traveling by wagon, packing enough nonperishable foods for a four-to-six-month journey was a major consideration. Sometimes a stove was added to the collection, sometimes a plow—rarely, a sewing machine.

Despite the constraints of weight limits, most women managed to pack at least a few things having more sentimental than practical value. Lenore Gale Barette used her mother's "gay colored quilts" to cushion her "few cherished dishes and other treasures" in one of the trunks that went west to Oregon with her. And once she had moved into her new home, she brought out other keepsakes from "the old home three thousand miles away" and placed them on the cabin's crude shelves: "a picture of grandmother's parents, a few books, the family Bible...." Among the items Mary Ellen Pease tucked into her trunk while packing for her 1888 journey west were willow shoots from her Eau Claire, Wisconsin, home. When she reached her Montana homestead, she saw to the planting of those shoots before she undertook any of her other settling-in tasks. For many homesteaders, such items, carefully chosen in preparing for the trip across the plains, became tangible if tenuous connections to families and homes left behind.

The *Frontier House* pioneers were equipped for their "journey" with many of the same goods described in the letters and diaries of those who went west a century or more before them. Their modes of travel were also designed to reflect the experience of their real-life predecessors. And the cost of their transportation—as well as the cost of the food, clothing, household goods, tools, books, and livestock they would need in the West—was based on extensive research in vintage sources: an 1883 Montgomery Ward & Co. catalog; records from an 1884 estate sale in Gallatin County, Montana Territory; 1884 and 1885 probate records from the same county; an 1881–1882 ledger from the Bruffey Mercantile Company of Fish Creek Station, Madison County, Montana Territory; and letters and diaries of actual homesteaders. More modern sources were also consulted: the National Railway Historical Society of Philadelphia, a consumer price index (CPI) conversion scale found on the Internet and used to establish the value of the 1883 dollar against that of the 2000 dollar, antiquarian book dealers, and the *Frontier House* assemblage of experts on nineteenth-century life in the West.

4

The Promised Land

aving been lulled into a false sense of security by two weeks of shorts-and-shirtsleeves weather up at Virginia City, we woke up in horror on the morning of May 20, the eve of our departure for Frontier Valley, to three inches of snow. Even with a fast thaw it could amount to a sticky journey through a morass of mud. Yet everyone was itching to keep to schedule. With three pairs of horses to haul the wagons and professional teamsters to pilot them en route from Idaho, plus a hundred other arrangements made to tie us in to a departure the next day, we had little option but to pray for the weather to turn in our favor. After our having driven two hundred miles east toward the homestead site, a day marked for relaxation became one of tense endurance for the families, occasionally punctuated by meetings guaranteed to raise the blood pressure. George, the local fish and game warden, warned how black bears and mountain lions in Frontier Valley might be on the lookout for an easy meal. Everyone was then introduced to the local doctor and emergency medical team who would be on standby in case of any accidents. Outside, snow turned to rain.

At 5 A.M. on Monday, May 21, the Grand Hotel in Big Timber was alive with a sudden burst of activity as our families prepared to leave the twenty-first century behind. A last chance to taste sugar-saturated cereals and drink decaffeinated coffee went largely ignored in the rush to be out in time. In the back bedroom the Glenns' video diary camera was whirring.

KAREN: *This is our last morning. Just had a shower and shaved those areas that need doing. Everyone is worried. Our clothes feel heavy. How is Logan going to pee? I can deal with everything—the food shortages, the bugs, the bears—but I cannot deal with this corset!*

Conor Clune watches as the horses are hitched to the wagons.

LOGAN: *Aíne says she is going to sneak in her makeup and hair dryer. I heard about this on the phone when she was talking to her boyfriend. Aíne is going to try and sneak in everything.*

By seven-thirty everyone was ready. The final encounter with the modern day was a twenty-mile journey by vehicle to the trailhead. Magically the weather had cooperated and a glorious spring morning was already doing a wonderful job of drying out the mud. Disembarking from the four-hundred-horsepower vehicle, our families were greeted by the sight of the three teams Rawhide Johnson had scoured the West to find. Magnificent tall horses that would, in just a few hours, convey our families toward their destiny on a two-day, fifteen-mile journey. Before departure, three "prairie schooner" wagons had to be loaded. From lists of possessions most commonly taken to the frontier, our consultants had made three stacks of goods, one for each family. Cast-iron skillets, galvanized buckets, wash boilers, saws, axes, storage barrels for food and water, the chests containing the families' newly acquired personal belongings, their clothes—each homestead required a considerable quantity of food. With the piles clearly exceeding the capacity of the wagons, the first job was to work out which would be the most valued possessions. A swift ransacking followed as brisk decisions were made and sharp debates held on what few items were essential. In the rush to be ready, Karen smashed two of her six eggs. Gordon, attentive to everyone else's needs, forgot to pack himself spare underwear. What quickly became clear was that the wagons that look so sizable through the wide-angle lens of a movie camera are in fact tiny. "We could fill this with just our books from home," observed Mark Glenn. Careful packing quickly filled the wagons to the brim. Small wonder that accounts of the era record how stoves and other heavy goods littered the settlers' trails as their bulk swiftly outweighed their usefulness.

Nate and Rudy faced their pile in quiet contemplation. Demonstrating methodical planning, a quality that quickly became their trademark, they approached the exercise like a mathematical equation. Having chewed over their priorities and carefully weighing (both metaphorically and literally) the importance of each item, they eventually managed to squeeze the vast majority of their provisions into the tiny wagon barring the stove and mattresses, which they chose to have delivered once their cabin was under construction.

BROOKS FAMILY SUPPLIES

1. Household furniture
woodstove, small
large traveling trunk, used

2. Kitchen and cooking supplies
cast-iron skillet and lid, 8.25"
cast-iron skillet and lid, 6.5"
tin skillet, 8"
Dutch oven, 5 qt

The Clunes look over their
worldly goods.

Mark Glenn struggles to
get everything loaded.

Dutch oven with feet
tripod with chain (outdoor cooking)
pot-lifter
stove shovel
stove scraper
tin bread pans
flat-bottom kettle and lid, 4 qt
large teakettle, 2 qt, blue enamel
cutlery—1 set for 4 people
cups, tin enamel
plates, tin enamel
bowls, tin enamel
tin plates
tin cups
maple-wood bowls, 12"
crockery mixing bowls
flour sifter
leather hot pads
wool hot pads
cheesecloth bag
butcher knife
paring knife
boning knife
skinning knife
can opener
ladle
wooden spoons

rolling pin
milk buckets, tin, 2–3 gal
cheesecloth
milk cans, small, metal
tin funnel, small
wood spatula
2-gal crock and lid for pickling
6 3-gal lard cans
water bucket dipper
broom
dustpan
thunder pot, tin

3. Laundry equipment
buckets, galvanized, 3 gal
washtub, galvanized, 11 gal
washbasins
washboards
hand washbasins
clothesline
clothespins
clothes bluing
rapid washer
starch
hard lye soap
soda

4. Bedding, tents, and tarps
feather mattress
pillows
quilts, cotton
wool blankets
double sheet
traveling tent

5. Crates, boxes, and barrels
wooden barrels and lids, 15 gal
wooden barrels and lids, 10 gal
burlap sacks

6. Lighting and fire
wall match-safe
matches
candle lamps
candle molds
candles
oil lanterns
oil lamps
wicks for oil lamps
replacement chimneys
kerosene cans, 1 gal
kerosene

7. Writing equipment
diary
account book
ink

lead pencils
steel pen nibs and holders
letter paper
envelopes

8. Fishing gear
fishhooks
fishhook holder
line, cotton
lead sinkers
pocket knives, Barlow style
knife-sharpening stone

9. Grooming supplies
castile soap
comb
toothbrushes
tooth powder
sponge for bathing

10. Men's grooming
men's hairbrushes
straight razor
razor-sharpening strop
shaving mugs
shaving brush
razor-sharpening paste
shaving soap
small shaving mirror

Most precious in the packing was food. Records of the day minutely detail just how much was recommended with careful reminders to travelers of what would be required to sustain their family. It was often many weeks before they could purchase essential supplies. From reading those accounts, food and hygiene consultant Sue Cain had worked out just how much each of our families should have allocated to them before their first visit to the store, planned in five weeks' time. Alongside the hardware necessary for frontier life lay those provisions: giant sacks of flour, beans, and cornmeal, with frugal amounts of luxuries from the day, sweet commodities such as honey and sorghum syrup. As the diet would prove a departure for our modern participants, it was decided to provide what, Sue anticipated, would be adequate amounts for the first phase. But Adrienne wasn't happy.

It seems that the food is to tide us over for five weeks. We were all surprised. I had thought it enough for two, maybe three weeks. After careful study of the list, I think we will have just barely enough of some items to last, provided we don't lose any to rodents, pests, or mold. Some items seem very sparse, one carrot per person, per week. [Vegetables out of season would have been rare in May of 1883. Our allocations were withered from months of lying over winter in a root cellar.] *There are little or no herbs; without many fresh vegetables the food will be very bland. I hope I can find some wild plants, herbs, and vegetables to make up the shortfall. The list seems very limited. I've been spoiled living in southern California, with year-round fresh foods.*

Most of the anxiety being expressed by the Clunes was that they had six members in their family, including three hungry adolescents. But Karen Glenn wasn't buying it:

I just walked by and heard the families talking about the rations, and I understand their anxieties, but what are they thinking? It was not a soft, easy time, it was a struggle, cruel and mean. But it was a good struggle. That's what brings a family together. Families aren't made of good times. They are made out of struggles, hardship, and pain and doing without. There are a lot of things I would have liked to have had. I do not have a sunbonnet, which any sound Southern woman would have brought. But there is a difference between what you want and what you need. In our life we are used to getting what you want.

More worrying though for Karen was the news brought by Rawhide. Despite the best efforts of a vet, their cow was still sick and he'd decided to pull her out of the wagon train departure. (Interestingly, all of the cows were eventually trucked into the valley as modern breeding for maximum meat and milk production has, apparently, eliminated the instinct or capacity for walking any significant distance.) Mark was despondent, requesting that a new cow be brought at that moment for his family's needs. Like earlier pioneers who lost livestock en route, he realized the urgent need for fresh protein now that his family would be away from regular supplies. At this point the Glenns sealed a deal with Nate and Rudy to buy their cow and calf. For Nate it was a canny financial move, netting him $32. For the Glenns it could just be the answer to their problems.

Despite the extra layers of clothing the women wore, some members of the Clune family appeared to be carrying a little extra weight that morning. To avoid body frisks, an honesty box was placed at the door of the store. Shortly before disembarking, everyone was asked, "Have you anything to declare?" Consciences were pricked and soon the box was loaded with contraband. The majority emerged from under Adrienne's dress where secret pouches of makeup

had been sewn into the lining. Eyeliner, lipstick, and foundation tumbled out—
fascinating choices as essentials of twenty-first-century life.

Before departure, a tearful farewell for Tracey Clune. Having been excited
to join Aíne on the adventure, fifteen-year-old Tracey always knew the moment
would come to say good-bye to her mom and dad. Bill and Cindy had flown in
to join the closing days of the training session, but with the wagons about to
depart, the traumatic moment was upon them when they'd have to hand their
daughter over to the uncertainties of the experience ahead. Tracey would be in
the care of her aunt and uncle for the next five months. "God only knows what
families must have felt to say good-bye to their loved ones in the past," said
Cindy as the last boxes were piled on top of the Clune wagon.

With Rawhide anxious to hit the trail the families were hurried into a hud-
dle. This was the last opportunity to get a group photo before the journey. But
coordinating twelve people, four dogs and puppies, eleven horses, and three
fully laden wagons for the pose took a lot of work. Ten minutes went by before
the shots were finally achieved. Throughout it all Rawhide watched nervously.
From our very first conversations about restaging a wagon train journey he
had warned that our biggest danger in the whole enterprise was the risk of a
wreck when bringing inexperienced people in contact with the powerful beasts

Poised for departure, the
families of *Frontier House*.

that would have to pull fully laden wagons. Having witnessed a number of fatal accidents, Rawhide, as the photograph was captured, was deeply worried, particularly as one team of horses was looking restless. His anxiety was shared by the professionals he'd hired to drive the three wagons. Unwilling to accept any further holdup, Rawhide eventually hollered, "We have got to go."

Retiring to camera positions, the crew recorded the departure of the wagon train. Many of the adults were riding horses alongside. Adrienne had elected to walk. Just as in the past, the youngest and the oldest family members rode in the wagons, sitting up high beside experienced drivers. After months of anticipation we were finally on our way. Watching from the sidelines, the production team was about to heave a sigh of relief when we were brought to the brink of tragedy. The horses drawing the final wagon pulled out smoothly at first but, eager to keep pace with the two other teams, broke into a run. In their path were riders, cattle, dogs, fully laden wagons, and most immediately, Adrienne. Wearing her all-encompassing sunbonnet, she could only see what was directly in front. She heard the commotion behind her as two draft horses cantered toward her. The hundreds of pounds of goods in the wagon being shaken furiously as it hit uneven ground made an eerie rumble. Our driver yelled for her to clear the way, but with no peripheral vision, Adrienne could only guess what was occurring and ran, literally, for her life. Everyone else watched powerless as the team thundered forward. (Watching this event on

Useful for keeping the sun out, it also blocked peripheral vision.

video shows just how close we were that afternoon to catastrophe.) Eventually horses and wagon parted company, the driver and nine-year-old Conor Clune being flung from the seat. The team, now freed of their burden, picked up more speed and bore down on the fleeing Adrienne.

Someone was watching over us that day. The horses must have passed Adrienne by inches. Conor lay bruised but uninjured where he fell. As we began to thank our lucky stars, Rawhide screamed, "Runaway team!" to warn of continued danger. (Fatalities in such circumstances often occur when loose horses turn and charge back to plow down witnesses of their getaway.) It took another three heart-pounding minutes before the horses were safely harnessed. With all animals restrained, we started to pick up the pieces and count our blessings. By some miracle no one was injured, though both Conor and Adrienne were visibly shaken. The only real damage was to the wagon, from which Gordon plucked eggs remarkably still intact. For everyone it had proved a defining moment, a timely reminder of just how dangerous the undertaking we had all been eagerly racing toward really was. Gordon was admirably calm about the close call:

Wrecked in too close a call.

First day out with family on the way to our homestead and we have had a challenge. In the first few minutes the horses ran out of control. It so very nearly killed my wife and Conor, who was on the wagon. But the family is in good spirits. Those horses are really spooky. Hopefully we will keep safe. We are a lucky family. Lucky to be alive. What we are doing is real and dangerous. You get a bit desensitized when you see movies where they go to the bar and they jump off the horses. I have been in Montana one day and already want to invent the combustion engine!

What's bewildering now is that within fifteen minutes of the incident the wagon train (now down to two) proceeded on its journey. The Clunes, like homesteaders involved in such incidents, had no option but to walk behind. Had we taken time to reflect on just how close we had come to disaster that afternoon, we might have lost our collective nerve and called it a day.

"This Is the Awfles Mess I Ever Was In"
The Darker Side of Wagon Journeys West

Traveling west by rail—as our *Frontier House* families would have traveled in 1883—not only saved time but lives, for crossing the plains by wagon could involve serious accidents, illness, and death. Our romanticized view of a brave little family riding into the sunset in a covered wagon leaves little room for the harsh realities of life on the overland trail. The journey West by wagon was interminably long, consistently uncomfortable, and fraught with dangers. True, adult memoirs of those who crossed the plains as youngsters suggest that most children saw the journey as an exciting adventure, but most parents would likely have agreed with Montana pioneer Pamelia Fergus, who termed her 1864 journey "the awfles mess I ever was in." A large part of Pamelia's distress was her concern for the health and safety of her children, especially her two youngest, fourteen-year-old Andrew and seven-year-old Lillie.

The dangers of life on the trail became all too apparent to the Fergus family early in their journey when young "Bell[e] McGuire fell out of the wagon" and the wheel ran over her instep. The child had "not stepet [since]," Pamelia reported by letter to her husband, James, who was awaiting his family's arrival in Montana Territory. Soon thereafter, another member of the train, five-year-old Frank Gravel, "bar[e]ly escaped with his life" after tumbling out of his family's wagon and under one of its wheels. The little boy sustained serious injury to his leg, as Pamelia wrote James: "The cords are badly drawed up [and the leg] will kneed great care to come out all right."

Pamelia, like others traveling in her train, had heard numerous stories of accidents of this sort, for wagon trains had been rolling west along the Oregon Trail for at least two decades by the time the Fergus entourage set out that spring of 1864. Catherine Sager, who had traveled the same route with her family exactly twenty years earlier as a ten-year-old, had been jumping from the moving wagon with her customary bravado—despite repeated warnings from her parents against such recklessness—when the hem of her dress caught on an ax handle in the wagon bed, interrupting her leap midair and jerking her downward into the path of the heavily loaded wagon. Before her father could halt the oxen, a wheel had passed over and crushed Catherine's left leg, so she endured the rest of the journey in agonizing pain—and spent the rest of her life as a partial invalid.

The longer the journey, the greater the potential for accidents, since even the most watchful parents became less vigilant as tedium and fatigue took their toll. Nightshirts and long skirts could burst into flames if a child wandered too close—or stumbled into—a campfire. Hot cooking pots and even rocks holding heat from the evening's fire could inflict life-threatening burns. And swift-moving waters, so inviting after a day of dust and heat, took their share of young lives. Children who wandered away from the camp to climb nearby boulders or explore sandstone cliffs were subject to falls and rattlesnake bites. Briers and prickly pear cactus barbs had to be removed from little hands and feet, and cuts and scrapes of all sorts had to be carefully tended to guard against infection.

Even within the family wagon, danger lurked. Unbeknownst to her parents, little Salita Henderson found a bottle of laudanum—tincture of opium, a fairly common item in medicine chests of the era. After drinking its contents, she complained of being sleepy—and lay down for a nap from which she never awakened. Adults had their share of trail mishaps as well. Pamelia Fergus reported that O. J. Rockwell, the man her husband had sent to accompany the family across the plains to their new home in Montana, had "got kicked by a mule," an accident that "strained his an[k]le," though he was recovering well enough to "step slitely on it."

Those on the overland trail were beset by illness as well as accidents. Dysentery, or "bloody flux," claimed children and adults alike, and a cold caught in a soaking rain might turn into pneumonia or "lung fever" that could kill in a matter of days, despite all the physics in the medicine chests most families carried with them. Castor oil, essence of peppermint, and boxes and vials of patent medicines were perennial favorites, along with quinine to ward off malaria, hartshorn for treating snakebites, and according to one pioneer, "opium and whiskey for everything else." That last category included childbirth, a common enough occurrence on the trail, though men and women of the nineteenth century seldom spoke about a pending birth—not even to family members—until the new baby appeared on the scene.

In prehomesteading days cholera had been the most dreaded disease on the trail, where poor sanitation was the rule rather than the exception. In 1852, Jane Kellogg reported an epidemic of the disease: "All along the road up the Platte River was a grave yard.... Most any time of day you could see people burying their dead; some places five or six graves in a row, with [wooden]...head signs with their names carved on them."

Pamelia Fergus, at about the time of her 1864 journey West.

Gravesites along the way were gruesome reminders of the uncertainties of life on the trail. Frightened at first by the graves they found at various campsites during their journey to Oregon, Martha Gay and her siblings soon grew accustomed to the gory landmarks, though they continued to be both drawn and repulsed by signs that wolves had dug into the graves of earlier emigrants, exposing remnants of bodies, including "long braids of golden hair telling of some young girl's burying place." Human skulls "bleached by sun and storms" were scattered along the trail, some of them bearing verses scribbled by earlier passersby.

For some emigrants, gravesites immediately conjured fears of being set upon by whooping, war-painted, bloodthirsty Indians, though in actuality disease accounted for 90 percent of all fatalities on the overland trail, and accidents were responsible for far more deaths than were Indian attacks. Indeed, in the relatively few bloody encounters that have been documented, more Indians than whites were killed. Nevertheless, tales of Indian "depredations" passed from wagon train to wagon train. "We have thought of the Indians

The grave of four-year-old Elva Ingram, who died on the Oregon Trail far from her Iowa home, is stark reminder of the dangers inherent in a family's move West.

[*sic*] and I guess all are [thinking of them] if the truth was known," Pamelia Fergus wrote her husband as her train neared hostile-Indian country. The company had begun to corral the livestock at night and were assigning men— including fourteen-year-old Andrew Fergus— to guard duty. But the small band of Indians who wandered into the Fergus family's camp one evening posed no threat to their safety. As the curious natives peered into her wagon, Pamelia, on impulse, "drop[ped] her teeth," startling the visitors, who had never before seen dentures. Though they ran off "screaming and yelling," they soon returned with more of their number, hoping to see her repeat the feat. When she did not oblige, the Indians eventually moved on.

Understandably worried when problems with their equipment caused them to fall behind the train they'd joined not long after leaving their home in Michigan, the Brooks family was assisted rather than attacked by a band of migrating Crow, who fell in beside them and kept them company for a week. Years later, Elisha Brooks, who had been eleven years old at the time, could still see the "old ox team with six wild, ragged children and a woman once called white" who straggled along behind their "colorfully dressed, well provisioned, and peaceful" Indian escort.

Such stories were largely the lore of the past for homesteaders bound for claims in Montana Territory in the 1880s. In fact, the overland trail itself had mostly been abandoned by then in favor of travel by river or rail. But the wagon continued to play a crucial role in most journeys West. When Emma Christie, her five little boys, and newborn daughter completed their October 1885 train trip from Minnesota to Montana Territory, the family was met at the station by David Christie, who was eagerly greeted by "a host of little chaps with rolls of Blankets and valises and Baskets and all saying at once oh here is pa." But the Christie family wasn't yet home. After an overnight stay in Bozeman, David hoisted Emma and the baby and then each of the five boys, aged ten to nearly two, into the farm wagon in which they would make the final leg of their journey—a day's ride through the narrow mouth of Bridger Canyon and out onto the site he'd claimed for them.

When Clark Shipman's two oldest daughters, Winifred and Gertrude, both in their midtwenties, decided to join him on his claim in the Judith Basin in central Montana, they made their way by carriage, boat, and train from Bethel, Vermont, to Bismarck, North Dakota, where they boarded a river steamer bound for Fort Benton, the head of navigation on the Missouri. A little more than a month after they'd left home, they were surprised by their father at Claggett Landing, some fifty miles shy of Fort Benton. But their trip was far from over. They still had to cover fifty bone-jarring miles in their father's farm wagon.

Like the *Frontier House* families who would emulate their journey over a century later, Winifred and Gertrude Shipman found that walking alongside a wagon wending its way across parched plains and through rocky gullies was sometimes more desirable than bouncing along on a wooden seat that grew harder with each passing mile, that handling a team of horses pulling a heavily laden wagon across roadless terrain could be a risky business at best, and that cooking an evening meal over a campfire after a day on the trail, then stretching out for a few hours of sleep on the hard ground, wasn't exactly what they'd bargained for in signing on as homesteaders in Montana Territory.

From out of the frying pan, into the fire. Six miles farther on, the *Frontier House* wagon train encountered a second major challenge that came as a sharp lesson in the hazards of life on the trail. Reaching the Boulder River, now in full flow from the winter snowmelt, we discovered our way forward blocked by a burst in an irrigation channel. Hundreds of gallons of water were pouring from a rupture high up on a hill, tearing out huge chunks of rock. A gaping hole now lay across the road; every minute we watched, the devastation grew worse. Our planned route was now impassable; the path to the river crossing was almost completely washed away. If our families had any suspicion that this had been organized as a test of their endurance, they soon realized it was otherwise as they witnessed the production team looking on in total bewilderment. After the wagon wreck, this second potential disaster looked set to put an end to our first proper day of filming. For Rawhide the recognition was equally hard to take. "This just isn't our day...I guess life doesn't change, 1883 or now." Now all eyes turned to him for a solution as, until we got to the land, Rawhide was in charge of the wagon train. Running way behind the anticipated schedule, he was faced with a dilemma. We still had a way to go before reaching the site where we could pitch camp for the night, and daylight would soon begin to fade. Thinking on his feet, Rawhide chose a risky option: he would take the more dangerous path by attempting to take the wagon train across a lower route that was badly flooded from the burst. Our families would have to walk a different route, high over the hill above the flood. Before the wagons could set off, however, a twenty-first-century solution appeared when a local rancher's bulldozer came to the rescue and cleared the piles of rubble blocking Rawhide's path. After seeing one team being spooked earlier that day, we watched in fear as Rawhide and Amber, the driver of the second team, cautiously approached the flooded road. After pausing for a moment to allow the horses to accustom themselves to the roar of the water, the two wagons pushed forward through the morass of rock and churning water. Having forded the river they were safe and dry.

Believers and nonbelievers alike all said their prayers that night. On the first day of our adventure proper, we had already powerfully experienced the pitfalls of life on the trail. Having witnessed the agonizing spectacle of the

Wagons roll—the journey begins.

wagon wreck, everyone must have reflected in their tents that night, What next?

ADRIENNE: *Quite a day. What an introduction to the hazards of the frontier. It was a little more real than I had anticipated and had wanted to get. It was close, I tell you.*

The anxiety of that first day was replaced by other feelings the next. Rising high over the saddle of land that overlooked their destination, our families had their first glimpse of the promised land. "It's humbling," said Nate. "A heaven on earth," thought Adrienne. Shafts of light bursting through the clouds did indeed lend the scene a biblical feeling. As they traveled farther down into the valley, a closer assessment could be made. "Good timber, water, and land," judged Gordon. "A great choice." (Had he seen the land two days earlier crisp with frost and snow, he may have felt differently.) Discovering her built cabin (an abandoned miner's plot was our model for one of the homes being complete upon arrival), Karen exploded with excitement. "You got to come and see my stove," she screamed from the window. "I have bragging rights!" After the tours were completed, the realization hit everyone that after this second exhausting day of travel, the light would soon dwindle, a cue for all to make ready for their first night spent in Frontier Valley. A communal meal of cooked ham and cabbage brought Karen's stove into much appreciated first use while tents were pitched outside. The horses were fed and watered. The dogs hurtled across the valley in packs, freed at last from the leads that had constrained them on the journey. Everyone was happy to be "home." As the temperature dropped, Karen offered overnight accommodation to the children in her, by now, snug cabin, but the Clunes chose instead to be squeezed, sardine-like, into their canvas tent.

Watching the families explore the valley with satisfaction made us ponder the hand we could have dealt them. Some settlers' diaries talk with excitement about the discovery of their land after the seemingly endless trek to reach it. Yet many record disappointments at the arid, flat, and featureless stretches inherited upon arrival after the best sites had been taken. Simply walking to haul water home took some homesteaders in dry-land stakes hours of travel each day. We could have based our project in such a site on the plains, leaving our participants high and dry without water or timber. Efforts to work the land there, without irrigation, would most likely prove fruitless. Like their counterparts who arrived at such places, our homesteaders may have found their enthusiasm blunted almost as quickly as their plow first bit the unforgiving soil. But here, despite our families' initial excitement at seeing green meadows, forests, and generous water, we felt sure our chosen site would soon reveal its true nature. The question in our minds that first evening was "How quickly will heaven turn to hell?"

The Glenns' homestead has a completed cabin.

"This Was Not the West as I Had Dreamed of It"
The Homesteader Faces Reality

For many a westering family, safe arrival at the homestead was cause enough for celebration. They had survived the journey, and come what may, a new life lay in front of them. But for others, arrival in the promised land brought tears of disappointment.

When Fanny Malone and her husband, far from their native Michigan, first saw their "home on the range" in central South Dakota, Fanny's heart sank. "I shall never forget the utter loneliness which almost overwhelmed me as we drove under dark skies...over the prairies with no path to follow...[watching] the buggy wheels...[gather] gumbo," she recalled in later years. Reaching the homestead site, her only impression was that of "prairie and sky"—and total lack of human habitation.

Similar reactions were recorded by Edith and Ida Mary Ammons, two sisters from St. Louis who were following the family tradition of "pushing back the frontier" when they took up a homestead in South Dakota. Unlike the Malones, the Ammons sisters went West expecting to find far more than "prairie and sky" awaiting them, having purchased, sight unseen, a relinquished claim complete with a partially furnished house. When that "house" turned out to be little more than a "packing-box tossed haphazardly on the prairie," its furnishings limited to a small, rusty stove, a homemade bunk, two chairs, and a wooden crate that served as a cupboard, the sisters were more than disappointed. "We were frightened and homesick," Edith Ammons recalled. "Whatever we had pictured in our imaginations, it bore no resemblance to [that] tar paper shack without creature comforts; nor had we counted on the desolation of prairie on which we were marooned.... This was not the West as I had dreamed of it." Indeed, their first thought was to return to their family in St. Louis the very next day—if only they could find someone to take them to the nearest train station.

Unable to find immediate transport out of their predicament, the Ammons sisters dug in and, in time, prospered in their new environment. Turning homestead into home, they discovered, took "backbreaking labor, and time, and the actions of the seasons." Gradually, as the sisters watched—and worked—the "drab and gray and empty" space took on new character. The "stubborn, resisting land" began to bloom. And as the land bloomed, it began to fill up. With the opening of "surplus" Indian lands that began in 1904 and continued on through the first decade of the twentieth century, the population on the plains of South Dakota increased dramatically. Fanny Malone, who had felt so disconsolate and isolated upon her arrival, soon had the comfort of seeing a neighbor's "lamplight shining through [a]...window through the night."

Long before the Malones and the Ammonses arrived in South Dakota, Julia Krattcer of Missouri had brought her own set of expectations west to Montana Territory. Having been left behind for six years to tend five children and manage the family farm in a border state torn by the Civil War while her gold-seeking husband sought his fortune in the West, Julia was more than ready for a change when George finally sent for the family in 1866. After wandering from gold camp to gold camp, first in Colorado and then in Montana, he had settled on land in the Gallatin Valley and erected a home to welcome Julia and the children. The "home" that greeted them was a rude cabin with sod roof, open holes for windows, and a dirt floor covered with wild-animal skins. An elk skin stretched over a frame served as the door. Whatever her hardships may have been back in Missouri, Julia must surely have stood at that elk-skin door and longed for the comforts of the farmhouse she'd left behind.

When Martha Lick Wooden joined her husband at the homestead he'd claimed outside Fort Hays, Kansas, in 1878, she didn't even see, at first, the home that he and their two sons had built for her, though she must have passed scores of similar dugouts notched into the Kansas hillsides and ravines all along her route without realizing they were there. Alighting from the wagon and entering the underground room, fourteen feet square, Wooden turned around and around, reluctant to believe that this was her lot. The out-of-doors had no greater appeal for her. "Bleak and lonely," she reportedly muttered as she surveyed the landscape. Having expressed her opinion, she accepted her fate and took up the duties of the homesteading woman.

Though "bleak and lonely" was the initial reaction of many a female homesteader, rarely does one find recorded expression of a man's disappointment upon arriving at his claim. Perhaps that's because, far more often than not, he had chosen the site in the first place. And he thought not in terms of making a home but of staking a claim. A claim that would reflect his strength and ingenuity, his ability to "tame" the land and the landscape. All the better perhaps if there was no mark of beauty or civility when he arrived. The raw environment was the slate upon which he would make his mark. The harder the task, the greater the glory.

5

Home Sweet Home

The sun crept over the mountains in Frontier Valley a little after six-thirty the next morning. For everyone waking up to the new day, a recognition must have hit home. All the rehearsal and hand-holding was over. Each family was about to be allocated its own 160-acre quarter section, their home sites located along the creek, half a mile from one another. Suddenly the pressure of the training period began to look like a gentle exertion. Gone were the three generous catered meals that had been served every day; so, too, the basic but comfortable hotel bedrooms for retiring to. For the next four and a half months, twenty weeks, 136 days, 3,264 hours…no matter how you looked at it, our volunteers were now on their own. As Adrienne said, shortly after waking in her chilly tent that first morning on the land:

> I was looking at the sunset last night and thinking, "How more beautiful can you get?" Then I lay in the tent and it started to get colder and colder, and somewhere in the middle of the night I lay there thinking, "Why did I ever let Gordon talk me into this? Oh, God. Only five months to go."

As she walked to their homestead site shortly afterward, her anxiety over what lay ahead can only have accelerated when she saw the scant start that had been made on their home. Just five layers of logs had been laid, a vague outline of the structure they would all have to work hard to build. "We knew we would have help in the construction, but somehow we imagined our home would have been more advanced than this," admitted Gordon as he gazed at the gargantuan task ahead. Stacked alongside was a huge pile of logs and joists. Luckily for the Clunes, they were already cut to size, peeled, and notched. To lighten the load Bernie Weisgerber

had preconstructed the shell off-site in advance. It now lay in over a hundred pieces,
ready for assembly. At eighteen feet square, complete with a second-level sleeping loft, their cabin would be the largest of the homes in the valley.

For Nate and Rudy an even bleaker prospect stared them in the face. Arriving
at their homestead site, they inherited nothing, save a stunning view. Nate reeled
at the beauty of their land: "Looks like we got the crown jewel, Pop." But no
home, outhouse, or immediate water source had been provided. With such a
mountain to climb Nate blithely continued to explore his new home, racing up
the hill overlooking the site. "Kristen will love it here." He looked like a king admiring his land, and it was easy to picture the excitement and pride settlers must
have felt after dreaming of their home for so long. A heady moment before the
onslaught of taming the land began. Rudy gently brought Nate back to earth:
"See anywhere you might want to build a cabin?" While exploring their site that
morning, Nate and Rudy stumbled across one small piece of evidence of man's
earlier encounters in the valley. A curious arrangement of poles lashed into a tri-
angular tunnel six feet deep had them both mystified. It was big enough to crawl
into yet clearly not of sufficient size to offer shelter. A sheep's skull just outside
was the final piece of the conundrum. Local knowledge solved the mystery: this
was thought to be an early bear trap, probably from the days when grizzlies occupied the valley. The sheep's head apparently lured the animal toward the entry,
where a rope tied between bait and trigger would dispatch a bullet from the gun
suspended within the trap. Crude but apparently efficient in their day, such devices
were assembled by trappers in the nineteenth century, who hoped to sell both hide
and meat.

In the middle of the valley, Karen and Mark Glenn sat inside their cabin somewhat bewildered. Aware that their neighbors faced colossal challenges in erecting

shelter, they were still pinching themselves at their good fortune. A small dwelling, almost comfortably outfitted, had greeted their arrival. An "abandoned miner's cabin" was on their plot of land, a re-creation of the sort of shelters that had been established illegally in the days when Native Americans and land-hungry newcomers intent on cashing in on the discoveries of gold had clashed over territorial rights. Small homes like these had provided shelter while the miners panned riverbeds for gold throughout the West. Taking our cue from history, we had assembled the sixteen-by-fourteen-foot cabin down in a sheltered recess between the creek and a wide expanse of meadow that looked out on a stunning view of forests and mountains. Inside, the newcomers had greeted a small stove, a few sticks of furniture, and a bearskin rug as though they had struck gold.

It took the Glenns days to feel sure that this hadn't all been a huge mistake. Truth is, homesteaders were never equally set up. For some, life was a battle just to stay alive, while others arrived with greater resources, even buying an established home. As Gordon and Nate began to struggle in those first few days to create their homes, the Glenns had a head start, their stove already baking breads and keeping them warm by night. As rain dripped on the Clunes in their tent, the Glenns were snug and dry in their beds. As sixty-eight-year-old Rudy dug a hole for the Brooks outhouse, Karen had already devised ways of replacing toilet tissue in the small outhouse that sat alongside their home:

Jasper, the Glenns' puppy. Dogs were working animals expected to earn their keep.

We are not cheating with the outhouse, but we have taken a rag and cut it into four and we use it to clean up. Then we wash it out in the creek and hang it on the washing line. It may not be the most sanitary thing in the world but neither are leaves . . . and it's a whole lot more comfortable. Oh, and to keep the smell down we sprinkle ashes after ourselves.

As Karen began learning her way around frontier life, Adrienne was having a harder lesson. The most important and in many respects the most humane change that domestic technology brought to the home in the nineteenth century was the cookstove. Prior to that, women cooked in primitive conditions, often over open fires. Without immediate hope of a completed cabin, Adrienne could only dream of such luxuries as a stove. For now she was back to basics with only a campfire to cook over. Up at Virginia City she had enjoyed the lessons with the Dutch oven; a popular tool for settlers while en route to their new homes, it allowed basic meals to be cooked in the open. Even in the wildest of country, food could be baked inside a fully contained iron vessel, set deep in the embers of a fire. Hot coals covered

Erinn and Karen were soon
immersed in frontier life.

the lid to prevent heat from escaping. Within hours of their setting up camp Adrienne was excavating a pit and building a fire to get their first meal going. It was a grubby introduction to the technique, with smuts and smoke chasing her around the campsite. "I'm dreaming of a stove," she said as the first attempt at cooking on the frontier got under way. Experimentation was the key as she noted to herself in her diary: "When using the Dutch oven, keep the coals very hot on top, use only one layer of embers underneath. This batter corn bread likes a hot oven. Bake hot approx. 40 minutes or 50 minutes." With patience Adrienne was not only able to master the device, producing accomplished and popular results for her family, but after a few days, she found ways of introducing flavor to camp meals: "This idea was inspired by frontiersmen Nate and Rudy, who started out making bread and decided to add cheese before baking. It was delicious." The hot cheese bread soon became a favorite in the Clunes' limited culinary repertoire.

With the wagons unhitched and the horses happily grazing after their exertions, Rawhide was a new man. It was as though a great weight had been lifted from his shoulders with the most dangerous part of his endeavor now behind. For Bernie, however, the anxiety was just beginning. With axes and saws specially sharpened it was time to entrust the responsibility of their use to our families. Having agreed that, after training, we would gradually segue from his full supervision of the families to a complete handover of responsibility, Bernie was now faced with making the transition. With his lead carpenter Jason and able assistant Gene, Bernie would now work on the cabin construction for the first few days to get the families going, but in a little over a week they would pack their gear and depart. "I know that was our plan," said Bernie as he began to fell the first tree for Nate's cabin, "but I can't help worrying for them all. This is dangerous work and we're remote out here." Back at our production center, a mile away, our emergency medics, Sarah and Tressa, sat nervously alongside the radio as axes were first wielded, saws swung into action, and meals cooked over open fires. In a crisis each family could break the seal on their "emergency box" to access vital equipment, most importantly a two-way radio to sound an alert. (With the nearest hospital almost an hour's drive away, compromising on safety would have been a recipe for sleepless nights.)

Thankfully, barring dozens of blisters and a few splinters, everyone stayed out of harm's way as the cabins began to take shape. Punishing days of long hours and exhausting tasks battered bodies more accustomed to the gentle exertions of our modern work. As demands grew in those first few days, the men took turns working at neighbors' cabins, heaving brace joints high onto roofs, hauling logs and hewing timbers daily with growing confidence and ability. At the Clunes' a staggering pace took hold as the precut pieces slotted into shape. But Nate, nicknamed the Timber Beast to mark his proficiency with the ax during training, had to learn the hard way. Every stage of his building was being done from scratch, and before long a myth of pioneer life was shattered. In movies, barns and buildings are magically erected in one day as the community turns out for a "raising." In reality

though, and despite the best efforts of all the men on the project, days could go by when it appeared as if nothing had moved forward on Nate's cabin. Progress was painfully slow, despite our having opted for the fastest building techniques. Instead of peeling the logs, we had decided to leave the bark intact, a shortcut in its day. The notch used on the corners was a simple but crude square tenon, devised for speed. (Bernie had copied it from similar joints he'd spotted on a group of intact pioneer cabins located nearby.) Every technique to cut back on time and effort, short of using modern power tools, was utilized to give Nate a fighting chance of having his cabin ready for the wedding, scheduled for just five weeks after his arrival. The incredible effort involved made us begin to doubt accounts in history books that suggest such shelter could be built in as little as three days. Watching Nate and Rudy at work was like observing an exercise in time management and diligent endeavor. They paced themselves for the marathon ahead. It wasn't long before Montana was throwing them extremes of weather. Days of rain pinned them to their tent. Heat would follow in ninety-degree blasts. Freezing nights followed at the end of the day. Throughout it all father and son grew closer.

Without a stove or cabin, Adrienne had only an open fire for her kitchen.

NATE: *It's really been great working with my dad and having this opportunity. I can't remember the last time we camped together and listened to his stories. He's sixty-eight and these are going to be memories that I will remember of him, and you know you see your parents in a whole new light when you are with them twenty-four/seven. I watch him clean his teeth and the different mannerisms you don't see when you are living in the same house.*

LEFT: Nate and Gordon work together to raise the wall of the honeymoon cabin.

RIGHT: Each notch took hours of work; typically, Rudy took it in stride.

You are seeing your parents almost at their most vulnerable. At times I catch my dad and he reminds me of my grandfather and that realization that he is getting older and that is a new experience. As a kid you put your dad on a pedestal, and to see the signs of age showing with him...I'm just really thankful to have this time.

"Some Kind of Home of Our Own"
Big Dreams and Humble Beginnings

Though log cabins—like those of the *Frontier House* families—were home to many a Montana pioneer, the first dwellings built by homesteaders varied according to the resources at hand in the regions where they settled. Thus, it's little wonder that in Montana, a state so varied in climate and terrain, newcomers built dugouts, soddies, and tar-paper shacks—as well as log cabins. These structures—and all their many variations—were usually considered precursors to the "fine frame house" that was the ultimate goal of most of those seeking a better life in the West.

When the Curtis brothers and their father, Joseph, filed on homesteads in the Gallatin Valley in 1864, they were less concerned about building a shelter than they were about turning the stirrup-high grass that grew on their adjoining claims into ready cash. Only after cutting the grass with scythes, raking it with crooked willow sticks, allowing it to cure, and hauling it by wagon to Virginia City to be sold for $50 a load did their thoughts turn to building a shelter against the coming winter. Three log cabins were hastily thrown up for Joseph, Wolcott, and Robert, but Wallace, who had settled on a site devoid of large trees, chose to construct a dugout.

By digging into a dirt bank, installing a wood-burning stove or stone fireplace against the back "wall," building a front facing of boards or logs or mounded dirt, piling branches, bark, and wood strips—and sometimes bits of canvas—across roof poles, and then shoveling on a generous layer of dirt, a settler could build a dugout that provided shelter, even if it afforded little light. While most pioneers considered a dugout a temporary home at best, Wallace Curtis lived in his for the next twenty years, too caught up in the business of homesteading to take time to build any other house.

More elaborate than a dugout, a sod house offered many of the same advantages—shade from the summer sun and insulation against the cold winds of winter. A detailed description of sod-house construction, written by Albert Rowan, the son of a Kansan who was practiced in the art, cites the use of thick (four-inch) slabs of grass with abundant root fibers that helped keep the sod strips from breaking apart as they were placed one upon the other. The thicker the wall, the longer it lasted and the better it withstood the elements. Most sod walls were built of twelve-by-twenty-four-inch strips laid out in a square or rectangle of the desired interior dimensions. Once corners were squared, a second row of strips was laid out against the outside edges of the first, with the two blocks being placed as close together as possible to effect a tight fit—and to bring the thickness of the wall to two feet. Each succeeding layer of sod was placed perpendicular to the last to "break joints." According to Rowan, no mortar or mud was needed to hold the sod strips together, and no special tools were required—beyond "a hatchet, a spade, a plumb and a string, a strong back, and a will to do."

This 1890s dugout near McCook, Nebraska, not only kept the family cool in summer and warm in winter but had the added advantage of being virtually windproof, a major concern in an area where fierce winter blizzards were legendary and where summer "breezes" were so strong and steady that the laundry seen in this photograph (far right) is drying horizontally.

While sod walls were too weak to allow for large windows, prefabricated glass windows could be ordered and shipped to the building site. Interior walls, hewed smooth with a spade, were plastered with a mixture of clay and ashes or with a finer form of plaster made from

These homesteaders' "improvements" included installing a plank floor; papering walls—and ceiling—with thick layers of newspaper to seal out dirt and dust; using a fabric partition to create a second room; hanging photographs, etchings, and paintings; adding touches of color throughout; and a "mouser."

native gypsum. The roof was generally made of rough boards laid side by side across rafters and eaves, then covered with strips of sod, generally grass-side down. Designing the roof with sufficient pitch to allow runoff of rain was a major concern. Some homesteaders accomplished this with a roof that sloped from back to front, some built a gabled roof that sloped to both sides from a middle peak, and still others bent long boards into a slight curve, then secured the boards to opposing eaves.

All three roof types had certain traits in common. First, they all leaked to one degree or another—and since the thirsty sod soaked up water like a sponge, a roof could continue to drip long after the rain had ceased and the sun had come out. Secondly, sod roofs attracted all kinds of pests, including centipedes. Apparently nocturnal by nature, these creatures would inevitably end up falling on a person sleeping below. If Albert Rowan's father was an expert at building soddies, his mother was an expert at protecting her sod-sheltered family. After tucking the children into their beds, she would spread a layer of newspapers over their covers, then listen through the night for the plop of centipede onto paper, her cue to rise and brush the insect onto the floor before smashing it with broom or shoe.

While soddies were common across the treeless plains of central and eastern Montana, log cabins were most often built by early settlers who moved onto claims with plenty of timber to cut. When David Christie wrote his wife in 1885 of the cabin he was building for the family in Bridger Canyon in Montana Territory, Emma couldn't help but envision a fine new dwelling out West, one more comfortable than the converted silo she and her children called home in Minnesota. David had written of the work he'd done that summer, felling "trees sixty feet high as straight as a gun barrel" from a forest within a mile of his claim, then trimming the logs, "snaking them out to the road," and hauling them onto the site, working toward a house "about 16 x 20 [feet] inside with a good high chamber." Thus one can only imagine Emma's surprise when she arrived at the claim site that fall to find only a pile of unpeeled logs and a stack of rough lumber awaiting her.

With winter coming on, she'd either have to rent a place in the nearest town, paying "10 or 12 dollars per month," or move into a one-room cabin with a lean-to kitchen, the claim shack David had been sharing with a cousin whose land bordered their own. She chose the claim shack, confident that her husband would persevere in his dream of building "some kind of a home of [their] own." Fortunately, that winter of 1885–86 was fairly mild through

Christmas, and under the watchful eyes of his five little boys David continued to notch logs and set them in place. Though slowed by heavy snows in January, he managed to have the roof in place by early spring, and the family was well settled in their new home by midsummer.

The log cabin built by the parents of Pearl Connor near Billings, Montana, was somewhat more sophisticated than the Christies', boasting a stone foundation and a roof made of planks. The unpeeled logs that formed the walls were covered on the inside with "what they called a house lining. It was white and it was all tacked on and it looked neat and clean." Even though it was a mere twelve by eighteen feet, the cabin had three interior rooms—kitchen, living room, and bedroom. All the floors were made of "plain boards," but Pearl's mother scrubbed the kitchen floor with lye "until it shone all the time" and covered the living room floor with woven-rag carpeting. Such carpets could be found in many homesteader cabins, and Iva Van Loan King, daughter of Dakota homesteaders, recalled watching her mother "operate the loom and change the rags...into pretty rug strips that were... just the right length for the living room."

When Danish immigrant Bertha Anderson followed her husband to a homestead claim near Glendive in eastern Montana, she found herself living in a log cabin previously occupied by a flock of chickens. Distressed by the look and smell of "the old gray logs," she covered them with newspaper, then spread canvas, carpet scraps, and gunnysacks over the dirt floor. A few months later, when the family moved into a new log home with a sod roof, Bertha once again set to work, this time

Thora Sanda, who followed her brother from Norway to Northwood, North Dakota, stabilized her shanty with rows of sod to keep it from being tipped over by howling winds or curious cattle. Note the snakeskin trophy that decorates the entrance—and the dog that kept Thora company.

This eastern Montana homesteading family enlarged their original log cabin, then added a new wing, casement windows, and an entryway with a screen door.

creating "ceilings...made of muslin tacked up tight to look like plaster." Though their new cabin had a floor made of wood, the "rough, unplaned cottonwood boards" were so hard on the tender feet of her little ones that Bertha spent most of one winter "sewing carpet rags [from] every available scrap," dying old flour sacks "a dull brown in copper." By spring the Anderson children were "rolling and playing" on their rag-rug-carpeted floor. But then came heavy rains that soaked the sod roof, so that the muslin ceiling "hung like a sack of mud" and the new carpet was "a dirty mess." Bertha Anderson surveyed the scene, torn by conflicting emotions—gratitude for the rain, despair for her ruined furnishings.

In the late years of the nineteenth century and the early years of the twentieth, many settlers took advantage of the availability of planed lumber and tar paper and threw up homesteading shacks or shanties literally overnight. Having filed her claim in the land office at Williston, North Dakota, in 1906, Cora Barnfather decided she should sleep on her homestead that very night and visited a nearby sawmill in search of building materials. The mill owner quickly "dug up some green cotton-wood boards from under the snow and built a 6 x 10 foot shack right on his bobsled," then hitched up his team and delivered the shack to her claim site, where he "cleared snow from a little spot and set the shack on bare ground [and] tar-papered it." Her home finished, Cora moved in and rustled up a late lunch for the man and his helper.

The portability of tar-paper shacks made them popular with homesteading families eager to claim more and more land by loading the little shanties onto wagons or skidding them along from site to site in anticipation of visits from the land agent. Portability also made such homes easy to sell, second- or thirdhand, to newcomers like Clara Troska, who claimed a homestead near Minot, North Dakota, and "bought a second hand shack, 10 x 12 feet, with two windows and a door." She paid $20 to have the shack moved onto her claim, then "bought new tar paper, a cot and a laundry stove with oven, put shelves on the walls for dishes and pans, [and added] a small table and a couple of chairs."

The Tintinger family, who homesteaded out from Big Timber, Montana, had similar furnishings. There were "plenty of grocery boxes for chairs," and the six children shared "a couple of home-made beds." Privacy was a luxury in such small houses. Often a blanket or sheet would be draped across one corner to separate sleeping areas. Children and even adolescents generally shared whatever beds were available. Sometimes an entire family slept in the same bed. Trunks and chests that had carried household goods and clothing across the country became important items of furniture in the new home in the West, used both for storage and for seating.

Humble though these beginnings seem today, they show the wisdom of those who deferred their dreams of owning a fine frame house with comfortable furnishings until they'd achieved their paramount goal: proving up on the land they'd claimed as their own.

After just one week of living in Frontier Valley, a living nightmare was taking shape down at the Clunes' cabin. Quite simply, expectations weren't being matched by the experience. Scrubbing out Gordon's only pair of underpants down at the creek, Adrienne gave us a frank assessment:

Aíne and Tracey have been complaining a bit about work. It's tough for them. They've been saying they want to go to the beach. This morning they asked why did you sign up for this, and I said I thought it was going to be fun. They looked at me and thought, you were so far off!

Just a few days earlier the Clunes had embarked on their adventure in a buoyant mood. Now a dark cloud hung over their camp. Their clothes, so crisply worn on departure day, were caked in mud. After the long walk to their home in unforgiving boots, Adrienne had been tending a large blister on her heel that now looked set to turn septic. Without makeup and shampoo the women were fighting a losing battle with Mother Nature after a lifetime of grooming. (A second haul of cosmetics they'd smuggled in was surrendered within their first few days, after Aíne and Tracey realized that there was no one to wear it for out on the frontier.) The food was proving monotonous. More than anything, six in a tent was losing its novelty value, "especially when you've eaten so many beans," added Conor. And tummy bugs unleashed severe diarrhea on a family without toilet paper or even the foundations of an outhouse. Meanwhile, Gordon and Justin (only now twelve but handed the full responsibility of manhood) were working like Trojans night and day trying to get a roof over their heads. Speaking to his video diary in a rain-sodden tent, Gordon opened his heart:

I can't tell you exactly what night it is, sixth or seventh, and we have had a big rainstorm. I have not had a chance to clean up properly since I've been here. Working on the cabin gives you plenty of time to think, and today I thought of something that is interesting. I was the one who saw the

Making do—trees become
kitchen walls.

*program on TV asking for volunteers to do this, and I see Adrienne with a
big blister on her foot and working hard, the kids are all grumpy, and if
anything that makes me want to work harder to do more for them. If you
think about it, I have got my beautiful wife out here and I am doing my
best to impress her. But the bottom line is I feel guilt for bringing my family
out here, and I have a hunch that homesteaders in 1883 had the same thing
in mind.*

With feelings running high, every new challenge, no matter how small, became
a big issue for the Clunes. Buttons popped off trousers. Blunt cutthroat razors
refused to shave. Interruptions dogged their water supply (which was piped from
an underground spring to avoid bacteria, which nowadays pollute every creek).
The fish stocked in a newly made water hole refused to bite to the simple hook-
and-worm fishing rods provided. Everything took on gigantic proportions, with a
salvo eventually being aimed directly at the project devisers. Two weeks in, Gordon and Adrienne deflected their anxieties and frustrations onto a safe target, the
camera crew. There were probably a dozen complaints in their long outburst, but
the main accusation was that life was hard enough as a homesteader without our
putting more obstacles in their way. They complained that their extra clothing,
delivered following the wagon smash, was now dirty and creased. (How else would
clothes have looked after an arduous overland journey?) That safety considera-
tions had prevented them from building a fire where they wanted. (After the worst
fires in living memory our adviser was, unsurprisingly, cautious.) And that rain
had leaked into their trunk and ruined their personal possessions. Even that their
tea leaves were not provided in a box and had spilled as a result.

Like father, like son. Gordon and Justin finish the doorway to the Clune "mansion."

ADRIENNE: *All of my clothes got mixed up with everyone else's. The girls have taken them and destroyed them, they wore them through the muck and the creeks. The homesteader may have been poor, but they would have guarded them. We just discovered this morning that all our best things are in the trunk and the stuff is soaked through and mildewy and the dyes have run. I cried this morning, everything I thought was safe from the girls is now ruined because of the rain. Real frontierspeople would have been smarter than that. They would have known where their things were. They would have hung stuff up properly, not put them in a trunk that will get wet.*

Watching the outburst it was hard not to have some sympathy as the Clunes looked close to drowning in their problems. But the harsh truth is that homesteading was often brutally difficult. People lived in uncomfortable conditions, often enduring bleak lives as accepted consequences of their lot. Their concerns took us back to the conversation we had had with Gordon and Adrienne as we sat comfortably in their kitchen sipping a delicious wine: "How hard should we make this experience?" To be authentic required a tough regime, but where to draw the line? Would any of us accustomed to the comforts of the twenty-first century have acted any differently from Gordon upon discovery of such unhappiness within the family? Their anger was a logical explosion of their growing anxieties, which had to find an outlet. But to have stepped in to help and fashioned the experience more comfortably would have been to betray the real lives of those who struggled at homesteading—the vast majority.

Up at the Glenns', Karen was feeling disappointed. Her offer to Gordon of letting his children sleep in her cabin during the first nights had been declined. It

Karen takes advice on planting the garden.

was cold at night and the spring storms were clearly making life under canvas uncomfortable for all. "Gordon did not want to let them do that.... It seems that every time I try to do something it is met with such gruffness and friction.... He's very difficult to like, and I'm at a point where I don't know if I want to try anymore."

The comfortable regime that marked the opening days of the Glenns' experience wasn't set to last. For newly arrived homesteaders getting a crop in the soil was often more important than erecting shelter. So with each day gradually warming it was important for our families to take advantage of the weather and make a start on working their land, especially as they had been warned that Frontier Valley would have a short growing season. The Glenns were particularly keen to begin planting a kitchen garden and on the last day of May were pleased to welcome a seasoned expert in the vagaries of Montana's weather. "Combat gardening is what you have to do up here," said visiting expert Jack Heaton. "You've only got around one hundred and twenty days free of frost here. There's hungry deer, bear, and every varmint known to man eager to eat up your garden, so you have to have faith to garden in such places." Jack should know; at seventy-eight, he's spent every year since boyhood gardening in similar circumstances. "Just last week I thought I'd judged it right and put my early potatoes in. This morning I woke to find the frost has had them already." Arriving with small quantities of cuttings and seeds suited to hard climates, Jack was eager to impart the importance of the garden to all the homesteaders. In a life where fresh vegetables are available year-round, it's easy to see gardening as a chore, offering little reward. But fresh, home-grown produce was a lifeblood to the settlers. Even a small garden could yield large rewards, especially if a root cellar could preserve such a rare commodity as flavor in a Montana winter. The first challenge was to turn the soil.

Returning for the day, Rawhide hitched up a late-nineteenth-century plow to our team of horses and looked doubtfully at the task ahead. "Don't expect miracles," he said. Turning virgin soil was a grueling task. Diaries of the time record how the backbreaking task often ended up dashing the spirits of the fainthearted, sending them packing back to town. Our efforts to break the sod were, appropriately, first tried up at the Glenns', where Mark had commented in his first video diaries that one of his main excitements was to plow a field. "Think of the pride you'd take in turning a few acres," he'd confessed. Now, straddling the plow between his legs, he looked less than composed as Rawhide readied the horses. As the powerful animals took off across the meadow in front of the Glenns' cabin, Karen, Erinn, and Logan watched with eager anticipation. Their land was about to yield those gold coins so famously promised in the railroad poster.

A hideous whine rose from the horses as the plow sank its teeth into the land. Below the surface, hundreds of years of knotted grass roots, boulders rigid from glacial formations, and layers of frosted soil bonded in a hideous union against the metal blade attempting to rip it asunder. It laughed at us, grounding the action within moments. Another heroic heave from the team and the plow was spat from the sod, leaving it to skid furiously along the surface. A small rip in the surface was all that showed of the attempt. A bead of sweat crept down Mark's face, almost as quickly as his grin had disappeared.

MARK: *Someone is going to have to describe to me how a schoolteacher from Tennessee came here to run a plow and break sod. It would be easier to drive a Ferrari than run that plow. I would have to practice for the year. It was one of the things I was really looking forward to. It's just like everything else on this homestead, everything is incredibly hard.*

Undaunted, Rawhide and the team tried again. And again. Vague interruptions to the ground cover were all that could be discerned, balanced against the enormous expenditure of energy by the horses. With mouths frothing they plunged again, tearing at the earth. Either the plow held steady, moored in the ground, or the steel blade jumped out of the earth and skittered across the surface. Karen, Erinn, and Logan were enjoying the show with unrestrained giggles. With admirable patience Rawhide changed tactics. "Find me the biggest rocks you can haul," he commanded. He retaliated by hitching a disc behind the horses (a series of blades intended to score open the ground). Lashing the heaviest rocks that could be manhandled out of the creek on top of the contraption, Rawhide set off with renewed vigor. The result was equally tragic, and not a little comic. Bouncing up and down like a buckaroo on a wild ride, Rawhide finally lost his patience. The ground had won the battle…just as it had on countless occasions before. "You'll have to go to it with a spade" was his best advice as he led the horses off to water and well-earned rest. Meantime, Mark showed his mettle and set to it by hand.

Unforgiving sod frustrates
Rawhide's attempts to plow.

MARK: *All of this stuff you think you knew they had to do, but the one word
you never heard—and damn the history teachers I had in school—was you
needed talent to do this stuff. It was not just backbreaking stuff. This looks
like it does not need skill, but, oh, it does. You know, conceptualizing before
we came out here has proved fruitless, what we thought about who we were
or what was going to happen, thinking we could conquer this... My feeling
about this place is, it has common points with a fever. I love it, but you have
got to be slanted, you've got to have a fever to do it. If you don't, you are
gone, this thing will eat you up, spit you out!*

Without the benefit of the plow, everyone in Frontier Valley had to resort to
hard digging to get their gardens under way. Forks and spades gradually took over
the excavation of small plots at all three households. Piles of cleared rocks and
stones slowly grew higher as each member of the families took turns to clear
their space. Jack had researched the types of vegetables that were historically
available to homesteaders and distributed a small selection of hardy varieties of
salad and basic root vegetables to all three households: beans, beets, cabbage, carrots, kale, broccoli, radishes, lettuces, onions, squash, and potatoes. "Just for fun
you can each have a tomato plant, too...but I doubt the frosts will see any ripen
up here." Jack's general tone was skeptical as he watched the planting. "Home-

steaders were up against it in their first years. I have heard of people here who simply turned the sod and planted stuff on top because it was such brutal work. The work in getting a farm started was beyond belief. We have no conception today. But they've got one thing on their side, it's good soil up here. I'll be fascinated to see if they succeed."

As the start of June brought warmer weather to the valley, it was time for our consultants to start heading home. Their work was over, and now it was all up to the families to make it alone. Preparing to return home to neighboring Wyoming, Rawhide left with concerns. In particular he'd been annoyed to see that some of the families' animals were not being cared for as well as they should: "They are their number-one asset here, and they've got to keep their needs in the front of their minds. They need feeding and caring for just as much as their children." In particular he was anxious about the Clunes' livestock, which had the run of the valley as the family had not yet had a chance to build a corral to contain their cow, her calf, and the horses. As cabin-construction adviser Bernie Weisgerber was leaving, he had a more upbeat report: "I think they've all done well so far. Nate is a natural with the tools, and I've no doubt he'll make it. Whether he'll get his cabin up before his bride arrives, I don't know." Watching Gordon pound away applying the cedar shingles to his roof, Bernie found himself surprised at his assessment: "You have to admire Gordon for his energy alone. To be frank, I wasn't sure if he'd pull it off when I first watched him in training, but he's a dynamo out here." After the pivotal moment of completing the roof, everyone was eager to

Karen cleans her cabin.

move inside the cabin. Justifiably proud of their endeavors, Gordon reflected on what he had learned thus far:

Where I come from, a lot of the work around the home is done by outside help. I have not mowed the lawn in sixteen years, so the children have not done such work. A lot of the jobs we used to do are not available for kids now. There is too little to do for teenagers now. I personally like work. The sooner this house is done, we can be warm and dry. We have slept cold and wet and it is not fun. Nothing wrong with work. It is therapeutic. Not a bad ethic for us.

If anyone had any doubts about the selection of our participants in this already almost absurdly difficult enterprise, the evidence was clear. In a matter of days it became obvious everyone had found levels of energy and ingenuity that confounded even the most skeptical of onlookers. Cabins rose from piles of timber, Adrienne produced hearty meals over open fires. The Clune children dug and built a neat outhouse. Somehow basic cleanliness was achieved while living in a huge mud bath. Karen made scores of improvements to her home including devising a rodent-free storage area achieved by hanging bags of food from the roof. Mark built a simple refrigerator to chill their dairy products, a "spring box," a wooden trunk sunk in the creek through which icy waters circulated. Every other spare moment he spent gathering wood for his winter log pile, an activity that prompted amusement from those who felt it a strange activity for summer. Nate even constructed a raised garden to defeat hungry predators and early frosts, and Gordon was soon carrying Adrienne over the threshold of their nearly completed cabin. The arrival of a stove at the Clunes' could have been the delivery of a Rolls-Royce, such was the delight written across Adrienne's face. Most profound though were the rewards being experienced by every participant.

In all honesty we would not have been surprised to see the departure of Aíne and Tracey during this hellish phase. What sane teenager would not have thought longingly of a summer on the beach or hanging out with friends in the mall? Having been open about their dislike of milking and the dozens of daily tasks foisted on them, they were clearly deeply unhappy in those opening weeks. But almost imperceptibly, they executed a remarkable change in attitude. Tracey offered her new assessment of frontier life.

It's good for people to do this as so many people back home are really lazy. If I talk to them on the phone, they are never doing anything. If they are unlucky, they have to wash dishes and they say, why don't they use disposable dishes? They are lazy. Here we are not lazy, you always find something

to do. I think hard work is good for people. Now I feel a lot more confident as I know I can do so much more.

Aíne and Tracey in search of their cow, Blanca.

It had been a hard landing in Frontier Valley. Whatever perceptions people had brought with them had been challenged by events. In the first weeks of their endeavors there had been one casualty: the romance of the encounter had gone. Having initially been seduced by the beauty of their new homes, everyone was now much more wary of their environment. As Karen said surveying her land:

I think it sad but my relationship with this place has changed. It's beautiful, but I do not trust it anymore. It is like a siren.

But, after their rude immersion, everyone was looking forward to better times. A wedding was around the corner. The days were getting longer and warmer. Summer was in the air.

6

Meltdown

Late afternoon, June 11, a call comes into the production center from a colleague. "I've just heard there's a big storm coming. A foot of snow is heading our way." He is well-known for his sense of humor, and we laugh. It is, after all, mid-June. Besides, the weather was mild. Even the locals on our team agreed it was likely to be a cool night. But snow? Not likely. Up in Frontier Valley our families bedded down for the night, Nate and Rudy in their tent, the Clunes in their far-from-finished cabin, the Glenns snug in their retreat.

Five miles down the valley *Frontier House* producer Simon Shaw had an early-morning wake-up call:

At 6:30 A.M. I awoke. It was freezing, even beneath generous bedding, in a heated home. Outside a sound of cracking, followed by a deep thud, brought me to the window. A blizzard had already dumped six inches of snow. Another searing crack explained the curious noises. The weight of the snow on the trees was bringing down the largest branches. Huge boughs on the cottonwoods surrounding my home were crashing down. A massive limb was already covering my vehicle. As the person closest to the families, it was important I make it up to the valley. Finding the road was the first chal-lenge. Deep ditches lay on both sides, but with a wind starting to drift the snowfall it was hard to make out the route. A journey that should have taken ten minutes turned into an hour's trek as, at each new corner, large treefalls blocked the path. En route, behind my truck a small convoy forms of Fron-tier House team members, similarly panicked to get up to the valley. No one else was on the road that morning; all the really sensible people were taking cover.

At the Clune cabin the day had started lightheartedly with Adrienne making a video diary through frosted breath: "I see cold people." Their home at least now had them under cover, but they hadn't had time to fill the large gaps, or "chinks," between the logs. In some places spaces of two to three inches allowed the wind and blown snow to penetrate the shell. It was almost as cold inside as out. The stove was battling against the freezing conditions, but with so many openings, it was a feeble attempt. "We learnt a hard lesson that morning," admitted Gordon, reflecting on the day. "We were so unprepared. In every way. We only had a tiny amount of wood cut. The cabin was unfinished. Adrienne had washed the day before, and with the constant rain, very little clothing was dry. We're used to enjoying snow at places like Lake Tahoe. But this was no fun. It was a bummer." As Gordon acknowledged, a homesteader had to be ready for all possibilities. Whatever the weather, life carried on. Struggling into the limited clothing available to them, Aíne and Tracey headed out to find Blanca to do the morning milking. What started as an exciting adventure, tiptoeing in foot-deep snow between falling trees, soon turned sour.

Wearing only chemises and thin coats, with blankets wrapped around their legs (even their socks were wet from the previous day's washing, so they'd tried substituting gloves for footwear), the girls soon started to feel the intense cold. Blanca and her calf had wandered off from the Clunes' newly built corral and were

Frontier House crew, Micah Fink, Simon Shaw, and Allison Whitmer, attempting to clear the route.

The misery of the cold is magnified by the thought of venturing out to milk.

half a mile up the valley at the Glenns', which required the girls to wade through the freezing water of the creek. Instead of leading her back home, Aíne and Tracey chose to milk Blanca where they found her. Just moments into the task, Mark Glenn emerged out of the thickening snowfall. The Glenns had only recently requested that the Clunes remove their animals from their corral so they could concentrate on looking after their own cows. Mark was upset at seeing the girls milking there. "You cannot milk her here. I have told you before. Your calf is suckling on our cows. Lead them away." Hard-hearted as it appeared in the circumstances, Mark was frustrated having had similar requests go unheeded before. As he turned to go back to his cabin, Tracey's protests fell on deaf ears. Already fatigued by all the difficulties, this was her lowest point with frontier living. Six weeks into the experience found her weary from the endless chores that hadn't been anticipated when the adventure first started. More than anything she was homesick and desperate to see her mom and dad. Tension had gradually been building between the Clunes and the Glenns over small matters, and now Tracey found herself the brunt of a simmering dispute over a cow. Tearful from the encounter, and with her legs numb with cold, she could barely continue milking. "It was the worst day of my life," recalls Tracey. Interviewed shortly after, Mark was unrepentant about his actions:

> I let the girls milk at our place this morning because they said they were cold. It irritated me a little bit when I said it would be better if you milk at your pen and Tracey said she was going to milk there anyway. Well, I've got news for you, this isn't your property, it is my property, and we are trying to do what is best for our animals.

With the weather deteriorating it was fortunate that Nate found the milking party shortly thereafter. He found Tracey in tears and complaining that she was so cold she could no longer feel her legs. Seeing how inappropriately dressed the girls were, he recognized the danger of frostbite. In characteristic fashion he quickly took control of the deteriorating situation and took over the milking, then accompanied Aíne and Tracey back home.

The early encounter with winter had proved a real test for all the families. The jokes about Mark's obsession for gathering wood now fell somewhat flat. A stockpile of dried goods and canned food beneath Karen's bed suddenly made enormous sense. Like those in wartime, the settlers clearly had to be prepared for all eventualities. The event became a sharp learning curve for all; no longer would anyone be caught short by the vagaries of the weather in the Rocky Mountains. But if readiness was a characteristic our families were fast learning, a different trait, so often associated with early settlers, obviously wasn't being displayed within the valley: neighborliness. True, our men had helped one another at key moments in house building, but the spirit of a close community, so often associated with pioneers, was a rare commodity thus far in our project. Small matters were becoming inflamed, such as the Clunes questioning if the Glenns had one of their milk buckets. An early incident recorded in Adrienne's diary sums up the growing tensions:

Mark Glenn retreats.

The Brooks camp.

Logan came over and played for a long time with our children today. During one of the games he lost a button from his suspender. Karen actually sent him back here later to have me send her two replacement buttons. It's amazing how people can be so petty.

A larger sense of togetherness and mutual support was, to our surprise, not on the agenda. (Interestingly, Nate and Rudy chose to stay in their tent during the nights of snow, despite offers of accommodation with the Glenns.) The growing lack of cooperation took us back to the perceptive way Nate had pinpointed this possibility when the families had first met during the training session:

The word that just came to my mind is independence *and how our society puts a value on being independent in building up a status and looking after a family and being judged by our neighbors on who we are. Balancing independence with interdependence. So I wonder how much through challenging and difficult times a sense of community will emerge or how much of a sense of independence? Is it the strong who will survive? Will it be adversity or community? Which will succeed?*

As the emotional distance between the participants grew, it proved a timely moment to reflect on our expectations. Was the lack of interest in working together as a community a reflection of the selfish society we inhabit in the twenty-first century? Or had we been naive to expect it to become a central element of our experiment? Perhaps the culture of communities working to help each other was another myth of homesteading life, distorted by romanticized storytelling. Despite all the recorded accounts of neighborly support, it's likely that real-life suspicion and antagonism across barbed-wire fences really took place. Perhaps the very nature of homesteading demanded people place their own needs above those of a remote neighbor. Mark Glenn, himself a distant relative of the families at the heart of the strongest American legend in family feuds, the Hatfields and the McCoys, in which twelve men died over a disputed pig, summed up his feelings:

I am not buying into this good-loving neighborly stuff as much as everybody else does. I don't think a lot has changed since then. We hope for good neighbors today. In 1883 I'm not sure if it would be rivalry or not. If you even knew your neighbors, you would be lucky, as they would be down the road a ways. It's not like you ran into them every day.

Coming out here today, you do not have companions anymore, you have competitors. You don't have friends, you have opportunities. We have brought that filth and that negative aspect from 2001 with us to 1883. Rivalries and competitiveness. I am competing with this land and weather. I do not want to compete with anyone. Sometimes I think it turns into an ego contest out here. I think the energy is meant to be extended to the land. I thought I had got away from that. It's crazy.

"People Are Ill-Natured and Look Only to Their Own Advantage" Community Spirit Is Tested on the Frontier

The first few years in Washington Territory for the Ferrel family of Wayne County, Iowa, were hard ones. "We went to work," Mrs. Ferrel said, "kept at it from early morn till late at night." But in the end she saw the value of the struggle: "Those hard times seemed to bind neighbors close together."

Many a homesteader would agree with Mrs. Ferrel that good neighbors were a large part of the reason they survived in their new environment. Neighbors provided companionship, entertainment, and news. More importantly, they provided extra hands for heavy work and help in times of trouble. "It would be so much harder if it weren't for...good neighbors," South Dakota homesteader Edward Boyden observed, then went on to put his own twist on the topic: "The only time one would spit in a neighbor's face was if his mustache was on fire."

But as the *Frontier House* families discovered, relationships with homesteading neighbors could be tenuous, even fractious. Not everyone was willing to share in ways demanded of "good neighbors." There was as much self-interest to be found among homesteaders as among any other people of any other time. Ole Lima, a Norwegian immigrant who settled with his young bride on a farm near Cooperstown, North Dakota, in 1894, was disillusioned by his experiences. "Times are poor," he wrote his sister back in the old country, "people are ill-natured and look only to their own advantage, so that he who does not use beak and claws to grab things for himself has to satisfy himself with—nothing."

A neighbor's selfish or careless behavior could lead to disappointment and worse. Bess Corey, a single woman who took a teaching position to support her South Dakota homestead, once loaned a piece of salt pork to a neighbor to flavor beans he was cooking for company. When the neighbor's dog ate the valuable morsel before he could return it, Corey was understandably put out. "I try to be neighborly," she said, "but sometimes I get disgusted." Animosities were sometimes acted out. According to South Dakotan Winifred Reutter, "Occasionally, neighbors got along like two tomcats tied by their tails and hung over a fence."

The isolation of the homesteader could have the strange effect of making neighbors who lived miles apart feel uncomfortably close. One's anonymity was lost, and no one's business seemed private. A person's daily life could quickly become the news of the "neighborhood." Though there could be comfort in this, it also lent itself to gossip and rumor mongering. That one farmer had "ordered a tailor-made suit" at a store in town was reported in a rural correspondent's column in the local paper. Such a purchase "puts people guessing," the columnist wrote—insinuating what? Another poor fellow was taken to task for the clothes he wore while working his fields: "[W]hat do you think of a man... preparing the land for seeding with a pair of low oxford shoes on with sox to match,... a claw hammer coat,... clean shaved, and smoking a cigarette[?]" the ever-watchful journalist reported. Surely such invasions of privacy, trivial or not, rankled—and perhaps drew return fire.

But nothing drew return fire—literally and figuratively—like encroachment on another's land or a dispute over wandering stock. Antagonism was particularly strong between the large cattle outfits of the high plains and the "nesters" who filed claims on land that had been considered open range by the cattlemen. The Olney outfit of Stanley County in central South Dakota had particular trouble adjusting to the presence of the new settlers. Olney's free-roaming cattle threatened many a farmer's crops and haystacks. And the homesteader who objected was taken to task by gun-toting cowboys in Olney's employ or by sheriffs who saw things Olney's way.

In 1879 the cattlemen's association of the Sun River Valley in Montana Territory took a similar stand: "[W]e the pioneers of this Sun River Valley, having established ourselves here at an early day and prior to all others," their resolution began—and then went on to declare that, by rights, the range was theirs. The newcomers had no alternative but to challenge such proclamations. In the first place, there was no legality behind them. The land the cattlemen were trying to preserve as their own was public land, open to settlement by claimants under the Homestead Act of 1862. If the cattlemen had the heavier artillery, the homesteaders had barbed wire. And they, like the families of *Frontier House,* learned to use it effectively.

Ranchers competed with other ranchers as well as with farmers. Granville Stuart, a significant figure in early Montana history, established a large ranch in the center of the territory where he meted out his own brand of vigilante justice to rustlers and kept a wary eye on his neighbors. "Near our home ranch," he wrote, tongue in cheek, in his *Pioneering in Montana,* "we discovered one rancher whose cows invariably had twin calves and frequently triplets, while the range cows in that vicinity were nearly all barren and would persist in hanging around this man's corral, envying his cows their numerous children and bawling and lamenting their own childless fate." This state of affairs continued, Stuart wrote, until he paid his neighbor a visit "and threaten[ed] to hang the man if his cows had any more twins."

Western lore is, of course, replete with stories of range wars—between cattle ranchers, between cattle and sheep ranchers, and between cattle and sheep ranchers and nesters. But it's harder to find admissions of unneighborly conduct within homesteading communities and even harder to find written evidence of friction within the home itself. Even so, given the close quarters and daily pressures of homestead life, it was only natural that conflicts arose, even if they rarely became a part of the written record. One way or another, tensions built—between husband and wife, between parent and child.

Indeed, for many frontier youngsters the harshness of home life was an overriding reality. "At table we weren't supposed to talk," one North Dakotan recalled of his childhood on the homestead. Talk during meals "was a waste of time," according to his father. The eldest son of a large family, this man told of being beaten by his father well into adolescence. In attempting to rationalize the harsh maternal discipline she'd known as a child, another North Dakotan attributed her mother's impatience and temper to the "big load [she had] to carry." If some mothers offered little comfort, others were their children's only protection from an abusive, drunken father. Oregon pioneer Elizabeth Gay's first husband was decent enough when he was sober, but when he was drunk—"which was most of the time"—he would "worry" the couple's little girl, Jessie, "till she cried and then he would beat her for crying." After years of trying to hold the family together, Elizabeth finally filed for divorce, thereby removing little Jessie from her father's abuse.

Within the home and without, tensions arising from the many challenges facing the homesteader could bring physical and emotional pressures that strained relations between family members and between neighbors.

As the snow began to melt, a natural opportunity for neighborly cooperation emerged. Almost a month into living on the land and Adrienne's worst fear was about to be realized. The Clunes were running short on food. With another ten days before our specially provisioned store would open for business, the family were out of almost everything but the least popular of their supplies: ham, cornmeal, and beans. Susan Cain, our food and hygiene consultant, had drawn up for each family an allocation of resources intended to last five weeks, based upon records of the era and on the requirements for basic sustenance for modern people. The Clunes' supplies were all but gone.

CLUNES

Unbleached flour	49 lbs/1 sack	Bacon 2 sides	10 lbs each
Cornmeal	49 lbs/1 sack	Ham	2/19lbs each
Scottish oatmeal	15 lbs	Lard	25 lbs

Hard cheese	6 lbs	Dried currants	1 lb
Great northern dried beans	10 lbs	Raisins	1 lb
		Dried apples	2 lbs
Cranberry dried beans	5 lbs	Dried prunes	2 lbs
Dried lima beans	4 lbs	Coffee	2 lbs
Dried peas	4 lbs	Black tea	1 lb
Rice	10 lbs	Lemon extract	1 bottle
Canned peaches	5 cans	Rose water	1 bottle
Canned pears	2 cans	Worcestershire sauce	1 bottle
Canned tomatoes	12 cans	Tabasco sauce	1 bottle
Canned corn	4 cans	Peanuts	5 lbs
Canned salmon	4 cans	Salt	5 lbs
Canned oysters	5 cans	Black pepper	$\frac{1}{3}$ lb
Crackers	4 lbs	Allspice	$\frac{1}{4}$ lb
Baking powder	1 lb	Cinnamon stick	$\frac{1}{4}$ lb
Baking soda	1 lb	Cloves, whole	$\frac{1}{4}$ lb
Cornstarch	2 lbs	Ginger, ground	$\frac{1}{4}$ lb
Cream of tartar	$\frac{1}{4}$ lb	Nutmeg, whole	2 nuts
Vinegar	1 gal	Mustard, ground	$\frac{1}{4}$ lb
Olive oil	1 quart	Potatoes	20 lbs
Sorghum syrup	1 quart	Carrots	5 lbs
Sugar	5 lbs	Cabbage	2 heads
Molasses	1 quart	Onions	10 lbs
Honey	1 quart	Turnips	3 lbs

With three ever-hungry adolescents to feed, Gordon and Adrienne were worried.

ADRIENNE: *I am not overly happy; we are pretty much out of sugar. With the lack of sugar I have stopped eating most other food as I do not like it. It is really getting to me. I am an absolute grouch because I cannot get sugar. I just put on the last of the ham for dinner. We've eaten it for a week, so the thought of eating more ham is not overly exciting. Ham no one likes, only Gordon and the dogs will eat it. We have one week of beans left, after that it is bread.... When I volunteered to do this I never thought starvation was one of the things I had to do. I can handle a lot but I am not going to handle this for two weeks, it is not fair.*

Interestingly, sugar, or the lack of it, was behind the food fantasies most eagerly imagined by Aíne and Tracey. Faced with another plate of corn bread and beans, they dreamed of their ideal meal to the video diary:

California dreaming —
Tracey Clune.

This is our California salad, this is a cheesy burger, this is my Dr Pepper. We want our Cokes back. We miss it all. And chocolate, Nestlé and Hershey's, were they around then? We have run out of our only treats, the tins of peaches have gone. Do you think people did not eat sweets? I think it's harder for us as we know what we are missing. They did not know what Coke and burgers were. They just knew beans and corn bread.

The cravings of the Clunes prompted some intriguing comparisons. Research shows that the average American today consumes three times as much sugar and sweeteners as back in the 1880s. That's an average of 150.1 pounds a year, or a staggering thirty-two teaspoonfuls a day, compared to 47.6 pounds per year in 1883. It's surprising given that we believe we live in a more health-conscious world, but many of our ready-made foods, including much of our bread, comes infused with sugar. A single can of soda contains the equivalent of five spoonfuls of sweeteners.

Up the valley, the Brookses were equally low on sweet goods, but Rudy was more philosophical about the loss:

I think some community members have brought the twenty-first-century attitude into 1883, rather than developing the 1883 attitude. And by this I mean it appears that families have spent a lot of time trying to live as if they are in the twenty-first century, especially with food items where things like apple pies and breads are being made. I think that food is important to us in 1883, but I think it has taken on a higher priority than is necessary for survival. That process has contributed to a lot of frustration, anxiety, and finger-pointing.

Susan remained confident (barring an inconsistency in the provision of small quantities of some sweet goods). She felt the amounts provided were consistent with the frugal amounts that had sustained settlers, particularly during the spring months when fresh produce was impossible to find. The late spring particularly found homesteaders having to stretch out foods as winter supplies ran low; some accounts called it "a starving time." But most curiously, the Glenns appeared to have an excess of food. Indeed Karen had been hoarding supplies since arrival. With the Clunes publicly questioning the amounts of food distributed to them, Karen became annoyed by their protests and showed our cameras her haul of saved goods. "We still have half a bottle of molasses. Raisins, dried apples, prunes, and honey. You make it last, just like you do at home." Alongside lay unopened cans and a goodly pile of dried goods. The traditional neighborly response would have been to give, or loan, each other supplies. "If they can't make it, they need to ask for some help. If you are too arrogant to ask your neighbor for help, then you are either going to starve to death or go home.... You make it last, just like you do at home—if you're used to working on a budget," Karen commented.

The Clunes came up with their own solutions. By trading for flour with Nate and Rudy, Adrienne managed to stretch out a few meals by filling the family up on bread. Nine-year-old Conor meanwhile had other plans. Frustrated by the lack of success at the pond in our valley, he embarked on a risky mission. Clambering over barbed-wire fences and across three miles of neighboring land, he set off one morning, fishing pole in hand, intent on solving the family's dilemma single-handedly. He got lucky. Straying onto the site of an abandoned homestead, he discovered an enticing fishing hole, complete with jumping trout. Hooking a worm onto his line, he cast into the middle of the pond. The youngest in the family returned a hero that day. Six large trout meant the Clunes ate like kings that night. A return the next day, this time accompanied by all the Clune children, yielded similar results. Now a fifteen-inch trout took pride of place on the dinner table. But their luck had run out. The owner of the pond had spotted the cheeky raid. Late that evening the phone rang in the production center: "I just want to say that this has got to stop." Years of careful care and management of the pond by the local ranch owner was under threat. "And don't tell me it wasn't those kids on your project. No one else is dressed like that 'round here." At our next meeting with the Clunes, Gordon was eager to defend their actions:

In 1883 I would have been able to feed my family by going hunting. These meadows are full of deer, which could give us a good meal. But 2001 bureaucracy doesn't allow me to do that most basic of things.

Current gaming laws (the first laws, enacted in 1872, tried to control the decimation of wildlife by early settlers) don't permit hunting large animals, such as deer, outside the late-autumn season. Efforts to obtain an exemption for our project were rejected early on by the fish and game department of Montana. However, one exception allowed us to deliver the families freshly killed game and, by doing so, to explore a fascinating irony. Hunting of game is permitted year-round on Montana's Indian reservations. The fertile lands the original homesteaders had moved to, including Frontier Valley, had originally been the preserve of legendary hunters, the Crow, yet when they were forcibly moved to their reservations by the arrival of the new settlers in 1882, they became subject to a hunting ban. The buffalo, their principal food source, had by this time been largely exterminated, the very last in Montana having been recorded as killed in 1883. Instead the Crow were given strict rations that proved inferior and inadequate and resulted in large numbers of them starving to death. Nearly one in three of their number had died by the end of the 1890s. But in a curious twist, the Crow would now feed our homesteaders. Their team of professional hunters set off early one morning to kill a good-sized deer or elk that could be shared among our families.

It was appropriate that the man bringing the food had strong family ties to the area. Dale Old Horn is a professor at Little Big Horn College and is passionate about communicating the real and sad events of the Crow. His ancestors originally came from Greycliff, a settlement nearby Frontier Valley, but like so many, his family was forcibly removed from the district in the 1880s and taken at gunpoint to a reservation in the Absaroka Range, where hunting was prohibited, with disastrous consequences. So delivering the haul of venison to our new homesteading families found him straddling emotions:

I came here with mixed feelings. Here's homesteading and it reminds me of when my people were so put upon. When so much fear and suffering was happening. My first feeling is, "Look at this beautiful country rich in game and fruit. All of this used to be my people's land." It also reminded me of the treachery of the U.S. government and of the Christian churches who ran the agencies, and it was under their hand the starvation policies were formulated. My people did not sell, they were forced off this land. When the Crow people were moved off this territory, it was at gunpoint, so the concept that this was "free land" was a wide misconception. I have remorse and I am a little angry remembering how it was for my people. But we come to learn my people's story, not how a white historian would tell it . . . the more we learn about each other, the more we will understand each other. Even though there are people who are driven by greed and a need for power, there is a great force among humans, that is humanist, which says if you treat me well, I will treat you well. There is peace in that. Rather than wronging and angering you, which has no happiness. Human existence is always searching for peace and happiness. Maybe we will find that.

Savoring the opportunity to discover the real history of their new home, our homesteaders made an eager audience for Dale. The discoveries were sobering. Newspaper accounts in the 1880s in Montana reported that Indians were dying at a rate of three to four a day from starvation. Moved to reservations, they'd further become susceptible to diseases brought in by the white settlers. Today their lives are little better. Large numbers of the Crow now live in poverty. Dale explained that far from being "savages," as all Native Americans were depicted at the time, the Crow had befriended the white settler from the earliest encounters. Yet successive treaties made with the U.S. government left them in ever-worsening conditions. Listening to Dale's stories that evening, everyone in our families was prompted to reassess the way in which this land had originally been settled. Karen Glenn, herself part Native American, was most moved by listening to Dale:

I was so excited to apply to take part in this project, but as I did research into the background of homesteading, I realized that I was going to be representing the people that drove Native Americans from this land.... What makes me angry was that the U.S. government played the Indians and the settlers against each other. They wanted people out here to expand. So I believe we, the homesteaders, went in very ignorant to this. If I was in 1883, I would have been ignorant to their plight.

7

A Bride Comes West

Almost two thousand miles away in Boston, Kristen McLeod was getting ready to say farewell to the modern world.

KRISTEN: *June 24, 2001. Now it's all starting to feel much realer. I'm starting to have to say the strange good-byes. "See you in October as Mrs. Brooks. Sorry, I really don't think I'll be in touch much." I can't imagine really saying good-bye in 1883. I don't know if I would have been able to do it.*

For women heading West in the nineteenth century the stakes were high. Forsaking family and friends in the relative comfort of the city in favor of a new life on the frontier was fraught with risk. Chances are they would never be reunited with their loved ones back home. Often their vision of the future was of a romantic adventure. The reality was too frequently in sharp contrast, as they traded their former lives for a daily regime of drudgery and isolation. Yet countless women took the gamble, either as solitary homesteaders (many of whom proved successful) or by joining their husbands, who regularly went in advance to set up their new home. Twenty-eight-year-old Kristen was about to step into those shoes. Parted from her fiancé Nate for six weeks, now she was beginning to experience much of the anxiety and uncertainty faced by those about to embark on a journey of no return:

What am I doing? Why? I just want Nate. I am alone in my feelings. I am afraid to go.... My Nate is gone. I can't even talk to him. I don't want to go. I don't want to stay.

For Nate and Rudy the pressure was on. A month on the land and the cabin was far from finished. As the days lengthened, so, too, did their efforts to build the shelter that would become the honeymoon home. Aware of the urgency, Mark and Gordon became regular visitors, eager to hasten the construction. As a July fourth wedding beckoned, a concerted community effort began to take shape. Every man on the frontier was pitching in; even the boys showed up to lend a hand: hauling logs, cutting out windows, sealing the roof. Meanwhile, as the women in the valley planned their contributions to the big day (each planned a wedding cake as a gift to the couple), their thoughts were for the bride. Since the training program where they had met Kristen, the women had undergone a sharp learning curve on the reality of frontier living. What had seemed realistic in Virginia City had proved way off the mark, particularly for Adrienne. Her typical day:

Up at daylight to start the fire—not always easy, especially when you're freezing cold and your hands don't want to move. Use the latrine. Boil water for washing buckets, hands, and dishes. Make coffee—try to grind the beans the day before. Serve breakfast, usually biscuits or bread I make the day before. Clean up. Girls go milking at sunrise and take care of the horses. Skim the cream, wash buckets again. Begin preparation for lunch. Keep fire going all this time. Still early morning. Keep water boiling all day, not easy when all you have is one medium pot and one Dutch oven. I'm also really short of containers, buckets, bowls, etc. I spend hours a day shifting things from one container to another. Cheesecloth's sterilized each time I use it. I strain the milk through a cheesecloth folded four layers thick. This is done morning and evening when the girls return with the milk. By lunchtime I bake bread. Favorites seem to be buttermilk biscuits, scones, and corn bread. When there is time between meals, I sew buttons back on for the boys, most of whose buttons have fallen off. I also try to wash my face and moisturize and tidy my hair. (Moisturize with cream for cow udders.) We churn butter twice a week, Monday and Thursday. Monday is also laundry day. That is a huge chore; it takes all day, boiling water, washing, scrubbing, rinsing. Our clothes get filthy here in the outdoors, climbing in and out of the creek, up and down dusty trails, milking cows and tending fires. They stay clean for about half an hour. I've cheated and washed some of my clothes before laundry day, as I cannot bear to be filthy. After lunch it's clean up, start preparing supper. After supper, scald milk cans and buckets, strain milk, put in creek. Clean and season the cast-iron pots and skillets. Wash up and put all food away safely for the night. Leave kitchen ready for the morning. Wash face and brush teeth in the dark, usually very cold now. Go to bed.

And the next day saw the same activity, only this time it might be raining, which meant walking around in sopping wet clothes. With six people to keep fed, inevitably much of Adrienne's day was spent preparing meals. The moment the dishes were done, it was time to start cooking the next meal. There was little variety in what she could prepare. For a woman who took great pride in producing interesting and varied meals back home in the modern world, it was becoming a depressing chore to keep serving beans and corn bread. But it wasn't just the monotony of her existence that was eating at Adrienne; she was lacking any satisfaction in achievement:

> *For the men they have something to show for all their work. Look at all the work they have done building our homes. But I work all day, too, cooking and cleaning, but I have nothing to show by the end of it, nothing concrete to show for all my efforts.*

Compounding it all, she was now feeling lonely. Gregarious and popular back home, here Adrienne was desperately missing the company of women. After the tensions with the Glenns she wasn't feeling well disposed toward Karen. Feeling friendless on the frontier, Adrienne broke down to the video diary:

The simple joy of a window curtain flapping in a breeze.

> *I really miss my friends…I really miss my girlfriends… It is isolated out here. I love the Brookses, Nate and Rudy, they have come twice with firewood. I think the world of them, they are terrific neighbors… I miss people, having other women around, to confide in. It's lonely here. You are so busy doing these tasks that you do not have time to think about yourself. Which is probably good, as the minute you start to think about other women having easier lives, you start to feel sorry for yourself, and the moment you do that you can start crying. The moment I start feeling sorry for me I have to kick myself. This is a place where if you are the type of person who could get depressed or down, you would have a hard time getting above that. These had to be tough women.*

Only toward the end of the project did Adrienne confess to having experienced bad days of depression out on the frontier. Days when she could barely bring herself to get out of bed or afternoons when she felt so low she just wanted to lie down and cry. Recognizing the changes in Adrienne, Gordon diverted his energies shortly before the wedding to turning their cabin into a home. Windows were finally cut into the logs to allow light to penetrate the darkness Adrienne spent all day working in. She noted, "What a difference the window makes! This cabin was like a dark cave without it. Now we have light and a beautiful breeze that blows through the cabin. I feel quite lighthearted and happy. Amazing how such a simple item can change one's disposition." Spurred on by her reaction, Gordon swiftly followed with a series of work units, a table and chairs.

Women's labor was hardly glamorous. It was backbreaking, monotonous work. But it was Adrienne's efforts that fed, washed, warmed, and dressed her family.

Not for the first time, he questioned if volunteering his family for this hostile experience had been a smart move:

You have to ask yourself, what sort of a dumb fellow would have brought his wife out to this?

"I Don't Know How She Did It but She Did"
The Lives of Women on the Homestead

"Westward I go free" may well have been the cry of the pioneering male, but the jury is still out as to how westering *women* felt about that slogan—and as to how they would respond to a related question: Was the frontier experience a liberating one for women? Responses to that question would likely be as varied as the westering women themselves.

"One year this day I entered upon my new duties," Colorado homesteader Amelia Bus confided to her diary in September of 1867, "and when I look back over the past I have no wish to live another such year." Having been reluctant to leave her home in New York and follow her husband West, she'd found the transition difficult. "[I]f I could feel duty called me here I could be reconciled to [having given] up all my former privileges and the society of friends," she wrote.

In contrast, consider the optimism and enthusiasm of Elinor Stewart, a widow who had supported herself and her young daughter as a washerwoman in Denver before she took up a homestead claim in Wyoming. "Any woman who can stand her own company, can see the beauty of the sunset, loves growing things, and is willing to put as much time at careful labor as she does over the washtub," Stewart wrote, "will certainly succeed; will have independence, plenty to eat all the time, and a home of her own in the end."

"Willing to put...much time at careful labor" is certainly the operative phrase here, for the work of the homesteading woman—whether married, widowed, or single—was truly "never done." In addition to taking care of all their traditional duties, women on the frontier frequently crossed gender lines to assist in chores outside their own sphere. Often the woman was the major provider for the family's immediate needs. It was her garden, her milk cow, her hens, that put the food on the table and provided the cash (or bartering power) for trips to the store. "My mother was a hardworking person," the son of a Colorado homesteader recalled in later years. "She...kept us all eating out of that garden.... If it weren't for [her], we couldn't [have] survive[d]."

When Montana homesteaders John and Dora Mos and their four children moved onto a claim east of Sweet Grass Creek in 1896, John built a house and a barn of logs, and Dora started a garden. By 1901 they had seven children. While John plowed, seeded, and harvested, Dora tended those children, milked cows, and raised chickens and bees. She sold butter, eggs, and honey to neighbors and merchants for the cash needed to buy staple goods and whatever clothing she couldn't make herself. She wasted nothing: brown paper, string, buttons, zippers, old garments, cans, jars, mail-order catalogs, hand-me-downs, and made-overs were used and reused. Socks were darned, quilts made, mattresses ticked, pillows

The care of barnyard animals was generally the responsibility of women and children.

stuffed. Clothes were washed in a large tub filled with water heated on the cookstove. Laundry soap was made from lye and tallow in a soap kettle. Meats, fruits, and vegetables were dried or "canned by the hundreds of quarts"; cabbage was turned to sauerkraut in a large crock behind the cookstove. Bacon and ham were cured in a vat filled with brine "sufficiently salty to float a raw egg."

Stanton and Guadalupe Brannin settled in Sweet Grass Canyon, not far from the Mos family's claim, seven years after migrating to Montana from New Mexico in 1896. The Brannins had thirteen children, some already eligible to settle on homesteads of their own by the time the family moved to Sweet Grass County, and Guadalupe became the matriarch of an entire community as well as of her own family. "I guess you would call her the mother of everybody," Anita Brannin Hoyem, the youngest of the thirteen offspring, commented years later. "Anytime [anyone] came to their home up here in the Sweet Grass, it didn't make any difference what time of the day it was or night…she would feed them." Guadalupe Brannin also took over the care of grandchildren who were the same ages as the youngest of her own children. "I don't know how she did it," her daughter marveled years later. "She sewed [all our clothes] by hand…just sewed them. That's all there was to it. I don't know how she did it and did everything else." The "everything else" included not only the usual household tasks, but also tanning the hides of the family's herd of Angora goats. She was midwife to many an expectant mother, and she doctored her neighbors with her many herbal remedies—as well as her camphor and turpentine. "Anytime anybody got sick they would run to mama," her daughter recalled.

Chores might be never-ending, but a sense of playfulness could elevate one's spirits.

Just as Guadalupe Brannin was the center of her small community up Sweet Grass Canyon, Dora Mos could enjoy the company of other Dutch women whose families had traveled together to central Montana to take up homesteads. Not all frontier women had that good fortune. Minnie Craig was so isolated on her Colorado homestead that at times, overcome by sheer loneliness, she would step out onto the prairie that lay at her doorstep and yell into the wind "just to hear noise in [that] desolate place." The incessant wind and the vast emptiness of the plains took their toll on many frontier women. One homesteader described the landscape of eastern Montana—that fabled "Big Sky country"—as having the effect of an "upside-down bowl" that was gradually smothering the life out of her. A homesteader on the cold and windblown Dakota plains, where only the hardiest of flowers ever survived, once found a dandelion growing in her garden. Its brightness was such "a pleasant reminder of old home associations" that she "felt less lonely all that day," and she cultivated the odd little weed as carefully as she would have cared for a houseplant.

But to focus on fatigue, loneliness, and failed expectations is to cast too dark a shadow on the lives of other women who seemed to thrive on their homestead experience, women who could ward off bouts of loneliness by joining in activities with neighbors, even when their claims were miles apart. Quilting bees, barn raisings, even butchering of livestock, offered welcome opportunities for enjoying the company of other women. Dances, too, were a favorite and frequent excuse for socializing. According to one daughter of Dakota Territory, "everyone along the trail would climb into the wagon box that had been filled with hay or straw, old and young alike...[and] ride to some neighbor's house.... [T]he cook stove would be moved out along with other furniture, then with the violin the dance was on...minuet, waltz, Virginia reel, and polka until daylight when the stove and other furniture was replaced and everyone went home tired but very happy."

Down in Texas, a quiet, dark night gave special joy to homesteader Frances Clack, who, according to her daughter's memoir, would "take her astronomy book out into the moonlight" and teach her children "to recognize Ursa Minor and Ursa Major, and...to locate the North Star." Clack loved the landscape on which she'd settled and gave her youngsters daily lessons on "the trees, the flowers, the rocks, the birds, and the animals that lived up and down the creek." Clack's sister Mollie, who lived on a nearby claim, would gather all her children around an old plank on which she had painted a keyboard. Each time a little finger struck a painted key, Mollie would sing out the note. When the family was finally

Nora Clough, Arizona homesteader, saws a branch she'll split and dry for stove wood.

Carrie Dunn, a turn-of-the-century Montana homesteader, attends to one of her many indoor chores.

able to afford an organ, hearing her children playing a well-practiced piece on a real instrument was one of Mollie's greatest delights.

Small triumphs of this sort buoyed the spirits of many a frontierswoman, including a North Dakota homesteader who, upon finding a huge sandstone, six feet square, on the banks of the Knife River, hitched up a team of horses and hauled the stone to her cabin as a front-door stoop—after her husband had declared himself too busy in the fields to take time for the task. Though their own tasks were legion, homesteading women seem to have marched through their days—washing and ironing, cooking and baking, cleaning and scrubbing, mending and sewing, planting and harvesting, paring and preserving, bearing and tending children, and assisting friends and neighbors—with a can-do attitude that helped assure their survival and that of their families.

Few women left detailed records of their day-to-day activities on the frontier, and even those who did—like diarist Emily French of eastern Colorado, sought not "the aplause [sic] of the people" but asked only to be remembered as a woman who had done "what she could," leaving it to children like Anita Brannin Hoyem to marvel, "I don't know how she did it, but she did."

Karen and Mark encountered tough times on the frontier.

As anticipation of the wedding grew stronger, up at the Glenns' a different atmosphere took hold. Both Karen and Mark were working harder than ever in establishing their homestead, but often in isolation from each other. Marital relations were becoming strained and arguments were occurring regularly. Being boxed in by a sixteen-by-fourteen-foot cabin meant they had no hiding place when tensions brewed. By now everyone in the valley had learned that such close living required a lot more tolerance than in our modern lives, where we have dozens of escape routes to avoid family confrontation. Four people sleeping within toe-touching distance had brought the Glenns into closer daily contact than ever before, and both Mark and Karen were starting to acknowledge the cracks it forced in their relationship. For Karen it prompted recognition of just how far women had traveled in 120 years:

> *I am a woman of 2001 living in 1883, and I am as trapped as women then would have been, as I cannot do anything on these grounds. I can really empathize with those women, and I am sure there were the same problems and I am sure women were not pansies, but they could do nothing about it then if they wanted a way out. So I am trapped until I get back in my real world, where as a female I have equal rights.*

Although nowhere as prevalent as today, divorce was a significant factor in life back then, reaching an unexpected high in 1880s America when one out of fourteen marriages was dissolved. Statistics show that unhappy wives initiated nearly two-thirds of these divorces, most often citing cruelty, desertion, drunkenness, or neglect by their husband. Western states and territories were also gaining notoriety for what were perceived as broad-minded or, as some said, decadent divorce laws.

Mark, noticeably more withdrawn from family relations, was spending a lot of time working on his own. It left him plenty of time to think:

My perception of trying to bring a modern-day woman to 1883 is it is like trying to put a square peg in a round hole—it fits but you have to force it really hard. The morals have eased up. I think they have brought a little bit more power than was available in 1883 then. Do I think that was right for them not to have power then? No. Look what came out of this. The push for the vote started at this time, and it was from this generation of women that it came, so these were pretty strong women in 1883.

Karen found herself channeling her energies on the frontier, tirelessly pushing to improve the lives of her family. Since day one she'd taken on the challenge of establishing a homesteader's life in wilderness country on a limited budget with admirable sincerity. Late at night as Erinn and Logan slept she was to be found poring over their account books, constantly planning and revising their plans for survival. By day she was the hub around which the Glenn family enterprise revolved, assigning tasks, reviewing progress. After their first few weeks in the cabin, Karen designed and built a loft space for the children to sleep in. Hacking down the trees necessary for the structure, she joked, "And they said it was a man's world!" She'd known from day one that her role wouldn't fit the neat assumptions about the traditional mom:

I am not the most domestic of females. I find it a lot more appealing to go cut wood or do livestock things than making butter or knitting. That's kind of frightening, trying to be domestic. I am a good mom but not a June Cleaver mom. That soft, cuddly, embroidery type of person.

In reality though she had identified herself with many women leading pioneer lives at the time. At the birth of the twentieth century the newly established state of Montana was predominantly male, with women and girls comprising just 38 percent of the population. For every woman the unifying experience was hard work, whether trying to scratch a living out of the land or working in the boisterous atmosphere of the mining towns. From such circumstances came the instinct to succeed, which characterizes so many women today out

Erinn and Logan celebrate Karen's sleeping loft.

The best man, Alan, gives his brother a much needed trim.

West who are adept at every working role. Although in 1883 women like Karen lived in a society that often ranked them as second-class citizens, it's significant that the next generation of Montana women won a major victory on the road to female emancipation, gaining women the vote in Montana six years before all American women were granted the privilege.

One feeling united Karen and Adrienne: they were both itching for the arrival of Kristen. As diaries of the day record, having another woman within walking distance (even if that meant a long trek) was going to be a godsend in their small world.

> KRISTEN: 6/24/01. *I can't sleep. My mind is whirring. I can't stop thinking about the wedding, about seeing Nate, seeing the other families. . . . I can't wait to be there and yet I feel there's still more to do to prepare. Prepare for the wedding. Prepare for frontier life. For the time away from the modern day. . . . Seeing Nate. What will he look like, smell like? How can I arrive with everyone looking at me and see Nate for the first time on my wedding day. . . and then jump into frontier living? No wonder I can't sleep.*

As Kristen was trying to imagine simultaneously stepping into a time machine and getting married, Nate was working diligently trying to complete their home. Five weeks on the land and he and Rudy had three-quarters of the structure complete. The rigors of getting it to near completion had brought Nate and Rudy to an acceptance of a different order in life on the frontier. Unlike the modern world,

progress in any task, however simple, was proving painfully slow. Whereas Gordon continued to work hell-bent for leather to achieve his tasks, Nate and Rudy had taken the challenges at a more gracious pace. Small wonder that the arrival of Nate's brother Alan, a week before the wedding, was greeted with such enthusiasm as the job of affixing the roof and preparing the marriage site beckoned.

"10 cents a go."

Alan was eager to know the state of personal hygiene in our families. In short, "Did they smell?" Without deodorants, heavily scented soaps, mouthwash, whiter than white toothpaste, and toilet paper, you might imagine our homesteaders smelled. True, on hot days if you were to stand downwind of some of them, you might experience a little of the "funk," as Nate put it, that is the natural consequence when hard work meets unshowered bodies. It was all part of the conditioning everyone in the valley had had to accept, but with the wedding day looming, for the first time in six weeks thoughts were beginning to turn to cleanliness. For the men particularly, a tidemark of grime and sweat was hard evidence of their day's work. The beauty regime on the frontier for the women was a brief daily affair: sponge bath with hot water and castile soap, chapped lips and calloused hands smeared with Bag Balm (the same cream used to moisten cow udders). At the Clunes' and the Glenns', once a week the largest galvanized washing pail was filled with hot water for a family bath. Woe to anyone who went last as the water was thick with the detritus of dirt-encrusted siblings. At the Clunes', Aíne and Tracey had developed their own regime for bathing with a brief plunge into the ice-cold creek. Ever eager to take on another project, Gordon was making other plans.

The bridal suite.

At the families' departure on the wagon train, everyone had taken the opportunity to inspect the store, which had been outfitted to sustain homesteaders' essential needs. For the most part the contents mirrored the initial outlay of basic goods provided to every family. But nailed to the wall on the outside was a treasured commodity: a full-size tin bathtub. The families had compiled lists of goods for their next store visit. The bathtub was at the head of Gordon's list. A few days before the wedding day, the Frontier Valley residents awoke to the sound of the creaking of a fully laden wagon. Atop the delivery of goods sat the tub. Not since the arrival of their stove had any single item made such a big difference in the life of the Clunes. Like the ultimate Christmas gift, it was greeted with unanimous excitement. Carrying it as though it were a consignment of bone china, Justin and Gordon proudly set it up in their tent, alongside the creek. Not only was this the answer to their personal hygiene, now Gordon had his first frontier enterprise: the Clune bathhouse was open for business at ten cents a dip.

Back in Boston, Kristen was having sleepless nights:

Who is Tressa and why does she know more about my wedding than I do? I feel so alone in this, without Nate, without being able to call him in Montana. Just me, trying to fall asleep, replaying my wedding image in my head over and over again. It's an overwhelming image. I absolutely lose it. I haven't seen Nate, Rudy, the Clunes, the Glenns, and all of a sudden there I am with my whole family about to see Nate again. I have that funny airport feeling when I haven't seen him in a while and I am so nervous for him to get off the plane . . . so I lie in bed picturing it over and over until I am so churned up with emotion, anxiety, and excitement that I have to turn on the light and get up. Last night I called the main Frontier House *office number in Montana trying to intercept somebody, anybody. I get Tressa.* [The medic who was on night duty.] *Don't know her, but she knows me. Says everything is "great" (even though letters I get from the frontier families suggest things can be less than "great"). I tell her I can't sleep. She says, "Well, you'd better get some sleep while you still have a bed." That is* not *what I was looking for.*

Perhaps the hardest part of what Kristen was feeling was the inability to understand exactly what she was about to step into. Letters from Nate and the women in Frontier Valley had given her a small sense of their lives, but reading them from the comfort and pace of the twenty-first century made them hard to connect

Nate picked wildflowers and decorated the cabin.

with. As all of our participants knew only too well, values from their previous life had swiftly been revised under their new regime. Matters that had seemed important back in the modern world were now of minor importance compared to the necessities of finding food, water, and shelter. Adrienne's new perspective had wrought big changes in her priorities:

> *This is the first wedding I have been to without makeup, but amazingly I don't care. It becomes so insignificant. My goal on the day is to be clean, to wash my hair, have clean clothes on. That for us will be a huge accomplishment. I was worried I would have gray hair coming through, but it's so ridiculous.*
>
> *This has been a learning experience for me how unimportant it is. There are so many types of beauty. Being happy with yourself and your life and here, that's more the type of beauty you see. It's a big switch for me but a good switch.*

As Kristen boarded her plane to head to Montana, a rush of activity began in the valley. A meadow seductively surrounded by mountains and deep in hay and wildflowers, was being prepared by the men for the wedding site. At Karen's and Adrienne's, two cakes were being baked; as was matrimonial tradition in the nineteenth century, both a bride's cake and a groom's cake were being made. Elegant icing edged the bride's as a magical creation was completed at the Clunes'. Karen meanwhile was trying to find a recipe for an eggless cake, having used the last of her egg supply for breakfast. Her mind had been elsewhere for days, still grappling with the distance that seemed to be growing emotionally between her and Mark:

> *I think marriage is a wonderful union and it is such a shame Mark and I cannot come back on course. It's unfortunate, it magnifies our unhappiness here. Which is kind of sad, I think, seeing Nate and Kristen so happy, and it magnifies the things that are lacking in this house.*

Now just twenty miles away, Kristen McLeod was settling into her hotel room:

> 7/03/01: *Arrived and am thrilled beyond belief. It sounds like everything is well in order. I look forward to tomorrow.... It's feeling realer. I knew it would get better once I got out here. I am so happy it is here!*

Wedding gifts were thin on the frontier, but for Nate a luxurious experience awaited at the Clunes'. Gordon had filled the bath to the brim with clean, hot water. Fresh soap, a sharpened razor, and a beer cooled in the creek sat alongside. Such small pleasures from our everyday world were magnified a hundredfold after six weeks of basic living and hard toil. The experience had visibly changed Nate, now noticeably thinner and exhausted from his exertions, but Kristen's new home was at last ready. Immersing himself in a true luxury on the frontier, Nate reflected on his unique situation: "I don't know how many couples spend six weeks apart before walking down the aisle, but I feel really comfortable and at ease." Trying to shave himself with a cutthroat razor with six weeks of stubble was less relaxing: "This must be the most dangerous thing I have done on the frontier!" Sitting alongside the newly completed cabin that night, he and Rudy shared a last meal together.

NATE: *This is the finest dining for bachelors everywhere, eating popcorn and fruit out of a can. At home we would be watching* Sanford and Son *and having root beer floats and eating popcorn. Instead we are drinking peach juice, watching the fire in the full moon on my last night of bachelorhood. I think I am pretty fortunate to have found someone I am eager to spend the rest of my life with.*

For Rudy this had been an unexpected turn in his retirement years. The call to join Nate on this adventure had come out of the blue with just a few weeks' notice. Far from his daily regime of golf and tennis in Oakland, he'd found himself working physically harder than he had in years. For six weeks he'd slept rough in a tent, often in subfreezing temperatures. Despite the privations, this had been a fulfilling experience that had drawn him closer to Nate. Rudy, admiring the small, sturdy cabin he and Nate had worked so hard on, became philosophical:

I am glad the first part of this journey is over. Whether it is maturity or age, it is a finite amount of time and I am excited about it ending and about the approach of a new beginning. Because it also means acquiring a new family with Kristen becoming a daughter-in-law. Tomorrow there is a little thing that says finis to another chapter in my life. That's how I feel about it.

Regulars at the Grand Hotel in Big Timber witnessed some curious guests on the eve of the wedding. From all corners of America, Nate's and Kristen's closest family and friends had flown in. Eager to participate, all had gone to extraordinary lengths to outfit themselves in period attire. On the evening of July third the pageant began in the bar as visitors aired their glorious costumes. Kristen was overwhelmed by their efforts, but the gathering reminded her that the wedding outfit selected for her by the historians was to be a simple burgundy dress. Frontier women had sparse choices in clothing; having a dress to wear exclusively for a wedding would have been highly unlikely. As much as her participation in *Frontier House* was a dream come true, she couldn't forget that from her childhood she'd been anticipating the splendor and excitement of her wedding day, a vision that had always pictured her in a white wedding gown. By eleven the next morning she was trying to persuade herself that she could look good in "a burgundy and cream sailor's suit" when a surprise package arrived from Nate. Knowing how hard this moment would be for her, he had been unable to allow Kristen a disappointment on her big day. Secretly planning with the costume designers, he had requested the manufacture of a simple

A surprise package for Kristen.

but elegant white satin wedding dress complete with a floor-length veil. It had been made to replicate a design taken from illustrations of period wedding attire. The result bowled Kristen over. A small card attached to the box bore his message: "Now the fairy tale is complete my beautiful princess—The White Dress. The Prince is awaiting. All my love." Tearful but ecstatic she set off from the Grand Hotel ready to face life on the frontier.

"Absolutely Indescribable" Weddings on the Far Frontier

When Nate Brooks and his fiancée, Kristen McLeod, decided that he should go out to Montana Territory in search of a homestead and she should wait in Boston until he sent for her and they could be married in the West, they were following a well-established pattern for young couples who dreamed of starting their new life together on land of their own west of the Mississippi River. Indeed, during the California and Colorado gold rushes of 1849 and 1859, thousands of men left wives and sweethearts back East and set out in search of gold, land, or adventure in the West. The discovery of gold in Montana Territory sparked yet another rush in 1860, and by the time the Homestead Act became law a couple of years later, quite a few of the lonely gold-seeking men were ready to trade picks for plows and take up homesteading claims.

Reunions between sweethearts—and between frontier men and the wives they'd left back East—were cause for much rejoicing. In the years before rail travel, the womenfolk most often followed their husbands west in wagon trains or on Missouri River steamers. Captain William R. Massie reported that a bevy of brides-to-be were on board his steamer, the *Twilight,* in the summer of 1865, all of them bound for Fort Benton, Montana Territory. Some of the bridegrooms were so eager to see their sweethearts that they traveled down the Yellowstone in mackinaw riverboats to intercept the *Twilight* at the river's confluence with the Missouri. "The scene that ensued when they got aboard was absolutely indescribable," the captain recalled years later. "Such a sight I have never witnessed before or since." The men had brought a minister downriver with them, and that evening sixteen couples were married in brief ceremonies aboard the *Twilight.*

More often couples were wed on solid ground by ministers living in gold camps or in rural communities across the West. For farming communities such celebrations provided welcome breaks from the work of the busy summer season, and nineteenth-century rural weddings were most often held at the homestead itself rather than in a church. Pearl Anderson, daughter of homesteaders on the Sheyenne River south of Warwick, North Dakota, was married in a "big home wedding" in 1908. The bride's mother was still frosting the tiered wedding cake at midnight the night before the wedding, but at least by that time the baked turkeys and hams were all in readiness.

That same year, Eva Sparr and William Christie, children of two Montana homesteading families, were scheduled to be married at the bride's home up Bridger Canyon northeast of Bozeman. A few days before the June ceremony, a late-season storm dumped two feet of snow in the mountains—heavy, wet snow that melted the next day, swelling

Mr. and Mrs. L. N. Beager at their wedding on the open prairie north of West Union, Nebraska, in 1889.

Bridger Creek and its tributaries and turning roads into gumbo. Since the flood also washed out the bridge between Bozeman and the canyon, the minister and many of the guests coming from town had to abandon their wagons, climb the ridge, and cover the last few miles on foot. Even so, the sun shone brightly on a wedding scene all set about with serviceberry and chokecherry blossoms and flanked by gaily decorated tables laden with the good foods prepared by friends and neighbors.

But the flood that had knocked out the bridge did put a crimp in the plans of those who had looked forward to the shivaree that evening. Unable to reach the hideaway cabin of the newlyweds, the revelers were forced to pound their tubs and beat their washboards on the far side of the swollen creek until Eva and William Christie appeared at the door of the cabin, waved them their good wishes, and sent them off into the night.

July fourth was another beautiful day in Montana. Worried the guests would stifle in the heat, an alternative, more shaded site was prepared under a canopy of cottonwood trees. Simple benches sat either side of an aisle cut through a grass meadow near the Clunes' homestead. A harmonium spotted in the window of a local antique shop was the only other addition to the scene. Yet the setting had the atmosphere of a magnificent cathedral, surrounded at each side by forested mountains. As the small congregation gathered, a group of curious deer gazed down at

The groom and bride.

the ensemble as if eager to witness the event. Local pastor Jim Holmand paced the field quietly rehearsing the text of what would be the most unusual wedding he'd ever perform. Around him the guests buzzed with excitement, resplendent in their outfits. After six weeks of wearing dirty clothes it was liberating for the *Frontier House* families to finally have an excuse to exchange their grimy and tattered garments for their Sunday-best outfits that had lain dormant since their arrival in the valley. The transformation was twofold: not only were the families clean and smart but now their fine clothes hung loosely from them, evidence particularly for the men of just how rigorously they had been working since their arrival.

Nate and Kristen finally saw each other as the small wagon bringing the bridal party made its way over the creek. As the pump organ wheezed into life, Aíne, Tracey, and Erinn escorted the bride, scattering wildflowers in her path. As she approached, Kristen took in the faces of the guests and, amidst the excitement of the occasion, remembers being shocked at how a matter of a few weeks had taken a toll on the homesteaders. Everyone looked so different, noticeably thinner, their faces drawn. Having read letters of their experiences, Kristen was finally seeing for herself the impact of the encounter and must have wondered what she had stepped into. After six weeks apart the couple finally met and drew each other into an embrace that spoke volumes of each other's loneliness, having been apart for the longest time in their seven-year relationship. Everyone laughed and used the moment to wipe away tears as, after what must have been a minute of eager embraces, the two finally settled to take their vows. Watched by their closest family and friends, they were united in a simple service they'd devised in the months spent in anticipation of the day. Like the pure white wedding dress, there were a few departures from the reality of such ceremonies at the time when frugal living and a more traditional form of religious service would have been the norm. Their vows saw gifts of cayenne, vinegar, honey, and lemon presented to symbolize the challenges and rewards of their future lives. These small changes to the purity of the homesteading experience were made in recognition that this was a real wedding, not an event staged for television. As Nate recollected the event, "I saw Kristen walking toward me as my fiancée, and I knew in the back of my mind that we were going to be walking down the aisle as husband and wife, and there was something so right about that. It just gave me a feeling of security and a calmness." A new chapter on the frontier was about to begin.

ABOVE: The bridal procession.   BELOW: Kristen and her father.

ABOVE: The Glenns enjoy the day.   BELOW: Logan dances with the bride.

Although rare, mixed-race marriages and unions were occurring out West during the era. Part of the appeal of such remote areas must have been the possibility of escape from the mores of the day, which would have been more strongly felt in towns. Yet shortly after the turn of the century Montana, along with many other Western states, passed antimiscegenation laws that would have stopped such ceremonies from occurring. Enacted in 1909, Montana's law declared a marriage between a white person and a black, Chinese, or Japanese person null and void. For a pastor, the penalty for solemnizing such marriages would have been a fine of $500 or imprisonment for one month. Even attempting to marry out of state and to return as a married couple was forbidden. It took until 1953 for such acts to be repealed.

Amidst the happiness of that day came one sad moment. Nate's dad, Rudy, was heading home. Sitting alongside him at the wedding, Rudy's wife, Eileen, must have been curious about the experience as she gazed at a changed man. Since she'd waved good-bye to him in California, he was visibly leaner, his beard now sprouted more gray, his eyes were shrunken from the exhausting routine necessary to complete Nate's and Kristen's home. Yet, saying good-bye to Frontier Valley was a hard moment. Despite the rigors and the tensions that had defined the experience thus far, this unplanned moment in Rudy's retirement had proved a rewarding challenge. Rudy noted, "I doubt many sixty-eight-year-olds came out to help their sons build a new life on the frontier. But I'm so glad that I had this chance." At the wedding feast he bade his farewell and thanked all in the valley for their friendship and support. Throughout the early endeavors everyone had found Rudy a gentle but important presence in the valley. Amidst the clamor to succeed and the raised temperatures those efforts wrought, he was always a reserve of calm and sound thinking. His departure would mark a turning point in the experience for all. We would all miss Rudy.

Farewell to Rudy—he'd be missed by all.

8

Do or Die

As Kristen awoke to her new life on the frontier full of excitement and anticipation, a different set of emotions were beginning to take shape farther down the valley. The buildup to the wedding had proved a wonderful distraction from the everyday grind. As the sun arose that morning, it was back to wearing shabby and dirty work clothes; the delicious meal of roast chicken and spring vegetables enjoyed so heartily at the wedding feast was traded for the regular fare of beans and corn bread. Most sobering of all was the recognition that suddenly there was no bright star on the horizon, and even the end of the project, in three months, seemed an eternity away. Moreover, the glory of the summer's day they woke to could only serve as a reminder that time was running out if our families were going to triumph in their endeavors. And there was so much to do. Everyone was conscious that in October they'd see the return of our consultants, who had promised that their final act would be to judge the likelihood of the homesteaders' chances of survival throughout the winter. Would they have enough food to sustain them across what might be months of freezing weather? Could they cut the formidable amounts of wood required to keep their cabins warm? Would they be able to feed their livestock when snow and ice could blanket the ground for up to half of the year? With Midsummer Day already long behind them, the residents of Frontier Valley were only too aware of the advance of time.

Everyone was growing anxious, too, about running short on money. Our families had each inherited a credit at the start of the project, drawn from records of the era by our historians. Although the families understood that the backgrounds they had inherited for the project were fictional, the adults were all growing incredibly serious about their finances and started to micromanage their limited funds as though they were their real-life resources. With the purchase of foods, building materials, and other family supplies, each household had, by now, eaten well into its reserves. One-third of the way through their experience the Brooks household had spent $121, a little over a third of their finances. At the same point the Glenns had spent $144, almost half of their funds. The Clunes, after two large food orders, were already in debt, having spent $272, $37 more than they'd started with. With the goal being winter survival, everyone clearly had a pressing task at hand. Just as the original settlers, the families were finding that the setup costs of their new lives were in danger of wiping them out, even before they got their first year of crops under way. As those homesteaders had also learned, the key to survival often lay outside their homesteads. Saddling up for a long ride, our heads of household—Gordon, Karen, and Nate—set off early one morning in search of solutions to their financial worries. They were about to meet a man who they hoped might help them, Hop Sing Yim.

At the end of the nineteenth century a remarkable number of Montana's population were Chinese. Figures vary, but Asians numbered between 5 and 10 percent of the community. Drawn by the lure of work on the ever-expanding railroads, they poured into the West, eager participants hungrily employed at rates often a fraction of those paid to their white counterparts. Along with the rail workers came Chinese merchants, initially keen to serve the needs of their countrymen, who with time integrated themselves into the new towns and homesteading communities, often running grocery stores, restaurants, and laundries. The nearest town to Frontier Valley, Big Timber, had just such an enterprising character at the end of the nineteenth century who appears in many homesteader diaries as a lifeline for supplies, Hop Sing Yim. One hundred and twenty years later the same name was being painted above the entry to our mountain store, a hastily converted cabin that had once seen a family of five raised within its tiny confines. Located a ten-mile ride over three mountain passes from Frontier Valley, it would be a major trek for our families, similar to the arduous journeys undertaken by early settlers on their rare trips to the nearest store. As the families headed over the first range, our storekeeper was putting the finishing touches to the cabin: tins of salmon and tomatoes in seductive wrappers were stacked at the window, pots of rare commodities such as black tooth-powder were arranged on the counter, while frugal amounts of newly ripened fresh vegetables graced the counter. Every item on sale was replicated from store ledgers found from similar small frontier outposts. Likewise, prices were all in accordance with costs of 1883, which revealed some surprising discrepancies. Eggs then were a highly valued commodity and sold at eighty-five cents a dozen; look hard today and almost the same deal can be found.

Running our store and playing the role of Hop Sing Yim was Montana resident Ying-Ming Lee. Watch his assured performance as our pioneer storekeeper and you'd have trouble acknowledging that in real life he is about as far removed from the role as he could possibly be. Lee is a rocket scientist, working out of the old mining town of Butte. How a NASA programs manager came to be our storekeeper

stems from Lee's keen interest in the history of the Chinese community in the West. As an active member of the Mai Wah society—the group specializing in the study of the large community of Asians who settled in Butte—he was eager to run our store. Once a month he turned his back on thoughts of interplanetary exploration and traveled back to the frontier of 1883 to open trading at Hop Sing Yim's. Just like storekeepers of the era, he was a sharp businessman, ready both to sell the array of goods available and to make deals with our homesteaders.

Gordon had barely arrived before he offered Hop Sing a taste of Adrienne's baking, eagerly produced in the hope that he might trade food in exchange for credit at the store. Karen, too, had entrepreneurial ambitions, requesting to sell her homemade butter and offering to take in laundry. Nate was keen to explore carpentry work he might perform, having honed his skills during the weeks of cabin construction. Each offer was eagerly explored as our families grasped the opportunity to do business at the store. In 1883 a real marketplace would have existed with the growing community of miners and other settlers for home-produced foods, clothing, and crafts. Another valuable trade made that day helped to put the Clunes back on course. Only too aware of their financial concerns, Gordon sold his team of horses for $160.

The long journey to the store.

GORDON: *It was vital for us to make that store visit. Not only was my family hungry, but we needed to manage our money, which meant it was good-bye to the horses, who had been used to haul our wagon. With the wagon smashed from the accident, we had no need for them, so they became a valuable trading commodity. They saved the day for us.*

KAREN: *I really enjoyed trading with Hop Sing Yim. It made you think so differently about how valuable a store would have been to settlers. Today a single member of the family can do the week's shopping in the blink of an eye, but back then you would have gone so rarely people would have planned such a trip for weeks and traveled for days to get there. Going over those mountain passes was amazing, but what an exhausting journey.*

"The Big Outside World"
The General Store and the U.S. Mail

For almost every homesteader the trip to town was a well-planned, much anticipated event. Lists were made and revised with "needs" winning out over "wants" as final preparations for the trip were made. Mattie Oblinger, a homesteader in southeastern Nebraska, wrote home in 1876 to her mother in Indiana of her preparations for her husband Uriah's trip to town. Since they had little cash and since credit was "pretty hard for anyone to get in Sutton," Mattie planned "to send a little butter and potatoes and corn and pickles" with Uriah, counting on him to barter such homegrown products for some badly needed staples.

While some homesteaders necessarily relied on their small local establishments, settlers close to larger towns served by railroads could find almost any item on their shopping list in stores like Langohr & Schmacher's, located on Main Street, Bozeman, Montana, in 1893.

If he could drive a hard enough bargain, she hoped he would also be able to bring home a few yards of calico "for the girls' dresses."

From the earliest homesteading days well into the early years of the twentieth century, merchants in small frontier communities stayed in business by being willing to bargain on prices, to accept barter, and to extend credit to customers hard-pressed for cash. "We charged most of our groceries," recalled North Dakota homesteader Flora Whittemore. "You were supposed to pay when you got your first crop.... [But] my first crop froze. You were not supposed to buy groceries that you didn't need. That was for sure."

Though some rural women like Whittemore, who was single, did their own shopping, the men of the household generally assumed that duty. Margaret McLeod Bryan of the Boulder Valley, the mother of nine children, once went five years without ever leaving her homestead, explaining, "It took two days in the wagon...to go to Big Timber and get supplies and come back and that was just too much...to do." When Kate Adams, who had fewer children to manage than Margaret Bryan, piled the kids into the wagon for the annual autumn trip to Big Timber with her husband, Ed, it was the beginning of a two-day event. The family would make the long journey into town, spend the night at the "elegant" Grand Hotel, purchase their winter supplies and retrieve the "big box" from Montgomery Ward the next morning, then pile into the wagon again for the slow trip home. "The big box was a magic container," the Adams children remembered, "holding special dainties, all sorts of dried fruits, raisins on long stems, special clothing, and mysterious packages that later appeared on the Christmas tree."

For the Lundberg family of eastern Montana, as for many a frontier family, mail-order catalogs were "a source of dreams and wonder." Whether from Montgomery Ward or Sears Roebuck, they came twice a year, bringing the pioneer "up-to-date on what was going on in the big outside world." For Sarah Ware and her siblings "the big outside world" was the railroad town of Huron, forty-five miles distant from their South Dakota homestead on the James River. And their annual shopping trips to Huron, where they "procured all…provisions," could take days, depending upon the weather and road conditions, the road being "an Indian trail [that] ran through the farm [and] could be seen for miles across the prairie."

This child of Nebraska homesteaders enjoys some of the long-anticipated pleasures of a trip to town.

Montana roads were no better than those of South Dakota. According to Milton Shatraw, who grew up on a ranch near Dupuyer in the early years of the twentieth century, local roads "were hardly deserving of the name." Most of them "were never laid out…they just happened. Ranchers would drive back and forth to town following the path of least resistance, and after a while these well-worn ruts across the prairie became known as 'roads.'" Shatraw knew those roads well, for it was traditional for his family to make the ten-mile trip to town together, and he held vivid memories of "shopping days." Shatraw recalled such days as "big events—breaks in the long stretch of lonely days on the prairie." The trips, of course, were subject to the weather, and "three or four hours in an open wagon during a driving rainstorm or a blizzard could pretty well dampen [a young boy's] enthusiasm for any kind of trip."

Sometimes a boy's enthusiasm was dampened just getting ready for the trip. As the oldest boy in the family, young Milton was expected to catch the horses that would pull the farm wagon to town. Trying to catch "a half-wild horse that didn't want to be caught" was not pleasant. "Eventually, with a pan of oats and a mouth full of sweet talk, I could manage to seduce the critter I was after," Shatraw remembered. Once haltered, the horse presented another problem, becoming "so amiable that he would step all over my feet and slobber down my neck, and I would have to go back into the house and change my shirt again."

While Milton was changing his shirt, the rest of the family were readying themselves for the trip, too. His father was shaving and "forcing his unwilling limbs into his one and only suit," his mother and oldest sister were readying "squirming small fry,…threatening dire punishments if they…got a speck of dirt on their clean clothes." Her youngsters dressed, his mother began the fascinating ritual of heating the curling iron to turn her own straight, red strands of hair into corkscrew spirals. To go to town without those curls, she often told the boy, "would be like going half-dressed."

Finally, it was time to "stow away anywhere from two to six kids in the wagon," which often "led to some friction. But after…a few healthy wallops to assorted small rears, things quieted down and we were on our way." To a child, the ride, no matter the ten miles, never seemed long enough, there was so much to see—the curlews wheeling over the prairie grass, the occasional great bald eagle, "a coyote…trotting across a distant coulee…. The horses trotted leisurely along, the steel rims of the wheels clinking against the stones, until the last turn came in the road, and there was the big bridge and, across it, the town."

Town. It still held magical memories even after the farm kid had grown to adulthood. No matter that "Main Street was simply a wide space of trampled dirt between two rows of buildings…four saloons, a livery stable, a blacksmith shop." And then at the very end of Main Street, Harris Brothers' General Store. Here, as his father brought the wagon to a halt, Milton and his siblings scrambled down and trooped into the store. Every item on the family's shopping list could be purchased within its walls, "from twentypenny nails and gum boots to flour, dress patterns and fabrics, dishes, shoes for us kids and—for the treat of the day—some bars of Hershey's chocolate." While their parents went about the business of selecting the goods, the children wandered the aisles, "smelling the strange smells of pickle barrels, kerosene, and new cloth, and looking at all the wonders on the shelves."

Harris Brothers' was more than a store. It was a community gathering place as well, and here the Shatraw family greeted neighbors who'd also come to town to shop and, just as importantly, to meet friends and exchange news and gossip. The store served another important function, for it was also the town's post office. Here the Shatraw family retrieved all the mail that had been held for them, as well as the mail addressed to neighbors they would pass on the way home. "This was the only R.F.D. there was in those days," Shatraw recalled, "and when the weather was so bad that no one was [going] to town, several weeks went by when no one got any mail at all."

For families who homesteaded in earlier days, mail service was even less reliable, and some were willing to pay for the services of those who became the unofficial postal carriers for isolated communities. In the late 1860s, George Krattcer of the Gallatin Valley in Montana supplemented his farm income by delivering letters to Virginia City, a nearby mining community, for fifty cents each. Even without such "special delivery" charges, postage rates could tax the resources of families with little or no cash income. Karen Olsen, a widow who homesteaded in North Dakota, once had "to wait six weeks until she had the two cents to buy the stamp" for the letter she'd written to cherished friends back home in Minnesota.

Mail was a lifeline for many homesteaders, and the postmaster was an important figure in any town. John Barrows held that position in the 1880s in Ubet, a small community whose singular importance was as a crossroads at the center of Montana Territory. Stages bringing passengers and mail—from White Sulphur Springs to Fort Maginnis and from Billings to Fort Benton—crossed at Ubet. The Billings-Benton line handled "considerable traffic" in Barrows's day, mostly four-horse Concord coaches pulled by "decent stock." Many of the coachmen were old-timers who remembered the days before the railroad came through when they drove six horses instead of four, and they grumbled over the loss of status, hardly realizing that the days of the stagecoach itself were numbered.

Shortly after the store visit, Hop Sing Yim arranged for a new series of faces to appear in Frontier Valley. With 160 acres of land to utilize, each of our families had made their most important purchases of the entire project. Staring intently at the For Sale board at the store, nurse Karen, chief executive Gordon, and teacher Nate all put on their new hats as farmers and made their decisions. First came a reluctant herd of sheep that tore off toward the mountains the moment they were released. Eventually most were rounded up and were divided between the Brookses and the Glenns. Next came Jo-Jo, the dancing pig, who swiftly assumed near human qualities in befriending her owners, Mark, Karen, Erinn, and Logan. Finally the valley welcomed Rachel and Glo-bug, a curious pair of earless goats who stole the hearts of newlyweds Nate and Kristen. Along with the chickens that had been delivered shortly after the families arrived (the Clunes had opted to raise thirty-five chickens in their ambitions to go into the egg business), these newcomers soon brought their owners face-to-face with the reality of running a farm.

Within days of the animals' arrival the perils of agriculture were being felt. One of Nate's sheep died and had to be swiftly disposed of for fear of drawing bears into the valley. Up at the Glenns, the sheep were making numerous escape bids that found the family having to ride horseback for many a mile to round up their new charges. At the same time, Gordon's chickens went on strike and refused to lay, leading the Clune children to explore whether their egg-laying vents were blocked by probing them with their fingers, a humiliating ritual that can only have prompted the poor creatures to continue their protest. With the animals came new daily responsibilities of providing food, shelter, and care. For the frontier children this added new chores, and the adults soon realized that each of the animals would need to be fed throughout the winter, something our homesteaders would have to make provision for if they were to satisfy the inspection when our consultants returned. For the Glenns, who had purchased the most animals with five sheep, sixteen hens, two cows with calves, two horses, and a pig, this came as a sobering recognition.

MARK: *We face needing tons of feed for our animals, and right now I can't see us satisfying that. Especially when you consider how we are going to have to go about this monumental task. You hear how animals die out here in the winter. I can see that happening here.*

Finding the winter feed wasn't going to be a problem: Mother Nature had provided. But gathering it would be another matter. A single scythe was all that each family had in their efforts to harvest the generous crops of natural hay that now grew in tantalizingly deep meadows outside each of the cabins. Harvesting it was a punishing challenge as the temperature rose throughout a blistering summer. Yet without it everyone knew their animals wouldn't make it through the winter. What began as a fun task soon required agonizing endurance as, after hours of toil, such meager yields of cut grass were carried back home. Sinking exhausted into a hay pile, Karen reflected on the seemingly hopeless task:

Gordon and Aíne hay their meadow.

It is hot as hell out here. This huge haystack that has taken all day to collect probably weighs nothing. It's very frustrating trying to squeeze a year's work into six months, but if homesteaders had arrived here in May just like we did, that's what they'd have had to do. It's very unique and challenging. I just can't imagine what a woman of over a hundred years ago would have felt like knowing that she would have to work in these fields from daybreak to nightfall. As well as feeding her family and knowing that what you were gathering was just not going to be enough. I don't know if I could have survived this. I think I am tough but I don't know if I could make it out here.

The toll was being felt most powerfully at the Clunes'. Gordon was finding himself weak with the combination of daily endeavors, and the impact on his body was worrying him. As hay making continued, he found himself becoming lethargic and reported having to sleep for hours in the day while every joint in his body ached remorselessly:

My strength diminished to a point where I was half the person I was.... I still believe it is either lack of protein or iron. The beans we ate went right through us. Our bodies were losing nutrients. I even experienced dizziness.

Gordon pointed to his weight loss, which, checked with a modern scale, was indeed dramatic. Like all the men in the valley he'd dropped a significant amount. Having arrived at 178 pounds, he now weighed 147.5 pounds, a loss of over two pounds a week. He was convinced that his health was being adversely affected by the limited diet available on the frontier and visited each family in the valley to voice his opinion that they were in danger of being "malnourished" and pointed to protein as the missing factor. Yet protein had been available in rich quantities in beans, ham, eggs, and especially in the fresh milk available twice daily from the cows. Gordon, however, had not been drinking the milk, their eggs were in poor supply, and he found beans disagreed with him. In particular Gordon felt he needed fresh red meat. Alarmed by his weight loss and continued weakness, Adrienne took drastic measures. On Friday, the thirteenth of July, unhappy with the provisions available and with the charges imposed by the store for buying her baked goods, she and the children ventured outside Frontier Valley to trade with modern neighbors. The purity of their experience was soon over as Aíne and Tracey sat inside a house watching MTV while Adrienne swapped fresh baked breads for elk steaks and fresh vegetables with intrigued local residents. Sitting down to dinner that night, the Clunes celebrated in front of the video diary what they saw as their entreprenurial zeal: "Meat, potatoes, carrots, onions, and more where that came from." In 1883, however, the lack of fresh vegetables in early summer would have made such a meal impossible in Frontier Valley. Further trading plans with the neighbors for ice cream and fresh fruit for the weekend were also being eagerly anticipated.

Elsewhere news of the Clunes' departure was spreading like wildfire.

KAREN: *It bothers me that they turned to the outside. Maybe that is their culture. If only we had all gotten together. That's what would make this community stronger.*

MARK: *As far as I am concerned, they could just keep going down the road.... I don't think Gordon sees what he has done is wrong, and to me it is very wrong.... Instead of spending a day running around this community trying to get support for this malnutrition thing, he should be cutting wood for winter as a day lost here is important. What will be the next issue?*

Nate and Kristen distanced themselves from passing judgment, but they agreed with the Glenns that they felt far from malnourished. A few days later a visit from local doctor Ace Walker brought a medic's perspective. Instead of malnourishment he saw the men in excellent health. Having met the participants before their arrival on the land, he was fascinated by their experience:

When I saw Gordon, I was surprised at how fit he was. The comment I made was, he was lean and mean, he looked in good shape. Listening to his symptoms of aching joints, it sounded probable to me that he'd suffered from dehydration, not malnutrition—that would take much longer to be felt. In fact my impression when he first came in was he had the body weight of a typical American male: that's to say he was in the overweight or obese category that a third of us fall into. Now he falls into a healthy lean category. I'd encourage him to carry this regime on when he gets home.

Comparing Gordon's weight with statistics from the era is fascinating. Having arrived within two pounds of the average weight of an American male today (180 pounds), he found himself at the average weight of an American male in the 1860s (145 pounds). Evidence from the period shows, too, that our food intake, despite the decline in manual labor, has increased substantially. Small wonder that obesity is so evident in our lives today.

The Clunes' actions to declare independence resulted in tension for days in Frontier Valley. Everyone was edgy about the action. Gordon and Adrienne saw it as characteristic of the initiative shown by homesteaders in having to find their own way out of difficult times. Others saw it as a clear violation of the rules they had agreed to. Rumors were starting to fly that modern food and drinks were being covertly brought into the valley. A clandestine rendezvous a few days later over the fence between Aíne and Tracey and one of the neighbors showed the purpose and integrity of the experiment was truly being tested. Most fundamentally for the other participants, it prompted an unwelcome reminder of the modern world and created an uneven playing field. Without wishing to turn Frontier Valley into a prison, it was clear that some boundaries needed setting, and in a series of meetings with Gordon and Adrienne appeals were made for them to honor the intent of the project. Having considered their actions and having been reassured by our visiting doctor, they eventually promised to stop trading with the neighbors.

"The Man Became a Landowner, and...the Landowner Became a Man" Men's Work on the Homestead

When Henry Ronish came to Montana in the early years of the twentieth century, he was a week shy of his twenty-first birthday and, by his own report, "healthy and single, a hard worker full of ambition and plans...a friendly type of lad...wanting a home of his own." Henry came with more than mere ambition and plans, however; he came with a milk cow, thirty-five chickens, eight horses, and various farm and household implements. With the help of his older brother, who had just proved up on a homestead of his own in western South Dakota, he filed on a plot of ground in the Judith Basin. Life seemed easy to the young man—until he "got to proving up." But Henry, the son of a farm family, had the requisite skills and energy, and five years after his arrival in Montana, he'd gained the deed to his homestead. And he'd gained some wisdom as well, reflecting years later, "After proving up, the man became a landowner and perhaps the landowner became a man."

Whether those words were Henry Ronish's own or whether he borrowed them from the lore of the era, they certainly spoke to the reality of his situation. No matter how enthusiastically a man might have looked forward to a new life on the frontier, his lot was not easy as he took up the tasks of the homesteader. Given the tenor of the times, failing at the manly task of homesteading was unthinkable—and virtually unforgivable for married men, who had, in effect, gambled the health and well-being of their families against their abilities to "tame the land." And while the hard work of a man's wife and children contributed greatly to his chances of success, ultimately the heavy responsibility of making a go of the enterprise rested squarely on his shoulders—as did the majority of the heavy labor needed to support the enterprise.

Both because of the strength required and because of the weight of custom, most of the initial tasks of establishing a homestead, from putting up the house and outbuildings to digging the well, fell to the man. Like Henry Ronish, Howard Ruede was young—twenty-two years old—enthusiastic, and ambitious when he homesteaded in Kansas in 1877. His beginnings would have discouraged many another man. His first sod house collapsed under heavy rains, and he was obliged to build another. He dug for water over and over, but found only shale beneath the hard-packed earth. "There's $3\frac{1}{4}$ days' work for nothing," he wrote after one failed attempt. Yet failure did not discourage him "in the least." With no plow, no plow horses, and no cash with which to buy them, he took a part-time job at a print shop in a town thirteen miles from his claim. He also worked for neighboring farmers—digging wells, quarrying rock, cutting firewood, plowing, hoeing, harvesting—all the while looking forward to the day when he could begin breaking his own ground.

Breaking ground was work that typically required—and often taxed—a man's strength. But as Oscar Micheaux, who filed on a claim in south-central South Dakota at the turn of the twentieth century soon discovered, strength alone was not enough to ensure success. Having come to the task with no farming background, Micheaux lacked the skills and experience needed to plow his land. He knew nothing of driving a horse; he had no sense of "plotting" a field or of the importance of running that first furrow straight and true. And when he began breaking up the sod, he could not keep the plow in the ground. "I hopped, skipped, and jumped across the prairie," he later recalled, "that plow hitting and missing, mostly missing.... Well, I sat down and gave up to a fit of the blues." But the blues gave way to determination, and after much trial and error, he began to learn the art of plowing. First he managed to move thirty or forty feet down a row without losing control of the plow, and soon he was able to keep the blade in the ground for the full length of a row—some five hundred, six hundred feet. Slowly, methodically he kept at his task, breaking ten or twelve acres a week. By the end of his first summer Oscar Micheaux had broken 120 acres. In doing so, he figured he had walked fourteen hundred miles behind the plow. Though he "was about 'all in'... when it was done," he was proud of his accomplishment. A neophyte—and the only black man in the entire region—he had broken more land than any of his more experienced neighbors. He had done what he'd set out to do: he had proven himself worthy of the task he'd undertaken.

The construction of the home and outbuildings was primarily a male responsibility.

Managing a two-bottom plow took skill as well as strength.

The tasks on the homestead that fell to men were more seasonal than were those performed by women. While "her work" was carried out day to day, season after season, year in, year out, "his work" was most intense during spring planting and fall harvest, leaving time for building and repair jobs during the rest of the year. But what of homesteading men who had no wife to see to "woman's work"? Of necessity, the young bachelor Howard Ruede took up sewing and biscuit making. "I got out the needle and thread, and then 'stitch, stitch, stitch' till my back was nearly ready to break," he confided to his journal. Having left his wife in charge of matters at home in Minnesota, David Christie was obliged to do her work as well as his own out in Montana Territory. "I have just got my Team turned out and have cooked my Supper and eat it and got my Dishes washed up, the room swept out, and some fruit on the stove to Stew," he wrote Emma. "I suppose Dear you would laugh if you could see me liveing this old Batch life."

Uriah Oblinger, a Nebraska homesteader, also faced the necessity of taking up "woman's work" in the absence of a distaff member of the household. But Uriah saw relief in sight. His wife, Mattie, and their young daughter were to join him on the homestead. "I will build my cage soon and then send for my birds to come," he wrote home to Indiana. "I want you to cook, wash, iron, scrub, bake, make & mend—and do many things too numerous to mention." This laundry list of the chores he intended his wife to assume gives evidence of how carefully Uriah had to schedule his days in her absence. When winter put an end to his field work, Uriah hauled ice and railroad ties to Lincoln, putting the $3 a day thus earned toward paying a lawyer to do the paperwork needed to legitimize his claim and saving the rest for his wife and child's passage to Nebraska.

Many another man had to take outside work to support the homestead—even men whose wives were contributing to family finances by selling butter and eggs, taking in washing, and preparing baked goods and handiwork for barter. Henry Ronish's father, who farmed in southeastern South Dakota, not only raised corn, wheat, hogs, and cattle and planted and tended an orchard, he supplemented his farm income with his carpenter's skills—making cabinets and caskets and building houses and barns for his neighbors. A native of eastern Europe, Ronish could speak and write four languages—German, Czech, French, and English—and he put these skills to use in the county courthouse, mediating legal difficulties between his neighbors and local officials.

Phil Philipson, an English immigrant, supported his Boulder Valley claim by "moonlighting with a butcher wagon that delivered fresh meat" to miners in the area and to other homesteading families on all three drainages of the Boulder River. While meat, fresh or dried, was the basic sustenance of the homesteader, it was more often procured by slaughtering one's own livestock—or by hunting or trapping wild game—than through purchases from a butcher wagon. When Phil Philipson's Boulder Valley neighbor William Fuller needed meat, he retreated for days at a time to one of the well-hidden hunting cabins he had built in the foothills of the Absarokas. These low log structures had a single opening in one corner of the roof, providing a space just big enough for him to crawl through—and not quite big enough for a bear to follow.

While Fuller hunted alone, it was common for men to form hunting parties in search of larger game. As his children grew, the homesteader introduced his sons, and even his daughters, to the hunt, vital as it was to their subsistence. This was only one of the many activities that rural children traditionally learned under the guidance of their father. As youngsters engaged in their outdoor chores, whether helping with the planting, hoeing, and harvesting or hauling feed, wood, and water, they were often supervised by their fathers. In this sort

Heavy timber on a homestead could be both advantageous and disadvantageous. It could provide materials for construction, but it could also hinder planting. Here, a homesteader, his wife, and child join in removing a tree.

of understated nurturing, the homesteading father performed a vitally important, if often overlooked, role—parenting.

As engaged as a man was with his own family and with the activities necessary to the success of the homestead, he was also frequently called upon to help in building the frontier community. Even Howard Ruede, the young bachelor who claimed land outside Osborne, Kansas, became involved in the activities of his rural community. When his neighbors came together to discuss the need for a schoolhouse, Ruede was one of many men who each pledged to give six days of work to putting up the building, which would also serve as church and community hall.

Though women were often the driving force behind the construction of schools and churches—and later, libraries and hospitals—and though their dedicated fund-raising and other behind-the-scenes work were crucial to the success of such projects, men were more often involved in the heavy physical labor required for the construction of the buildings. And as the major holders of capital, they were often the primary donors of the cash and supplies on which such endeavors depended. However, despite men's highly visible role in the molding and shaping of community, and in the homesteading effort, cooperation between the sexes was the best guarantee of success on the frontier.

In between the hay making the women of Frontier Valley were hard at work running their new cottage industries. Each Friday, Hop Sing Yim sent in a wagon to pick up the fruits of their labor, with Adrienne baking delicious breads and pastries. Karen was churning butter and baking, too, alongside ferociously tackling up to thirty pounds a week of heavily soiled laundry. Eggs were traded, too. These enterprises were helping keep the families afloat financially and mirror accounts of the day when women kept homesteads running, particularly in the early years of the enterprise, by bringing in a small but significant income: twenty-five cents for a fresh-baked loaf, eighty-five cents for a dozen eggs. (These goods made by Karen and Adrienne, along with the fresh eggs, were eagerly awaited each Friday evening by the retired community of Big Timber, many of whom had grown

Churning butter required hours and patience.

up on homesteads and remembered with affection the simple pleasures of tasting Mom's home-churned butter and baking.)

Up at the Brookses' an experience radically different from an idyllic honeymoon was taking shape. Kristen had been propelled into frontier life without mercy. Lacking the gentle buildup of the training sessions experienced by all the other participants, she had been dropped headlong into the new lifestyle. Surrounded by alien technology, rudimentary foods, and a radically new environment, she was trying to come to terms with her role:

> I got here for the wedding and everything was fun and exciting, honey-moonish. It was fun and I was clean. But it's been a tough time adapting. You just feel so dirty out here. I feel stinky, reeky greasy, and there is no way of feeling cute. If you feel nasty at home, you can freshen up, but there's no way out here. You just feel ugly and it stinks. I have highs and lows and feel a little psycho. It's hard; there are so many different levels of hard. As well as feeling dirty, I feel I am incompetent. I get mad at myself as I do not know how to do the basics like light a fire.

Shortly after her arrival Kristen recorded her immediate impressions of frontier life in a diary article entitled "Words to Describe the Frontier":

1. Greasy
2. Sooty
3. Hot
4. Buzz/hum (of flies)
5. Breezy
6. Tired
7. Ugly
8. Moments of utter joy at how lucky we are to have been chosen to do this
9. Reward/huge sense of achievement
10. Black dishrags
11. Diarrhea
12. Flies

In their modern lives she and Nate had enjoyed sharing responsibilities in their home, little differentiating their efforts in their enjoyment of life together. Their first challenge on the frontier was to sort out who did what.

KRISTEN: *One of the hardest things in the first two weeks was duking out our roles. I wanted to be useful so I cut out a window in the cabin, but all the calculations were hard so I now leave Nate to do that stuff. I am definitely the wife, I do the dishes... usually I am in charge of food and he does the labor.*

Kristen found the transition a struggle.

Nate and Kristen milk their goat, Rachel.

After three difficult weeks Kristen was starting to find ways to feel more productive. Adrienne had helped her master the campfire and the cookstove. Excited by the arrival of their goats, Kristen had also begun experimenting in ways of making cheese and saw a chance of making a little income from selling it. She was also starting to knit hats as another moneymaking venture, but even with all her new interests it was a hard lesson for Kristen that women on the frontier didn't assume the same roles as in her modern life:

> I'd say there is less work satisfaction for a woman out here. The most I can do is work out are we going to have onions in the omelet. I wake up and I know what the day has got to be…I know the first thing is empty the chamber pot, the same every morning. At home I will do anything to shake up the routine. Out here though there is no variety—at least Nate has different jobs. That's what I like about knitting. You can say, look what I did, whereas if you wash the dishes, there is nothing to show for it. I like being productive, artistic, or putting work into something that has a result.

On the morning of July twentieth, each of the families woke up to find a letter awaiting them, a short note that caused a shiver of anxiety:

Dear Homesteaders,

In good conscience I thought it fair to alert you that on the first of August I shall be driving 400 head of cattle near your homestead. Failure to fence your land will result in damage to your gardens and cabins.

Under the Montana Law of Open Range—both in 1883 and today—it falls upon you to fence them out should you not wish them upon your property.

Furthermore I have noticed that you have not harvested your hayfields, and if you don't do so by the time the cattle arrive, you may not have enough hay for your own livestock over winter.

Cordially,
Your neighbor Ken

The letter came from the owner of Frontier Valley and the surrounding acres of grazing land. Like all ranchers, Ken was facing another severe drought and was looking to move his cattle to higher pastures, which offered good grazing. En route lay the homesteads, and anything that wasn't fenced, such as the maturing gardens, would be trampled underfoot. It was a bolt out of the blue and found

BELOW, LEFT: Kristen at the water flume. This is the closest she got to piped-in water.

BELOW, RIGHT: Despite the uneven start, Kristen eventually took pleasure in her new role.

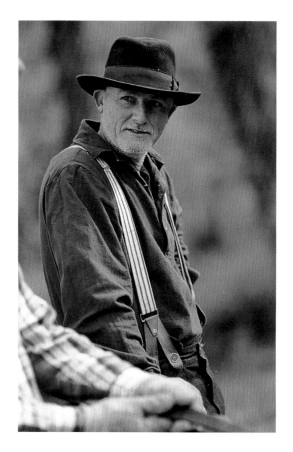

Mark Glenn found rewards in pioneer life.

each family lost for words. With their efforts to harvest the hay already hopelessly behind schedule, now they had an even more pressing task. Tales of wars between cattle barons and the homesteaders now made sense as the families got a vivid picture of how emotions could get out of control when your land came under threat. In this case they had at least been given the courtesy of advance warning; in the past many ranchers had simply driven their herds over the homesteaders' land, often in an effort to drive the newcomers away. The law of open ranges, then as now, required them to protect their boundaries. Now our families had less than two weeks to get their land adequately fenced.

With the deadline of August first looming, fence posts were being pounded up and down the valley. Gordon had recruited Aíne and Tracey to help create a protective barrier around their garden and cabin. Mark Glenn meanwhile had bolder plans, with a hundred fence posts being erected to make a much larger compound around their home. Despite the intensity and ambition of his plan he was finding great comfort in the joint tasks of haying and fencing, utilizing every minute of the day to try to beat the arrival of the cattle. From dawn till dusk his was often a lone figure working in the fields, and he admits that at these moments he came closest to truly connecting with the homesteader in 1883 and felt he truly understood the combination of pride and panic that spurred on settlers. With his relationship with Karen still fragile he was often isolated in his tasks but found the time alone incredibly valuable, thinking more deeply about his life and direction:

I think it is a matter of pride trying to live this life the way that it was. In choosing to do this project I do believe I have lost more than anyone else. I don't know what I have to go back to. My life has changed as a result of this. I do not know if I will go back into teaching, even if I have a job waiting for me. Relationship-wise I am so up in the air. On the face of it I have lost everything by coming out here, but I found me. I have figured out some wrong turns I took in the past. Out here I realize anything that happened in the past I must let go of. I am not trying to prove anything to people but me. If you cannot find yourself out here, you are not looking very hard.

The energy required to fence the land was formidable. After the pounding of the stakes came the stringing of hundreds of yards of barbed wire, which had to be cranked taut to keep out the cattle. Combined with the unrelenting heat of the high summer, it was exhausting. In a few days Mark Glenn laid almost a thousand feet of barbed wire around his home. "When open range starts, you can stand on the other side of this barbed wire and just laugh at the cows. I'm looking forward to that." Now, as in the past, this simple yet highly effective barrier was about to prove its worth. Barbed wire revolutionized farming when it first came on the market back in the 1870s, particularly for those settlers who were moving onto the plains of the West where, without access to large quantities of wood for fencing, effectively fencing your land had been impossible. Though viewing it with suspicion at first, farmers found its advertising claims were true: "It takes no room, exhausts no soil, shades no vegetation, is proof against high winds, makes no snowdrifts, and is both durable and cheap." Such was the demand for it that over 530 patents were eventually produced in the creative frenzy that followed its introduction.

In the early hours of August first the thundering of hooves could be heard approaching from miles off. Four hundred cattle were slowly climbing up the hill toward Frontier Valley. An avalanche of dust was left in their wake. As the cacophony of the arrival increased in volume, all the homesteaders were eagerly checking their fences. If they didn't hold firm, their gardens could be trampled underfoot within seconds, their homes desecrated, even damaged, in the onslaught. It was a tense moment as the first sighting was made. Each cow brought hundreds of flies buzzing angrily around it. Life was about to change in the valley with a plague of biting insects brought in by the herd. Above the din of the cattle came the cries of the ranchers pushing them toward the brown gate that would set them loose on Frontier Valley. Assessing their fences for the last time, Mark, Gordon, and Nate must have been silently praying that morning. To everyone's immense relief, the fences didn't collapse. The most testing moment came shortly after arrival as the fatted modern beasts eagerly pushed toward the fences as if to examine our homesteaders' curious, bony milk cows. All those hours of hard labor had paid off as the fences held back the advance. But that succulent hay, unharvested in the rush to build fences, was being eagerly consumed. Now the homesteaders would have to look harder for their winter feed.

9

All Work and No Play

If our experiment had somehow allowed us to reverse time travel and bring people from the past to inhabit our world, the revelations would be deeply fascinating. Imagine our great-grandparents performing the simplest daily tasks: watching television, driving a car, cooking in a microwave—every chore today has been eased beyond comprehension. If such a feat were possible, it's likely that the most bewildering change in lifestyle would be for the young. A child's life on the frontier was shaped differently from the everyday experience of so many of our youngsters as to be barely recognizable to the children of today. From the moment our half dozen younger volunteers arrived in Montana, they were propelled into encounters that forced them to continually reappraise what had previously been taken for granted. If the experience had been anticipated as a long summer vacation spent on horseback, hunting, fishing, or playing cowboys and Indians, it was time to think again.

The first bombshell hit fifteen-year-olds Aíne and Tracey as Sue Cain announced during training period that makeup would be forbidden. "We look plain and ugly without makeup. We look like four-year-olds." Shortly after, a demonstration in feminine hygiene of the era with washed-out rags pinned to a sanitary belt came as another hard lesson. During those first two weeks the biggest reeducation for all was in the expectation of just how much work they'd have to do. Buckets of water and stacks of wood for the fire were continually needed; the ashes in the stove had to be removed. Conor, Erinn, and Logan found themselves during those first two weeks doing dozens of tasks from pot washing to coffee grinding. And those cows needed milking day in and day out. After the initial excitement of rising with the dawn and staying up for late-night ghost-watch vigils, a growing fatigue began showing itself even on the youngest of our volunteers.

For twelve-year-old Justin Clune the training session at Virginia City marked an important moment in his life. Poised at an age that found youngsters in 1883 given almost the same responsibility as adults, he was eager to prove that he was ready to make the leap to manhood and demonstrated he had what was required as he learned carpentry skills alongside his dad, Gordon. His coming of age proved deeply frustrating for younger brother Conor, who, at nine, was deemed too young by the consultants to start using period tools. To add to his disenchantment everyone used his inability to join the carpentry class as an opportunity to send his young legs on less glamorous missions. By the end of the two weeks of training, all the youngsters were acknowledging that life was going to take a huge turnaround on the frontier. This madcap scheme their parents had signed them up for was going to be an adventure the likes of which none of them had anticipated.

Perhaps the hardest adjustment of all was for the youngest, Conor Clune and Logan Patton, who both turned nine while in Montana. On day one of the experience, Conor had been thrust back in time with an intense immersion into the perils of frontier living. Thrown from the seat of the wagon as the horses went out of control, he had recovered sufficiently to walk the rest of the journey to the campsite that first night. Eager to turn his back on the events of the day, he chose to go fishing but found himself frustrated by the dozens of fish that disregarded his crude willow fish pole, simple hook, and worm. Returning cold and empty-handed to the campsite, he was then bitten by the Glenns' dog Duke. Tearful with the frustrations of the day he faced the camera: "In one day I got thrown from a wagon, I catch no fish, then I get savaged by a dog. You call that fun?" Two days later, as the Clunes began to build their new home, he turned to the video diary camera in similar mood:

> Yesterday I was waking up and my dad said, "Why are you sleeping in?" And I said, "I wish I could hibernate all the way to October fifth." He said, "Why?" And I said I would not have to do any of the work. It's too hard. I think it would be pretty hard for a kid on the frontier.... Today I did not like it much. When I woke up, I found my hat under a ton of clothes and now it is destroyed. I thought Sunday was a day off, and the next thing I was in trouble and had to do lots of work.... The only thing good happening today is me trying to set a world record for the world's stinkiest kid on earth. I am not going to take a bath or shower for five months till I get back. My friends may have to wear a gas mask when I get back.

Around the same time, Logan Patton lay on the floor of his cabin hoping his mom, Karen, wouldn't spot him and assign him another task. Turning to their diary camera, he unburdened his feelings five days into their new life:

> I don't know why I did this project. I miss my friends so much. If I were here for a year, I'd die of friend loss. Just one day, that's all I am asking for. I miss 'em too much. Man, it hurts too much. I wish I had some friends. I've been

here one week and I'm already dying of friend loss. Not one letter, not even a little thought. It's so bad. Bye.

His feelings weren't being helped by the fact that his sister, Erinn, had apparently taken to the whole experience like a duck to water. She'd proved herself handy with the animals during training and was now caring for the family's horses, cows, dogs, and puppy like a natural country woman. Pausing momentarily to explain her feelings to our camera, she looked radiant in her new role:

I'm really enjoying the frontier. I thought I would never live without my television and video. It's more fun hanging out here without TV. Actually I think I should have been born in 1883, I think I got mailed wrong! I like working. It makes me feel like I really did something.

Her take on the lifestyle couldn't have been in more marked contrast to that of Aíne and Tracey Clune. Within days of arrival they felt trapped in the valley and talked about missing going to the beach and trying to adjust to having no stimulation for the next five months except from their animals and the myriad jobs aimed in their direction. Only later did they own up to creating in those early weeks a smoke screen of appearing busy to avoid Gordon and Adrienne's giving them more tasks. Without a corral to contain their animals they had to spend each morning and evening walking up and down the valley to find Blanca, who invariably wandered off in search of company, usually the Glenns' cows.

AÍNE AND TRACEY: *We hate milking, the cows smell, we step in their crap, all they do is moo, and they have to shoo their flies away. It takes an hour to*

Conor Clune had a narrow
escape on the wagon train.

milk. Then we walk for an hour and it spills all over our dresses. Then we have to do it again and we have walked four miles by the end of each day. We have to look after the horses, too. We walked six miles yesterday.

Within a matter of days Aíne and Tracey had worn every garment available to them and even taken to wearing Adrienne's while a bundle of grime-encrusted outfits piled ever higher. While Adrienne slaved at cooking up hearty meals to keep everyone happy, Gordon was working hard on getting the cabin under way. Watching the children as he pounded away at the roof, he found himself losing patience with them in those opening days. Aside from Justin, who was spending every moment helping on the construction, Gordon saw idle hands and realized that it was time to change his attitude. "Drill Sergeant Dad" was born:

I worry I may be too severe on my kids and worry that I may drive them to hate me and hate this place. But in order to get things going I need to bark orders. They may respect me more for it, but what worries me is I do have a family of individuals and they have a right to go.

OPPOSITE, TOP LEFT: "Man, I miss my friends," a lonesome Logan remarked.

OPPOSITE, TOP RIGHT: Tracey Clune and "dinner."

OPPOSITE, BOTTOM: A natural, Erinn loved working with animals.

BELOW, LEFT: Aíne and Tracey set off for *another* milking.

BELOW, RIGHT: Aíne, Blanca, and Tracey—they finally made peace with her.

"Just Like ... [a] Tumbleweed"
The Magical, Tragical World of Childhood on the Frontier

The American homesteader's child grew up, by and large, in a world of blurred boundaries, a world where the lines between work and play, between formal and informal education, between childhood and adulthood were faint to nonexistent, a world in which "children learn what they live" was perhaps the one constant in the rich and varied landscape of family life on the frontier.

As children shadowed their parents around the homestead, they learned by observation and imitation how to care for chickens, herd sheep, milk cows, chop and split wood. By careful instruction girls and boys acquired both indoor and outdoor skills such as cooking, sewing, washing, tilling, planting, and harvesting, skills they were often called upon to master at an early age. R. D. Crawford of North Dakota plowed his first field at age eleven; Percy Ebbut of Kansas "plowed acre after acre from the time [he] was twelve." Too young to plow, the children of one Oklahoma homesteader did their part in breaking down the big clods turned up by their father's sod-breaker, following in the wake of their ax-wielding parents and attacking with butcher knives any clumps that escaped the blades swung by their elders.

Even so, most frontier children found time for play. Lacking the toys and playthings of their urban contemporaries, they used their imagination in amusing themselves with whatever came to hand. When young Pearl Anderson was growing up near Grand Forks, North Dakota, she and her siblings spent hours searching for "pretty stones" on the ridge behind their barn. Ella Montjoy, a child of Montana homesteaders, recalled that "from early March, when the snow was disappearing and the first flowers beginning to bloom, until October ... I with my brothers and sisters roamed the mountains and hills and explored the streams for miles in every direction."

Such meanderings were often carried out in the line of duty. Rolla Banta, who grew up herding sheep in West Texas, remembered how she and her siblings spent their evenings sharing with their parents the stories of each day's adventures, of "where [they] had been, to what creek, up what branch, and what [they] had seen." One ten-year-old girl drew the admiration of a traveler who happened by her Nebraska homestead one day in the early 1880s as she was "herding sheep ... handling her pony with a masterly hand, galloping around the herd ... driving them into a corral."

Frontier children also devoted many hours to play that mimicked the work of the adults around them. In late October of 1885, with his newly arrived family settled into a neighbor's small claim shack, Montana homesteader David Christie resumed work on the house he'd begun building for them earlier that year. Under the watchful eyes of his young boys he notched the logs and set them in place, hoisted and settled the rafters, and though slowed by heavy January snows, had the roof in place by early spring. His example was not lost on his sons, for by the time the family home was completed, seven-year-old Davy and five-year-old George were putting the finishing touches on a home of their own, a playhouse they'd constructed from short logs and leftover lumber and had roofed with branches and animal skins.

Little girls were equally fine mimics, sweeping with miniature brooms made of sticks and straw, cooking make-believe meals, and creating doll clothes with scraps from their

These children of Sweet Grass (Montana) homesteaders pause in their play to be caught by their mother's camera. The homemade wagon was likely used for chores.

mothers' sewing boxes. Little Urma DeLong, who grew up on the plains of Montana, entertained herself with a family of frogs who inhabited the root cellar on the homestead, diapering and dressing them as if they were dolls. "I would lay them down to put their diaper on," she recalled years later. "They just lay there and let me do it. When it got wet, I changed [the frog's] little diaper—we always had chunks of outing flannel.... I had more fun with my little frogs." Gophers, not frogs, were the playmates of Matt Jarvis and his younger brother, who grew up on a homestead in Dakota Territory. The boys actually trained those gophers to come when they whistled, and they dissolved into tears when a cousin, practicing his hunting skills, aimed a shotgun at one of their pets and killed it.

Olephia King, who grew up "just like an old tumbleweed" in the Monitor Valley of Nevada, spent her summer days playing "rodeo" with the Indian children who lived nearby. When a hard spill off one of the "broncs" resulted in a broken wrist, her mother buried Olephia's arm in mud for an hour and then splinted it with pieces of an old apple box from the barn. Having observed her mother's actions, young Olephia would likely have had few qualms about tackling such an emergency herself in later years. Montana pioneer Pamelia Fergus, in describing the way she'd cleaned and stitched her daughter's heel after the girl had stepped on an ax blade, noted, "If anything of this kind happens again, our girls will remember this."

If such lessons seem harsh, they remind us that, in the words of Fred Martin, a German-Russian immigrant who settled his family on a North Dakota homestead, "In those days it was customary to expect the impossible, especially from a girl." Indeed, in retrospect, this father realized that his eldest daughter, Magdelena, or Lena, had essentially "played the role of an adult since she was a child." With her mother pregnant again and weakened by the passage from Groszliebental, Russia, to Ashley, North Dakota, the care of her six younger siblings—and especially of the chronically ill toddler, Mathilda—fell solely to fourteen-year-old Lena. One evening, as she shifted little Mathilda from one arm to the other, she suddenly realized that the child's body had gone limp. Her baby sister had died in her arms.

The loss of a parent could affect a child even more deeply than the loss of a sibling. Delia Klaus, the oldest of three girls, was nine when her mother suddenly took ill and died in their farmhouse in western North Dakota. "That very night our dad and this good neighbor took lumber and made our mother a coffin," Klaus recalled some fifty years later. "The ladies washed her and with Dad's help they dressed her.... Very early the next morning Dad and our neighbor loaded our dead mother on the wagon [and] bundled up us three kids,...hitched up his faithful...team of horses, and started out for [my] grandparents," a trip of some fifty miles, "[crying] pitifully all the way," Klaus remembered, while she was left to wonder what to make of this sudden turn of events. The child's intuition that life would never be the same proved valid, as she and her little sisters were left with their grandparents while their father returned "all by himself to the empty sod shack."

Other children who found themselves caught in adult situations were able to carry through in ways they looked back on with less pain. When William Davis was thirteen, his father left him alone for several weeks on land

Joseph and Vernon Asbridge of Roundup, Montana, were put on horseback at an early age.

the two of them had been working in Montana's Gallatin Valley while he crossed back over the Madison Range and into the Ruby Valley to bring the rest of the family to the new homestead. Left in charge of the place—including milking the cows and keeping seventy-five cattle within the unfenced pasture and out of the garden—the ingenious boy soon struck a bargain with the hired hand on the neighboring farm. In return for William's help in plowing, the hired hand cooked his meals and helped him corral the cattle at night. By the time his family arrived, William had not only kept up with the cattle and protected the garden from marauding cows and other critters, he had also earned some $50 for his work in the neighbor's fields.

Herding stick in hand, this Bonner, Montana, child is already learning the responsibilities of livestock care.

Even as children were engaging in the work that prepared them for adulthood, they were also being formally educated in the three Rs, either at home under the tutelage of a parent or in hastily organized schools. "I have learned my letters and can spell," little Ella Oblinger wrote from her family's eastern-Nebraska dugout in January of 1874 to her grandparents back home in Indiana. "I will be ready for more books pretty soon. I can spell Ax & Cat & Dog & Girl off the book when Pa or Ma give it out to me. I love to spell so well...[and] I bother Pa and Ma considerable to get them to learn me."

With children like Ella "bothering" them for an education, parents in most homesteading communities organized schools that would provide formal instruction beyond that which their youngsters could receive at home. In the autumn of 1885, the settlers in what would become Douglas County, South Dakota, met in the home of the Meade family to organize the region's first school. It was agreed to hold a three-month term in an abandoned claim shanty central to all the homesteads. Seven families enrolled a total of sixteen children—including four little Meades—and hired a teacher at $15 a month. The teacher provided her own desk, and the fathers built crude benches and desks for the children. A stout piece of "red building paper" was the blackboard, and the erasers were pieces of old cloth. Pupils furnished their own books, a great variety of them: Appleton's and Swinton's readers; Ray's, Robinson's, and Appleton's arithmetics; Harvey's and Read and Kellogg's grammars.

There was, however, only one history book to be shared by all sixteen students. No matter their grade level, they studied from that one text, the teacher reading aloud from it every day and expecting her students to be able to recite what had been read the previous day. Emily Meade Riley recalled in later years that they never seemed to advance beyond the chapters on the discovery and exploration period and the Revolutionary War, since the

The children of homesteaders who settled near Grassrange on the plains of central Montana pose with their teacher in front of their school.

term was but three months long and it seemed that each succeeding teacher started the new term on page one. By the time she had finished her formal schooling in the claim-shack classroom, Riley said, she had memorized the first two chapters of that U.S. history book.

Lessons, whether learned from a teacher in a one-room school, from a parent at home, or in the course of work and play, were long remembered by those who, in the words of historian Elliott West, "gr[ew] up with the country." And though the learning curve could be high and the lessons harsh, children tended to be remarkably resilient. Most of them not only survived but also learned important lessons in *how* to survive, lessons they passed on to future generations for whom the homesteading adventures of their parents and grandparents would become the stuff of family legend.

Acceptance of their new lifestyle eventually crept into the lives of all the children. As food ran short at the Clunes', Aíne and Tracey threw themselves into the rigors of digging up the land for cultivating vegetables. Digging a latrine for the much-needed outhouse, Conor was up to his neck excavating soil. His next enterprise was a homemade mousetrap, created out of tin cans suspended on string over a bucket of water, and the family of mice inhabiting the Clune cabin soon met their maker. At ten cents a mouse it proved lucrative. The arrival of farm animals brought out new qualities in the younger homesteaders, with Justin and

Logan each proving his worth as the "chicken man" of his family. What didn't alter, however, was the amount of work required; as soon as one task was completed, mom and dad always found a new one. Small wonder the shoes worn by many of the children fell apart midway through the experience, hard evidence of their arduous lifestyle.

As the frontier children discovered, play rarely happened. In their breaks from work Conor and Logan keenly fashioned brutal-looking axes from rocks. A fishing hole created and stocked especially for the project higher up in the valley proved an ongoing challenge for all the boys. Equipped with a rudimentary rod, line, hooks, and home-dug bait of worms, they spent hours trying to entice the trout to bite. Frustrated video-diary reports pointed fingers of suspicion that somehow they'd been badly equipped and that surely tackle in the 1880s was more sophisticated? Despite reassurance, try as they might, the fish continued to avoid the juiciest lures, even ignoring small pieces of succulent corn available in the canned food supplies. Worst of all was returning home empty-handed to families eager for a modicum of flavor in their bland diet. After weeks of patient

BELOW, LEFT: Conor's better mousetrap.

BELOW, RIGHT: Logan heads for garden duty, *again*.

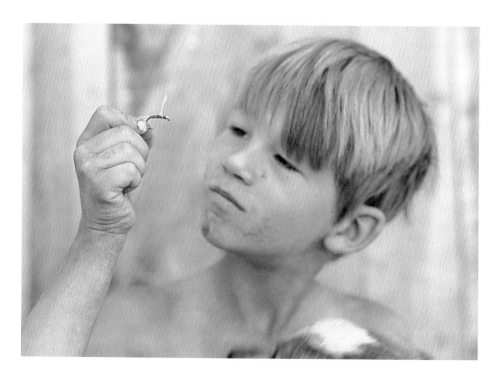

Conor Clune examines a homemade fly.

endeavor, Justin and Conor finally found the secret, painstakingly crawling on their bellies toward the hole so as to give no visual warning to their prey. Their first haul was eagerly distributed up and down the valley for all to celebrate their achievement.

Meanwhile, Tracey and Aíne built an escape from the rigors of their everyday experience with a fort in the woods where trespassers were warned of severe consequences. On the warmest of nights they chose to sleep out, suspended on a sleeping loft halfway up the tree. What they gained in extra privacy, however, was paid for in mosquito bites. Tracey counted over a hundred on her at the worst of the season. Without complaint it seemed, twelve-year-olds Justin and Erinn temporarily suspended their childhoods, both spending much of their day working hard alongside their parents.

ERINN: *I get here on day one and look around. I love my homestead already. Yes, I miss my daddy and yes I miss my best friends but that doesn't mean I can't enjoy five months of no loud racket from civilization. I can just celebrate the mountains and sunsets of Montana.*

Rather than wake and wonder what to wear, I glance in my trunk and realize there's only one thing I can wear today . . . and for the next five months. The worst part is, it's a dress!

Are you gulping down an ice cold soda right now? Or just gobbling up ice cream? I don't think I'll ever shovel down ice cream again. I haven't had ice cream in such a long time, the taste and sweetness of it now would probably overcome me. My mom bought an ice cream maker from the store but here's one problem with it. We can only make ice cream when it snows, and who

Logan's chore was to remove mice and bugs from the vegetable patch.

wants ice cream when you're ice yourself? We get about one piece of candy a week and we try to make it last till the next piece. Can you count the times you've got a butterscotch candy and chomped it up and never acknowledged the sweet flavor?

You know the frontier American Girl dolls that look so happy and clean? They aren't the real thing. I am! I am dirty and tired a lot but I am just as happy as they are if not happier.

My only physical work back home was sports. At seven I can be found milking my cow, Crystal. Milking is relaxing because I can watch the sunrise and the beautiful sunset in the evening. It's fun because I have one of my best friends, my mom, milking with me. We have milk squirting wars, deep conversations and tell each other what the cows and horses are saying and thinking.

I know what you are probably thinking, don't you miss the computer, television and radio? Actually all I miss out of the three is the radio. If you want to know the truth, my mom's nightingale voice is better than any radio. I really miss my waterbed and shopping in a mall, but they're not needed I know.

I will cry when I leave my small quaint cabin. I'll miss my five sheep, two horses, two cows, two calves and my eleven chickens. I'll miss all the 1883 things I've grown to love. Then I'll cry when I get to Tennessee for happiness. I'll get my dad, family and friends back. Let's just say it's a catch-22.

Just as life settled into a daily ritual of farm chores and homemaking tasks, a newcomer arrived who was to transform the lives of the children. Early one

August morning, smartly dressed in a fine Sunday-best suit and sporting a handsome felt hat, a stranger made her way slowly up the path leading to the Clunes', where a special meeting had been called for the parents. Her arrival was eagerly anticipated by all, especially by the children, who had been told to wait outside. The elegant newcomer soon won her way into the hearts of the curious youngsters as she handed out round, tasty, home-baked cookies. Inside, following introductions, the business of the day began: "I understand you folks want to start a school, and I'd like to offer my services as a teacher." For Judy Harding teaching in a one-room schoolhouse was an unfulfilled wish in a distinguished career in education in Montana. Having grown up in a rural community in North Dakota, she'd attended a small school where one teacher had overseen the studies of all ages. With a lifetime's interest in the history of schooling, Judy couldn't have been better suited to fill the role that the parents in Frontier Valley now sought. In recognition of the tough living demanded from working the land, original homesteading communities were quick to recognize the importance of educating their children, often in a hope to open the door for a better life. The parents in our valley were keen to start motivating their children's minds, after almost three months of little stimulation, but education in 1883 out in rural communities brought parents new responsibilities. Judy noted, "As you aren't paying taxes yet in this community, we cannot join a school district, so you'll have to work out my wages, but I'm cheap. In 1883 a woman teacher would average a monthly salary of fifty-four dollars and fifty cents. Had I been born male...you would have to pay me seventy-one dollars and forty cents. One change that is interesting... if I were teaching now, I would be making fifty-one thousand dollars compared to six hundred and fifty-four dollars in 1883."

Judy had been diligent in unearthing the educational regulations for public schools in Montana in 1883, and her research had yielded some fascinating and equally uncomfortable facts. Schooling was compulsory even in that era, when just ten pupils were sufficient to start a district school. But children of African descent were not permitted to be educated alongside white students in Montana's public schools. Instead separate arrangements had to be made, which, in practice, often saw black children educated later in the day. As Judy explained the details, everyone sat quietly in acknowledgment that if Nate and Kristen were parents, their children would not be permitted to sit alongside Aíne, Tracey, Justin, Conor, Erinn, and Logan.

TOP: Erinn gained an appreciation of frontier life.

BOTTOM: Schoolteacher Judy Harding.

Agreeing to pay Judy's fee for an initial five-week term, the parents struck a deal. "On August twentieth at eight-twenty the bell will ring. You will just have to come up with a building in which to hold school," Judy noted. As she departed, the parents looked to each other for inspiration. They had just two weeks to build a schoolhouse.

"A Teacher Must Expect Hardship"
Winifred Shipman and Her Chicken-House School

In the summer of 1882 when twenty-five-year-old Winifred Shipman traveled from her childhood home in Vermont to her father's newly established homestead in Montana Territory's Judith Basin, she was bent on obtaining a teaching position in one of the schools springing up in tiny farming communities in the area. In addition, like many other single women who went West, she planned to spend a part of each year living on and improving a homestead claim of her own.

Having spent several years teaching in common schools in Vermont and New Jersey, Winifred Shipman was well qualified to teach in the rural schools of the West. However, she soon learned that establishing the very first school in a frontier community was a far cry from teaching in well-established school systems in the East. She had to adjust quickly to life on the open plains where houses were often miles apart, trees were found only along the banks of creeks and rivers, and school buildings were virtually nonexistent. If there were as yet no buildings, there were at least plenty of parents who wanted their children educated, and Winifred Shipman, who came from a long line of teachers and felt that "a teacher must expect hardship," took her new situation in stride.

Even so, the challenges she faced during her first assignment—in the tiny community of Philbrook—might well have defeated a lesser educator. Located about seventeen miles west of Lewistown and some ninety miles due north of the *Frontier House* site, the town had but one house, one hotel, one store, one saloon, and one blacksmith shop. Most of her pupils lived on farms or ranches and traveled to school on horseback or on foot. "My school house had been a chicken house," she later wrote. "We had no seats except boards and no books, one window and one door. We had a blackboard but no chalk." Having signed a contract that paid her $60 a month for a three-month session and having made arrangements to room and board with a family named Porter, to whom she paid a total of $40 for her three-month stay, she set about getting ready for her first day of teaching.

Finding the interior of the school too dismal, Winifred asked for help in whitewashing the inside of the building to make it lighter. With no books on hand for the first half of the term, she wrote out stories on brown paper so the children could begin their reading lessons. To illustrate lessons on history and geography she scratched out maps on the floor. "We looked at stars," she noted to family members back East. "We studied rocks. We dissected a hawk and other birds that had been killed and did anything we could think of in the way of learning something."

At the end of the term, Winifred Shipman and her Philbrook students—like Judy Harding and the pupils from *Frontier House*—prepared a special program for their parents. "We had a Christmas tree and a few exercises," Winifred recalled. "Then I went home [to the Judith Valley]"—where she spent the rest of the winter preparing for her spring teaching assignment by the flickering light from a rag "wick" that hung from a nail suspended over a cup of hog grease.

As primitive as frontier living and teaching conditions were for Winifred Shipman, her students, like those of Frontier Valley, must have found going to school a welcome diversion from the monotony and drudgery of their daily chores at home. And although the tiny settlement of Philbrook "went to nothing" after the homesteading boom turned bust, old-timers in the area still recall hearing stories about a "chicken-house school" and the New England schoolmarm who taught students to value the hours they spent within those whitewashed walls.

A quarter of a mile from the gate leading to Frontier Valley stood a long-unused sheep shed. A rusted iron roof was the only recent addition to a precariously balanced log shed with two large openings welcoming wind, rain, hail, and snow freely inside. Years of decayed manure and foliage lay piled on the floors. At first sight, it was not a promising building to think of as a schoolhouse. "Looks like it's pretty old…are we sending our animals here or our children?" asked Karen as she looked around inside. Huddled under the low roof, the adults from Frontier Valley were assessing the potential. Even Nate had come to take a look and offer his assistance. It was dark inside, despite a bright summer's day. Windows would need to be added, doorways properly built, the flooring cleared and leveled. And if the children weren't going to freeze come the turn in the weather, a stove would be essential. "It's a lot more work than I expected, but it has potential," acknowledged Adrienne. In the past, any abandoned building had been pressed back into action when pioneers first established schoolrooms. Tents, old barns, rooms above taverns, all had doubled as schoolrooms. Following in that tradition, the families decided to attempt to convert the old sheep shed to fit their children's needs. As Karen noted, set in a small clearing outside a wooded area, complete with a creek running through, it would make an idyllic spot for the children to come every day. Work schedules were hastily assigned: the men would restore the building and make doors and windows, while the women would make the school furniture and clean up the floor.

If we needed a yardstick to measure just how their experiences had reshaped the children so far, their reaction to the start of school in Frontier Valley couldn't have been more revealing. They were thrilled at the prospect. As Adrienne put the finishing touches to one of the crude school desks that was being made from wood salvaged from a nearby abandoned homestead, she reflected on the change: "It's interesting to see our children appreciate their education as a result of what they have experienced here. They see school here as a vacation from the chores they have to do." "I think going to school will be good," said Logan. "It will give us a chance to rest our muscles. Now the parents are going to have to muscle up!" Aíne, who admittedly had never been fond of school, was eager to start, too: "I always thought that physical work would be preferable to school, but now I definitely think school is easier." As the first day of school grew closer, the children were all encouraging the adults to work harder to get the school building ready. Perplexed but excited about the new enthusiasm, everyone put his or her back into the project as windows appeared, a stovepipe was run through the old roof to accommodate a small stove, and sturdy doors were fashioned to close up the building. In the corner of the room curtains were hung around a small area where a crude bed and washstand were set up. School was also home for the teacher.

Once a home to sheep, the schoolhouse needed a lot of work.

Judy was clearly thrilled by the progress when she arrived on Monday morning, August twentieth. "It's just perfect," she declared, gazing around at the neat desks and benches lined up in anticipation of classes. Distributing slates and chalk to each desk, she heard the approach of her class. Erinn and Logan had ridden their horse, Snowball, the mile and a half from their cabin. The Clune boys had walked, and Aíne and Tracey brought up the rear, clinging together on Cowboy, their horse. The school day was divided into two halves: mornings would see modern studies essential to keep our youngsters up to speed with their current curriculum, while afternoons would take the students back to the classes of 1883. Excited at the prospect of schooling in period style, Judy had been researching the techniques recommended to teachers at the time. Although she had only six students, she faced the same challenge as her predecessors in having to devise lessons that straddled a wide age range. She would have to keep two nine-year-olds moving forward while ensuring the older children didn't feel left out. It wasn't an easy task. Judy decided to break the ice with a musical introduction to class that saw her accompany on the guitar a group chorus of "Polly Wolly Doodle." A shared counting lesson followed. Clearly bored, Aíne and Tracey later declared that first day had reminded them of going back to kindergarten. Erinn, too, wasn't happy; a star pupil back in Tennessee, she returned home to the Glenn cabin concerned that she was going to fall behind in her education.

The absence of the children soon began to be felt back on the homesteads. Even the simplest tasks, such as watching that the sheep and chickens didn't invade the gardens, now fell on the adults, and both the Clunes and the Glenns had to revise their working patterns to cover all bases. Karen was most deeply affected; having worked so closely over the summer with the children, she now found the days dragged. By the end of the day she was longing for the return of Erinn and Logan and would sit watching the horizon to see them being brought home by Snowball.

However, Gordon and Adrienne were enjoying the peace: "We have so much privacy now it's just wonderful. For the first time in three months we have the cabin to ourselves. When they come back at night, it's almost like an invasion we get so used to the quiet by day." On the second morning of school Adrienne took a long wash down by the creek. The extra privacy afforded with the children at school allowed her to remove her clothes, rather than taking her usual sponge wash, which led to a worrying discovery. "I found I had a lump in my breast and wondered, how long has that been there? It shows just how little chance you get to be private out here." Rightly concerned, she called in on the two-way radio to ask for a visit by the medical team, and Sarah, our EMT, confirmed Adrienne's concerns. Forty-eight hours later Adrienne was in the nearby town of Livingston to have a checkup: "I was pretty nervous. It all happened so quickly." It was a doubly anxious time as not only was she concerned about the diagnosis, but she found herself having to adapt to the modern world. "It was ridiculous, but I couldn't get used to the simplest things. Like having to flush the toilet!" Even a small Montana town felt frantic with the unaccustomed cars and rush of daily life. Luckily for Adrienne the checkup quickly confirmed good news: the growth was benign and she returned

home full of relief. "You think about a woman's options in 1883, though, and she'd have been so busy, what are the odds of actually seeing a doctor? What could he do if he found anything? I'm so glad I could come to 2001 technology. This was not the time to put myself last."

After the first week of classes, school was getting better. Instead of devoting the day to teaching one group, Judy had broken her instruction down into separate, smaller lessons. The older children started to take on some responsibility in assisting with lessons, so Tracey might be helping Logan with his sums, while Aíne was assisting Conor with spelling. The work gave the two girls an extra interest in school, while Judy could focus on the individual needs of other children. In shared classes, everyone was discovering more about the history of the homesteading era, and not all of it proved popular. Judy had located a series of books and teaching aids from the period. To make children think about opportunities for work, an old teacher's manual had thirteen illustrations showing occupations ranging from farming to blacksmithing. Of thirteen pictures, only two featured women, one depicting a mother working in the kitchen at home, the other showing a young woman doing chores in a bakery while a man produced the bread. These were stark depictions of a woman's lot in the nineteenth century. As Conor observed, "In 1883 women did not have their independence yet. They weren't allowed to vote. They had no power as all the men in the world said, 'Feed me dinner. I am not going to kiss you unless you feed me.' So it wasn't really fair." Looking at the illustrations, Erinn was the most thoughtful, quietly assessing the world she would have been born into had she truly been a child of the frontier. A later lesson from a history book, circa 1880, found Erinn reading a passage aloud: "Let me tell you

Tracey was proud of how she picked up the guitar.

that our country was once a wilderness inhabited only by savage Indians and wild beasts until it was discovered and settled by Europeans.... Native Indians are copper-colored and warlike." Having recently met Dale Old Horn and heard his accounts of the treatment of the Crow people, the view of history from the past was met with curiosity and robust questioning. As Erinn said at the end of school, "It was really good to have to think about different matters for once. I was really worried about missing my real lessons, but Miss Harding was great in making us look at other things."

For all the students the greatest enthusiasm was given to Judy's guitar lessons. After the first day the repertoire had expanded. Many songs celebrating the history of the era soon became popular choices to learn. A friendly competition emerged to borrow the guitar so that it could be taken home. Practice was necessary as, by the end of school, Judy planned a concert to show the parents what the children had learned in a selection of short dramatic historical scenes and traditional songs.

Judy, too, was learning, finding the one-room schoolhouse experience fascinating. Retiring to her comfortable bed in the nearby town each night, she would often pause to look at the small living quarters and think about the lot of a woman teacher who would have spent night and day living and working in the school: "I think about those women, single women, and try to imagine what they gave up to come and teach in such places. Many came out of the cities back East and devoted their lives to teaching in what must have been quite lonely conditions. But they must have had hope because they would have seen that it was from education that some children managed to turn their backs on the hard lives of their parents doing such difficult tasks as homesteading. I'm just so glad I had this chance to get the experience."

For new bride Kristen, the activities three miles down the valley at the school-house were intriguing and, at the same time, frustrating. Having immersed herself in the realities of the frontier world, she'd been struggling to find a role for herself that would give her the same sense of satisfaction she had gained from her work back in the twenty-first century. Much of the homestead work found Kristen trapped in a dull routine of cooking and cleaning, while Nate ran the farm. It left her plenty of time to reflect on what a young woman joining her husband would have expected in such circumstances in the late nineteenth century:

I have thought about having a baby out here. I got married in July and I could have gotten pregnant and had a child in the dead of winter here in the cabin. It's made me think a lot about women back then. What if I had a child and it died in childbirth? It's terrifying. There was no birth control, you know. I probably would be pregnant by now. This is not the environment to be raising a baby.

A few weeks into the school "year" Kristen volunteered her services, eager to see if Judy could utilize her as a trainee teacher. In reality, Kristen would proba-bly have become a full-time mother out on the frontier. Not far from Frontier Val-ley lay the ruins of the Phillips homestead, a tiny collection of cabins in which ten children were raised.

Although birthdays on the frontier would rarely have been marked with the same emphasis as today, our parents were keen that the children should not feel disap-pointed—especially since they were far from friends and family. As late summer approached, Logan was the first child in the valley to reach his birthday, and Karen was eagerly plotting how to celebrate without departing from the era. She eventu-ally took her cue from a day at school that found all the children returning home particularly happy. In the lesson, Judy had vividly demonstrated how the connec-tion of the railroad in September of 1883 had brought great excitement to settlers' lives. The joining of the eastern and western lines of the Northern Pacific Railroad had brought new consumer goods speeding to the frontier from both coasts. To demonstrate the changes, Judy had presented each child with an orange, their first taste of fresh fruit since their arrival. "The opening of the railroad would have brought other things, too," mused Karen to her video diary camera. "People could travel farther." With the aid of the production team she arranged a special package to be sent to Montana, timed for Logan's birthday. "Mom says I have a secret for my birthday," said Logan, intrigued. On that morning, the mystery was solved as

Conor practices casting.

Grandma Lewis made her way up the path to the Glenn cabin. Karen was as excited as Logan to finally see her mother; with tears streaming down Karen's face it was hard to judge who was excited most about the arrival. Karen's written diary had signed off most evenings with the same words: "Miss Mom." Logan, more accustomed to presents on his birthday like Super Nintendo, was delighted as his grandmother pulled out of her bag a selection of exquisitely made toys produced by his uncle Tommy. A catapult, a domino board, and a small wooden boat took pride of place by Logan's bed that night. Hours of whispered conversation continued long after the children had fallen asleep as Karen and her mother, Martha, caught up after four months apart. Having grown up on a small farm herself, Granny Lewis paid Karen perhaps the biggest compliment of her entire stay:

Honey, I didn't think you were going to make it out here. But look at you, cooking fine, the animals look well, you're really getting into this.

With the five-week school term almost over, Judy would soon be heading home. The children in Frontier Valley would shortly return to the last few weeks of their homestead routines, a prospect viewed with disappointment after the popularity of Judy's classes. Before they said good-bye, there was still the evening of the school performance. Such a rare gathering for the adults merited their wearing their best clothes. Having all been nervous about the event, the children gradually found themselves enjoying the limelight as they recited the history of the area and sang a mixture of traditional songs and compositions of their own. Watching over it, Judy took great satisfaction from the progress they'd made in such a short time: "I've seen a big change in everyone here. I think we've all learned a lot from this." For the parents it was a good moment to reflect on the journey their children had taken and the changes the experience had wrought since arrival. Adrienne summed up the reactions to school: "We've been amazed at how our children have really grown to love their lessons, and to watch them enjoying studying is such a change. I can't think of a time when they spent such time poring over their books back home." All of the youngsters demonstrated shifting attitudes, new skills, and growing confidence. City ways had given over to the enjoyment of simpler pleasures: learning the guitar, riding horses, catching the occasional fish. Our two youngest contributors spoke volumes in their review of frontier life.

LOGAN: *I have discovered imagination out here and found out how you can use the surroundings to make fun things.... In the modern world kids have more than they need...as grown-ups work so hard we get more money to buy stupid stuff. When I get home, I am going to spend it wisely on things I really need.*

CONOR: *I have been proud of my mom and dad as they have been through a lot of things here. I am proud of all my family as we are hanging through this. My granny is a hundred years old and she lived the life we are living for more than five months and it was hard for them. We truly are in the shoes of our ancestors and these shoes suck!*

10

Downhill to Winter

A taste of the change in seasons showed itself as early as August 23. Karen had taken time to record it in her journal:

I saw the first yellow leaf drop off a cottonwood this morning—a harbinger of colder times to come. A warning to enjoy these last warm days. Lean times are ahead of us, not behind us, and challenges we only guess at are waiting around the corner.

Small clues were coming to light in all manner of places. The gradual sinking of the water in the creek, a frosted breath at dawn milking, a slow decline in egg production; everyone had noted the advance of days.

The late summer brought with it new opportunities; not only was there still hay to be cut from the higher reaches of the valley, so far unvisited by the rancher's cattle, but other natural riches were presenting themselves. The vegetables were maturing in the family gardens; come late August a glut of berries hung heavy in the chokecherry and gooseberry bushes seeded throughout the land. Armed with buckets, all the homesteaders were soon hard at it eagerly picking the unusually rich harvest, staining their hands. Watching them, you'd believe that a race was on, such was the energy invested. Truthfully, there was competition to get the berries. Not only were they going to make delicious pies and vitamin C–rich preserves for the families for the winter, but the four-legged inhabitants of Frontier Valley were also hungry for their share. Every day brought fresh sightings of large-animal tracks and piles of fresh manure, evidence of what the local game warden had foreseen: bears were heading back to our valley. A huge cinnamon bear accompanied by a family of smaller black bears greeted us early one morning, eagerly devouring the carcass of one of the rancher's cattle that had died just half a mile from the Glenn cabin. This led to a series of close encounters that made for an anxious time. It began with the day the children joined forces after school to go berry picking and, literally, stumbled on a mother black bear and her cub intent on the same mission. A few days later Adrienne was returning home one evening having picked up one of the consignments of fresh meat provided to the families to make up for the lack of hunting on the land. With blood dripping from a wrapper of a hefty buffalo steak, she walked within inches of a large black bear that must have found the smell tantalizing. In the tales of close encounters, Mark Glenn won the day with his story of "running into" a bear: "I was walking home in twilight when out the corner of my eye I saw this thing run at me from the woods. I don't think it was looking too closely either as we both collided. I was staring a black bear in the face…and he at me. He must have been as surprised as me because we both turned in opposite directions and ran!" Mark laughed off the incident, but none of us was to know just how close we had come to real danger until we finally left Frontier Valley.

The Clunes made the greatest effort to collect the fruits of the season. Adrienne was particularly keen to make preserves and lay down stores of bottled jams for the approaching winter. Gordon was eyeing the considerable yields, too, daily encouraging Aíne, Tracey, Justin, and Conor to gather more. Shortly after the first collection a mysterious series of activities occurred down by the creek, with a new burst of energy from Gordon, who was racing around his homestead with a glint in his eye. Plans were afoot and rumors soon began to wind their way up and down the valley. In the intense heat of the late-summer days Gordon had taken to wearing only a skimpy arrangement of cut-down underwear. This latest activity found him returning near naked and sweating from his encampment down by the creek to drag back large piles of wood. For Gordon this latest project was a potentially serious moneymaker. He was about to enter a new profession with deep roots in the homesteading era—bootlegging. To do so he was about to utilize his secret weapon.

Each adult had been asked to choose one item to bring on their time-travel experience. It couldn't be a luxury and had to be authentic to the era. The choices were intriguing, ranging from simple pleasures, such as Mark's pipe for smoking tobacco, to practical items such as Karen's bolts of cloth for making extra clothes. In the Clune household, Adrienne had chosen an early model of a sewing machine, a tiny and basic contraption compared to what's used today that had, so far, lain unutilized. Nate and Kristen had chosen a hammock. But Gordon had proved the most ambitious, requesting permission to build a still, similar to those that had been found in secret corners across rural America in a bid to produce profitable hard liquor. The rewards from sales of rotgut, however, came with risks. In 1883 such activities were illegal, with strict penalties for making alcohol without a license. Distilled spirits were then, as now, heavily taxed, and such taxes made up nearly half the income of the federal government in 1883. Until now, Gordon had lacked the raw ingredients to produce the necessary mash, but with many pounds of chokecherries in hand, he was in business.

Adrienne's chokecherry syrup, decked out for the fair.

This latest enterprise was characteristic of Gordon's spirit to continually innovate and seek new opportunities.

Homesteading is about survival, and I believe the spirit of America was shaped by experiences like this. Here we are competing with nature, and the pioneers had to respond in any ways they could to improve their family's lives and make a living. Sometimes that meant getting around laws. I'm hoping to sell this to the store.

As he assembled the necessary pieces, skillfully engineered by his company's workshop, Gordon was reminded of his student days when he'd first attempted such production. Screwing the copper kettle and condenser into place, he was excited to finally get the mash up to heat. Before long, the berries and wood smoke produced a heady perfume that started to waft up and down the valley. Watching the operation prompted thoughts of the early moonshiners who'd retreated deep into the backwoods to avoid detection. In their explorations of their land the families had stumbled across a tumbledown cabin tucked in the middle of a remote forest quarter. It was a mysterious place to have located a home. Boulder Valley is rich in local legends of illicit hooch production. Gordon clearly wasn't the first person to attempt home brewing within this very valley. After five days of eager experimentation, Gordon was frustrated; despite encouraging aromas, the spout at the end of the condenser remained dry.

I last tried this at fifteen and I sat here and thought I have forgotten an ingredient. I began to think I am not going to be able to do this, but then I realized I had a vapor lock. So I started to explore where the problem was

Gordon goes into business with his still.

and, bingo, I am suddenly having alcohol pour out. I was in business. In 1883 I believe I would be making more money out of producing liquor to sell to local miners than out of the whole of my one hundred and sixty acres. And why not?

As he eagerly watched the drips emerging, he reflected, too, on the irony of his encounter with the past:

It's funny, with all my business and social commitments I have no spare time in the year 2001 as I run from meeting to meeting, and with all the activities here, the same is true in 1883, where you imagine time ran more slowly. I have just the same amount of things to do.

"A Helluva Big Gamble"
Montana Moonshine

Many a night a grizzled and bedraggled Gordon Clune rose from his bed to walk bare-foot across his Frontier Valley acres to add more fuel to his wood-fired still and check that the chokecherry "beer" he'd drawn off the top of his fermentation barrel and poured into his still was boiling at a sufficiently high temperature to vaporize the alcohol in the beer and send it upward through the "worm," or cooling coil, where it would condense into a clear liquid destined to improve his sagging spirits if not his dismal finances.

Certainly Gordon Clune wasn't the first frontier settler to decide that the best thing to do with corn and rye, barley and berries, was to turn them into what old-timers still refer to as "white mule," because of the kick it carries. Unlike the commercially distilled liquor, home brew made without a license was illegal. It sidestepped both taxation and regulation, making its price a little lower and its health risks significantly higher. Brewed in stills sequestered in coulees and ravines by bootleggers who worked under cover of darkness and paid scant attention to quality control, moonshine whiskey could be contaminated by anything from pine pitch to lead solder, from convulsion-inducing fusel oils to unappetizing traces of insects, birds, and mice lured to their deaths by the sweet aroma of the fermenting "mash" with which the whiskey-making began.

A successful moonshine operation depended upon several factors. The right ingredients: some form of starch—usually corn, barley, or rye, though berries or other fruits were also used—plus malt, sugar, and yeast, all placed in a barrel or pot, mixed well, and liquefied with several kettles of boiling water. The right conditions: hot summer days in which fermentation—the process by which enzymes in the malt turn starches to sugar and yeast turns sugar to alcohol—could take place in as few as three or four days. The right kind of distillation apparatus: Gordon Clune's professionally engineered column still was far more sophisticated than the simple kettle and copper-coil devices used by most early Montana moonshiners. And finally: patience and perseverance, for neither Rome nor rye was built in a day.

But even if all these factors were in place and a bootlegger produced a smooth product that compared well with the brew from rival stills, one more element was crucial to success: a market large enough—and thirsty enough—to bring in sufficient profits to warrant the risks. In 1883 Montana Territory, where liquor flowed freely, what would motivate a buyer to choose rotgut whiskey over the government-regulated bourbons and ryes so readily available in the hundreds of saloons and bars across the region? Ever the entrepreneur, Gordon Clune would no doubt have managed to persuade miners farther up the Boulder of the advantages of buying strong, cheap whiskey they didn't have to go all the way into town to get. And had he hitched up his wagon and driven the backcountry, there would likely have been cowboys and soldiers working far enough from legal booze to find his wares attractive. But profits from such sales would have been slim compared to the gains to be had in the most profitable bootlegging activity of that era—selling whiskey to reservation Indians. For, after years of trading firewater of all sorts with the Native Americans whose lands it had systematically acquired, the government had outlawed the sale of alcohol to Indians, thereby all but guaranteeing a booming business for moonshiners and smugglers all across the West.

The law of supply and demand was soon to produce an even larger market, for as early as the 1880s organizations such as the Women's Christian Temperance Movement were citing Demon Rum as "productive of pauperism, degradation and crime" and urging people to "pledge...to abstain from intoxicating liquors." Perhaps the most notorious zealot for the abolition of alcohol was Carry Nation. Her hatchet-swinging visits to bars and saloons across the West were legendary by 1910, the year she called on the ladies in the red-light district of Butte, Montana, exhorting them to renounce their infamous profession and lead their wayward clients from sin to sobriety. Though a group of supporters cheered as the righteous crusader elbowed her way through the crowd, Carry Nation emerged from her visit of charity with no recruits and a badly wrenched elbow, testimony to how little interest those ladies of the night had in joining her campaign against alcohol.

In 1889, North Dakota entered the Union as a dry state, thereby creating an eastern-Montana bootlegging market beyond Gordon Clune's wildest dreams. By 1903, Jacob Seel, who owned a strategically placed piece of land on the north bank of the Missouri just over the Montana state line from Fort Buford, had joined forces with a couple of Montana ranchers and a lawyer from Minot to exploit that market to the fullest by establishing the border town of Mondak, a watering hole dedicated to quenching the thirst of North Dakotans left high and dry by their constitution's prohibition plank. For starters, Seel and his brother built a log tavern that straddled the state line. While liquor could only be bought on the Montana side of the establishment, it could be consumed in either end of the building—or smuggled out to be enjoyed later at home on the range. The resident population of Mondak never exceeded three hundred, yet many times that number of visitors regularly converged on this unique crossroads where ferryboats, railroad cars, stages, and farm wagons made for ready transport of customers, whiskey, ranching supplies, and farm produce. Games of chance made evenings in the bars all the more lively, and in 1919 the tiny center seemed destined for greatness as it was voted the seat of newly created Roosevelt County.

That same year the Eighteenth Amendment became the law of the land. With the manufacture, sale, and transport of alcoholic beverages suddenly banned nationwide, Mondak seemed doomed to become a ghost town. Big dreams die hard, however, and with taverns outlawed, enterprising bootleggers turned to making their own brew and selling it in less obvious venues. According to Dale Scott, the son of North Dakota homesteaders whose claim was some two miles from the Montana border, a retired Mondak madam proved to be one of the area's best brewers, making booze so strong that "one bottle and we just about would fall off our horses going home."

With the coming of Prohibition, the market for moonshine whiskey exploded. Soon stills were being run and liquor was being sold by men and women all across the West, and booze production boomed in Montana, where, according to the *Montana Almanac,* baffled federal agents "ranged this huge state in a vain effort to dry up millions of gallons of 'mountain dew' made for 537,606 prospective drinkers who had 94,078,080 acres [in which] to hide" their illicit operations. With the state's live-and-let-live attitude, the Feds had precious little help from Montanans—including officers of the law—in finding the stills or their owners. "It was no disgrace after Prohibition if you bootlegged," according to Cascade County resident Jeannette Bowen. "You could always get a bottle from somebody," agreed Pat Merva, whose father had made wine and white mule for family and friends throughout the long dry years and who later ran a bar in Centerville, Montana. According to Merva, nobody bothered you if you brewed for your own consumption, but selling moonshine liquor was "a helluva big gamble." And so was drinking the potent stuff. Sometimes home brew was smooth as could be, the former barkeep recalled, but some of it "damned near killed you."

Cheese production goes into high gear.

Up at the Glenns' the same intensity of activities was being played out. Now running their farm like clockwork, Karen and Mark found themselves busy at every minute of the day. As haying continued up in the top fields, Karen was tackling an ever-larger pile of laundry sent over each week from the store, taking satisfaction in bringing in a small but significant income to keep their lives afloat. Scrubbing filthy sheets and oil-stained jeans with only a brush and lye soap, she reflected:

I get twenty cents a pound for this and it is hard work, but I can make the money that keeps this farm afloat so Mark can keep haying. If I keep to my goal of cleaning six dollars' worth of laundry and I can bake and sell at least four loaves at twenty cents each, we can make as much as eight dollars a week, and that's keeping us alive. And it's legal!

She was not impressed by Gordon's latest entrepreneurial effort, seeing it as a poor example to his children.

By contrast, Nate and Kristen Brooks were taking a more cautious attitude to the spirit of enterprise engaging the rest of the valley. They had chosen not to trade regularly with the store, spending their time slowly refining their goat milking, haying, and preparing for winter.

NATE: *It's interesting. What we have found is that we are the same people here as we are in our modern lives. If you are a workaholic back home, then you will be that here. We could be doing laundry for the store, doing baking, chopping wood.... There is tons you can do out here, but it's down to what is*

important to you. So we choose to have some free time out here to enjoy the mountains. Why do more work than you need to? We are obsessed with being busy in the modern world. It's the same out here for some people.

They were suspicious of the idea that exhausting yourself to make an extra dollar was what should motivate everyone on the project.

NATE: *I'm not into the rat race. So I'm not into Hop Sing's laundry. There's even a rat race out here.*

On the morning of September 11, news from the modern world reached even our small corner of tranquillity. The terrorist attacks on America brought us a difficult decision: whether to break from the experiment, which demanded isolation from the modern day, and take the reports to our homesteaders. For the families, a welcome break from their regular routines had been planned, a day of hunting and fishing on a local ranch where they could shoot small game birds and catch trout. Having risen at six to walk to the site, Gordon, Conor, Justin, Karen, Erinn, and Logan must have been midway through the journey when the first news from New York began to filter out. Producer Simon Shaw eventually broke the news to the families. "By seven-thirty [Mountain Time], like most of America that morning, I had witnessed the first of the horrifying events on TV, and soon after the collapse of the first of the Twin Towers I set off to work. Driving up a quiet track in the middle of Montana wilderness was a bewildering contrast to the news that came in via the radio in my vehicle. Turning the corner, I caught sight of the party, excited in their anticipation for the day. By then the news was too momentous to hide from them. Stopping the vehicle, I approached them and started by making an apology for having to bring news from the modern day into their lives." At this point the families hadn't watched a news bulletin on television, heard a radio, or read a newspaper for over four months. They had all talked about the freedom they felt from not having to keep up with current events. That liberation was put on hold as the news was briefly outlined to them. Shell-shocked and confused, they decided to continue walking down to the site. "If I return to my cabin today, I'm just going to sit there and wonder what is going on in the world. So I'd rather sit and fish to give me something else to think on," said Karen. By the time we caught up with them a half hour later, the continuing horrors were unfolding to a point where it only felt fair to allow them to listen to the events by radio. "Are we safe here?" asked Logan as he sat listening. Awed by the news, they spent much of the remainder of the day in silence, choosing to contemplate events quietly while fishing.

In the uncertainty that surrounded the unfolding events, it was also difficult not to pass on an atmosphere of fear, even in the remote space we were so lucky to inhabit. Adrienne was particularly shocked, recalling having eaten in Windows on the World recently. For Nate and Kristen, the events prompted thoughts of how early settlers in remote areas would have been equally isolated from national events. The small fragments of news coming in would have traveled slowly, brought either by infrequent mail or in rare sightings of newspapers. Mark Glenn, who had become so immersed in the isolated lifestyle of the homesteader, had difficulty connecting the events with the life he was leading in the valley: "Hearing this kind of stuff just makes you appreciate the beauty of this place even more."

This news triggered a thirst for updates on continuing developments. So for the next few days, the families were offered the chance to read modern newspapers and printouts of the latest news downloaded from the Web, which were placed in a delivery box at the entry to the valley. Seeing the horrific pictures spread across the pages came as uncomfortable confirmation of what was really going on in the outside world and, for Kristen, triggered a sudden panic at being so isolated. Unable to deal with the fears in her mind, she and Nate walked the two miles down to the production center the next evening and requested to use a telephone to call home. Reassured by talking to her mom, they returned to their cabin, thankful to be away from the continual broadcasting of events. After four days, everyone felt keen to move on and requested that we only bring them news of significant magnitude in their remaining time so they could attempt to return to their daily lives. But like everyone else across America, the events continued to haunt them.

The long, hungry days of winter made protecting the garden's crop a high priority.

Gordon works on his root cellar.

GORDON: *Immersed in another century, living in a bygone era, I chop and saw wood. I contemplate the catastrophic reality of yesterday's carnage and I saw through fallen trees. I shoo chickens away from a fertile garden. I think of those countless Americans destroyed and crushed under the weight of steel girders. Entombed forever the innocence of a generation. I pause and feel the weight on my shoulders. My strengthened arms and shoulders from countless saw cuts and ax chops could not begin to lift the weight I feel. I listen to the silence in our 1883 sheltered environment. The wind rustles leaves and whispers sad thoughts and condolences. How can I help? What can I do? It's war without boundaries, an enemy without a face. An elusive target I don't know if my aim could hit. I saw and chop wood and shoo chickens away from my garden.*

Everyone responded by throwing himself or herself into another round of work. A flurry of snowflakes one September morning reminded everyone of the approach of winter and cued a new set of urgent activities. At each homestead the men began making serious excavations for root cellars, slowly displacing what must have amounted to tons of soil. At the same time the gardens were being picked over, yielding a summer's growth of vegetables, so eagerly awaited since their sowing in late May. Sadly, in most cases, the harvests were providing small return on the energies that had been invested. Every day dozens of buckets of water had been hauled from the creek to keep the crops alive. Many an hour had been passed diligently weeding the plots, never mind the long stints the children had spent patiently watching over the gardens to head off deer or cattle. "I'd dig a much bigger garden next year," remarked Karen, looking at the meager amounts of potatoes, turnips, carrots, and beets emerging from her plot. She knew that the harvest was one of the most important factors that would be considered by the *Frontier House* consultants in their assessment of whether the families would last through a winter. Accounts from homesteading days reveal how substantial kitchen gardens were considered necessary to produce the quantities of vegetables to sustain families through winter months. In *Letters of a Woman Homesteader,* Elinore Pruitt Stewart, a feisty newcomer to the hard life of the settler records how in one year she grew more than two tons of potatoes, half a ton of carrots, large bins of beets, turnips, onions, parsnips, and more than one hundred heads of cabbage. Plus a winter squash that was pickled along with beans and green tomatoes. Remarkably, Karen Glenn had managed to ripen a small but tasty handful of tomatoes from her plant lovingly cared for outside the cabin door—no mean feat given the short growing season offered at such altitude. Up at Nate and Kristen's, their returns were small, too. The Clunes had enjoyed better results, with larger growth and a bigger crop, a confirmation that Gordon's excavation of an irrigation ditch from the nearby spring and a later extension of the garden had paid off. Aine and Tracey, who'd had garden duty throughout much of the summer, took great pleasure in digging up the strong haul of produce, much of which was being pickled by Adrienne.

Meanwhile the backbreaking job of digging out the ground for root cellars for winter storage of crops continued, each man apparently eager to build a bigger and better model than his neighbors. Mark, Gordon, and Nate took on the guise of miners in those final days of feverish deep digging, returning grimy and sweating from their labors, each praying he would get the job done before frost turned the soil to concrete. The final results were admirable: each had been a mammoth task and resulted in a generous frost-protected storage area in which to overwinter their vegetables. Proud of pulling off his last big endeavor, Mark Glenn reflected on the marathon of activities that the project had seen him tackle:

Digging this [root cellar] makes you really reflective. Right now I begin to feel angry as I am leaving this place soon and I know we will prove that we could make it through a winter here and yet we don't get to stay. I am angry at how much of myself I have invested in this place. Leaving is going to be tough. I sat down yesterday and looked around at what we have achieved, and I am proud of what we have done. Nothing has happened here that I have not put my mark on. I don't want to go home. This is home.

As autumn arrived, another milestone approached, the first of the farewell ceremonies for the families in Frontier Valley. In the third week of September a small party embarked on the last visit to the store. Even though they would be leaving in a little over two weeks, this was an important trip as our homesteaders knew that they would soon face an assessment by the project consultants including how well provisioned they were for the winter. Each had been carefully planning his or her purchases and trades: Nate was eager to buy snowshoes, Karen was after more feed to see her chickens through winter, the Clunes had ordered piles more vegetables. A summer of trading had produced a mutually lucrative arrangement between the homesteaders and our store owner, Hop Sing Yim, and everyone was looking forward to the opportunity to say good-bye to him. But a shocking discovery awaited them on arrival. After a hard day's ride across the mountains they arrived to find the store sign had been painted over with a new name. Inside, Hop Sing Yim's personal effects had disappeared. The trader who had proved a lifeline for the families had sold out. The decision to end Hop Sing Yim's dealings was based on real events of the era, when local newspapers reported the circulation of anti-Chinese petitions. Active unions of traders began to gain strength in the 1880s, and boycotts were organized in many Western towns to curtail Chinese businesses. The Chinese Exclusion Act of 1882 became the most devastating blow of all, giving all Chinese settlers permanent alien status, barring them from becoming American citizens. It further placed the burden on the individual to prove why he should not be deported to China, and random arrests and interrogations at this time were frequent. Exhausted by such activities and being hit by higher taxes, the first of many Chinese merchants across the West were starting to give up their enterprises. The decline continued well into the twentieth century, by which time the numbers of Chinese residents were a small fraction of those who had come so eagerly to build the railroads. Our homesteaders were now experiencing the impact of such harsh legislation with the departure of Hop Sing Yim. Saddened by his departure, they reflected on the man they had come to see as a friend and ally. Karen said, "I saw Hop as a good man and employer. It is sad to judge a man by his background. It reminds me in some ways how we haven't come that far in a hundred years." Nate said, "I've become more interested in the politics of this area in recent weeks, and this is a sad lesson. Even though homesteaders had it hard, no one could claim to corner the market in hardships. It was everywhere."

A small consolation waited inside where the new owner (a role played by Virgil Gust, a lifelong trader in a modern general store in Big Timber) was eager to show off a new line of goods. The completion of the Northern Pacific Railroad in September 1883 was now providing a wider range of choices in our store. On this final visit, the new goods would have had customers drooling in their day. Fresh fruits and vegetables from California were now on offer, including juicy watermelons, oranges, plums, peaches, and lemons. On the top shelf new lines of fabrics and warm winter clothing caught the eye of Karen and her family, but most tantalizing of all, particularly for Erinn and Logan, was a mechanical contraption that promised new treats. Priced at three dollars, an ice-cream maker may have seemed a rash purchase at a time when all the families were taking great care in managing their finances, but mindful of how hard the children had worked all summer,

Karen was keen to reward them. With winter approaching she'd have had access to the ice necessary for production, so the purchase was made along with a generous amount of foods to go into her winter larder. Having balanced their accounts for the last time, the families took the long hike back home, their last journey back to Frontier Valley.

"Just What Is Needed in This Country"
The Completion of the Northern Pacific Rail Route

By 1880, the railroad, the most powerful force for change on the frontier, was stretching farther and farther into the West. Montana Territory had long anticipated its coming. For a region heretofore dependent upon freighters whose wagons were immobilized in winter, the train promised a reliable means of importing fruits, vegetables, and manufactured clothing and goods, plus a means of exporting cattle, sheep, timber, wool, grain, and ore to far-distant markets. Equally important, especially to homesteaders, the coming of the railroad meant greater availability of household goods and farming equipment—and eventually, lower prices on all imported goods, including those ordered from mail-order catalogs.

In the spring of 1880, when the Utah and Northern finally reached Dillon in the southwest corner of the territory, a Helena paper editorialized, "[W]e have at least one live railroad town within Montana.... Our people will be enabled soon to indulge their taste for fresh fruits without bankrupting their pockets." It would be another three years, midsummer of 1883, before the Northern Pacific reached Big Timber from the East and the settlers of the Boulder Valley could enjoy the benefits of produce "fresh and good...from St. Paul." The editor of the *Livingston Daily Enterprise,* the paper that served the citizens of Big Timber and the Boulder Valley, touted the "new refrigerated express cars" scheduled to run every other day as "just what is needed in this country."

On September 8, 1883, the ceremonial driving of the final spike of the Northern Pacific, the line that stretched from St. Paul to Portland, was cause for great celebration among all the settlers along the route connecting those two cities. There was hardly a homesteader who didn't realize the significance of that event, for the railroad would change forever the character of the frontier, tying small, isolated communities to each other and to the rest of the nation.

For frontier families, the completion of the northern rail route increased the reliability of mail delivery—including the delivery of goods ordered from the Montgomery Ward and Sears Roebuck catalogs. Urma DeLong Taylor, child of Montana homesteaders, recalled waiting impatiently for a new pair of shoes "bought out of the catalog" to arrive in the mail. "Oh, those leather shoes!" she remembered years later. "You know what new leather smells like. That was the best perfume I'd ever smelled as a child.... Every few minutes I'd take them out—ohhh—put them on and look them over, then put them back in the box." Had little Urma DeLong been old enough to appreciate all the factors involved in the delivery of her lovely new shoes, she would no doubt have agreed that the coming of the railroad was, indeed, "just what was needed" by homesteaders and merchants alike.

One bright prospect beckoned on the horizon. From the earliest days of their experience our families had been eagerly talking about celebrating their time on the frontier with a small fair—a chance to demonstrate their achievements to local people. Now plans were afoot for the event. Gordon, by now successful with a high-alcohol creation from his still, was planning to demonstrate it at the fair as a "tonic rub," similar to "cures" of the day sold by visiting traders. (Negotiations with the Bureau of Alcohol, Firearms & Tobacco, which enforces current regulations for alcohol production, had only enabled us to produce liquor for educational purposes, which to Gordon's dismay did not permit drinking it.) Meanwhile, Adrienne was achieving appetizing results from her home industry of bottling chokecherry preserves and was planning to run a stall on the day. At the Glenns', a measuring tape was put around Jo-Jo, the popular pig. Nervous conversations followed between Mark and Karen about whether they could persuade the children to accept the demise of one of their family of animals to sell for food as the numerous guests would need feeding. Up at Nate and Kristen's, the new home industry of knitting hats and the production of goat cheese were stepped up for sales at the fair. Everyone was excited at the prospect of a gathering as a guest list of consultants and local residents who had assisted the production was put together.

More than anything else, the event proved a welcome focus to take everyone's mind away from September 11, which, despite the suspension of modern news, continued to trouble the families. Sewing thirty-eight stars onto a homemade flag (in 1883 there were only thirty-eight states), Adrienne reflected:

> *In the wake of the recent tragic events, I feel everyone's pain as I sew this flag, but it's helpful in healing that hurt for me. And it makes me think how proud I am to be an American because, like many homesteaders, I came out here as an immigrant and this experience has made me think of the tremendous determination people must have had not to give up. It's a tremendous heritage which was passed on to their children and that's at the heart of the American people today.*

OPPOSITE, TOP LEFT:
Every member of the family pitched in.

OPPOSITE, TOP RIGHT:
Gordon expected a lucrative return on his "tonic rub."

OPPOSITE, BOTTOM: Kristen takes advantage of the natural light.

The Final Reckoning

Right to the very end the experience proved a series of contradictions.

ADRIENNE: *The moment I get off the frontier, I think I am going to be smiling. When I came out here, I thought I would not want to go back to the twenty-first century with all the stress of modern-day life. Well, I don't feel like that at all. It's been the opposite.*

I am so looking forward to the first day out of here when I will jump and scream. Walking out, I will have the biggest smile on my face!

KAREN: *As the time gets closer, I hope to bargain for a few more seconds in the day to absorb this place. I want a place when life gets real crazy in the twenty-first century that I can go to in my mind so I can visualize the mountains and all the peace we have come to associate with this. You'll have to tear me from these hills come departure!*

KRISTEN: *The other night I looked at the moon and thought about how far I am from home, and I was thinking how in 1883 I would have been wanting to go back home on the train. If we were staying for real, I'd probably have to talk to Nate and say that by now I'm not sure I am a Montana girl. I want to go back to Boston to do something more active.*

An Indian summer visited Montana for the last stretch of September. Warm days accompanied the gradual transition of the valley to a golden brown as months of drought began to show itself on the landscape. The aspens turned in tandem, edging the exhausted grassland with a brilliant lime-green border. Mark and Gordon made the most of the weather by finding isolated pockets of remaining hay to try to top off their winter stores. They were small dots on the landscape dragging piles long distances in this last effort. Nate was using the days to split logs into a pile that began to tower alongside his cabin. Every day was bringing them closer to the final assessment of their chances of surviving the winter.

The first to return of those who'd be making the judgment was Bernie Weisgerber, our cabin construction specialist. He'd spent all summer quizzing members of the production team via phone about the progress of the families and could barely contain his excitement at seeing the results of their endeavors. The last time he'd been in the valley, Nate's cabin was standing just eight logs high, and Gordon's had no roof, door, or windows. Now Bernie was keen to see if everyone had paid sufficient attention to his advice during training.

Sue Cain, our food and hygiene adviser, who'd waved good-bye to the families the day they'd departed from Virginia City, came next, eagerly anticipating the outcome of her teaching. With her were historians Linda Peavy and Ursula Smith, keen to observe firsthand the results. Rawhide Johnson, last seen driving the wagon that had delivered Kristen to the valley on her wedding day, was next and equally intrigued. "Are their animals still alive?" he asked with uncanny timing.

Up in the valley, Jo-Jo, the Glenns' "dancing pig," was slowly turning on a spit. Mark, who'd grown close to her with daily conversations about the ways of the world, had dispatched her just the day before, when a local butcher came to oversee the kill. She'd fattened up well in her time in the valley and was now about to feed the guests due for the "Frontier Fair." It had not been a popular move with everyone in the family: Logan had been equally close to Jo-Jo and found it distressing. Karen, though, saw it as an important lesson for her children:

People have got into a situation of not knowing where their food comes from. They get their dander up and say it is bad to kill, then run down to the market to buy a steak. No one realizes that someone raised it. This experience has put me much more in touch with animals, and my children are understanding those lessons, too.

As Mark barbecued the pig, finishing touches were being made in every cabin to cakes, jams, goat-cheese parcels, small homemade crafts, and numerous bottles of Gordon's "tonic." Each commodity would go up for sale, the last chance for the homesteaders to make a small income from their summer of endeavors.

Since their arrival, the modern pioneers had prompted considerable interest in the local community of the Boulder Valley. On the last Saturday in September the gates leading to the land were finally thrown open for visitors. Many of those arriving were descendants of the original settlers within the region and were fascinated to see how our families had coped. The morning began with a tour of each house led by the residents of Frontier Valley. Most intriguing was the reaction of the elder members of the community who'd been born in similar cabins built by their parents who had grown up in the same era being experienced by our families. The

hillsides and river bottoms are still dotted with their original homes, many abandoned after too many hard winters and summers of drought. Watching the register of memories on their faces was a joy, as they eagerly examined cookstoves, scrub boards, and the ceramic vessels for churning butter. It was the minute details that triggered reminiscences. Up at the Brookses', Nate's water flume and root cellar prompted reminders of the past for Big Timber resident Hazel Ewan, who had lived in a log cabin just half a mile away in the valley sixty-five years ago: "I think he's done very well. It took enterprising people to make it here, but he looks like he's well able to handle it." Moved by the occasion, Nate marked their visit as he made a speech down at the meadow where the fair was to be held: "Remember these people. They have endured more winters in Montana than any of us. These are the folks who were truly the pioneers." The oldest visitor, eighty-nine-year-old Isabel Berkland, was typical. Her father had arrived in a covered wagon pulled by two cows to set up a homestead in the Gallatin Valley. After being presented the 1883 cookbook the Brookses had been provided for the project, Isabel thanked Nate: "I learned to cook on a stove like yours, and I still bake my own bread today."

After the raising of Adrienne's hand-sewn flag, the fair could begin. Brisk sales of homemade goods saw everyone quickly running low on stocks while a hearty lunch of roast-pork sandwiches courtesy of the Glenns' pig was devoured by an appreciative crowd. Even Logan appeared to be coming around, but drew a line at taking a bite from the morsel offered. Meanwhile, competition for the most lucrative enterprise was keen: Aíne ran a fortune-telling booth, Tracey charged ten cents for haircuts, Justin and Conor had made homemade bows and arrows that proved popular with younger visitors. Perhaps the most profitable stalls were those offering alcohol. Nate had set up a sleight-of-hand card game at which dozens of customers lost a dime in their attempt to "find the lady" and win a bottle of beer. Gordon meanwhile had plenty of interest in his "tonic rub" and was eagerly demonstrating the apparatus in which it was produced. One of the most enthusiastic at Gordon's stall was Ying-Ming Lee, who'd taken the role of storekeeper Hop Sing Yim, and was back for the day with his family. Everyone welcomed the opportunity to say thanks and farewell. Ying-Ming had found the whole project fascinating: "It's been a great honor to be able to do this. The population of Chinese settlers in the West is a little-known story, and I hope this will help people understand that."

Traditional games that tested muscle power followed as the women tossed a cast-iron skillet to see who could hurl it the farthest. The men tried to prove themselves in a series of macho challenges, including a hair-raising round of ax-throwing at a distant target. A final challenge requiring brute force was introduced by our master of ceremonies, Bernie Weisgerber: "If you don't think this summer has been grueling for the families, I want you to know that Mark Glenn here has lost thirty pounds since he arrived and Nate Brooks has slipped over twenty pounds. You'll see why when you witness our last contest." (Gordon had chosen to pass on this last event.) Two hefty tree trunks set up on trestles were ready to test the men. The winner would be the first to saw through one single-handedly. At the sound of the pistol both Nate and Mark set to it, five months of muscle building at work in a furious burst of energy from both. Stripped to the waist, the men soon began sweating profusely. Nate maintained a sound rhythm, while Mark couldn't find the same momentum, his face soon turning crimson in the effort. The sound money was on the younger blood, as Mark quickly tired and Nate sank his saw through the foot-wide trunk in less than ninety seconds.

For the women, a different contest had seen them spend days sweating over their cookstoves perfecting breads, cakes, scones, and preserves for the "Best in Show" judging. A spread of delicious foods took center stage on the fairgrounds, displaying the fruits of Adrienne's, Kristen's, and Karen's work. From the start Adrienne had proved herself greatly accomplished in the kitchen, and she had now surpassed herself with an amazing feat, a perfect replica of the Clunes' cabin made from gingerbread, the individual logs held together by a creamy sugar paste. Kristen had made one of her favorite recipes, which had proved popular with everyone who'd visited their home, zucchini bread. Karen had entered a tasty bread-and-butter pudding, richly blended with her homemade dairy produce. Our panel of consultants enjoyed their judging, taking time to savor each of the items entered. Finally, they passed their verdicts to mark the end of the Frontier Fair. In the baked-foods category there were two prizes, one for best bread, the other for best sweet. Not surprisingly, Adrienne took the award for the best sweet food with her frontier-house cake. Kristen, who'd only recently considered herself hopeless in the kitchen, was delighted to take the award for best bread. Karen generously congratulated

ABOVE: Food at the Frontier Fair courtesy of Jo-Jo the pig.

BELOW: Nate shows his sleight of hand.

ABOVE: Tracey takes aim.

Ax throwing, a
frontier sport.

Mark sets to with
the crosscut saw.

Nate and Kristen,
a powerful team.

both women but couldn't hide her disappointment in taking no prizes in any of the games or Best in Show categories that afternoon. While the band that had proved so popular at Nate and Kristen's wedding played traditional songs, Karen reflected that the most important judgment of the whole enterprise had still to be made, the assessment for the families' winter survival.

"Step Right Up, Folks!"
Frontier Fairs and Festivals

In celebrating their first harvest by inviting friends and neighbors to a fair featuring plenty of good food, displays of fruits, vegetables, and baked goods, games of chance and skill, and lively music and dancing for young and old alike, our 1883 *Frontier House* families were following a well-established tradition, one stretching back to similar harvest celebrations in Europe and to town and county fairs held in states and territories across the North American continent.

Harvest fairs and festivals had been a part of Montana Territory since the first homesteaders celebrated their agricultural accomplishments back in the 1860s. At the first Gallatin County Fair, held in 1866, early settlers loaded livestock and produce, baked goods and and jellies, and kith and kin into farm wagons and headed to the fairgrounds, eager to see how their efforts compared with those of their neighbors. One of the most amazing exhibits that year was County Commissioner Philip Thorpe's decorative display of two hundred pounds of butter. Thorpe's booth drew widespread approval, for it was seen as a forecast of bright prospects for the valley's dairy farmers.

Gold-seeking pioneer James Fergus, who had taken up ranching after he and his wife, Pamelia, left Virginia City and moved to the Prickly Pear Valley, showed his top-grade bulls and raced his thoroughbred horses at fairs in Helena and Great Falls through the 1870s. As fairs moved beyond the homemade good fun of small community gatherings, games of chance as well as horse racing gained popularity. Over the years traveling medicine wagons, fortune-tellers, and hucksters of all stripes vied for the attention of fairgoers, with "Step right up, folks!" becoming as integral to a fairgoer's experience as the livestock, baked goods, and produce displays that had once been the center of attention.

The homesteading Shipman family of central Montana were major exhibitors at the first annual Fergus County Fair in 1893—where they were awarded highest honors for the largest variety of vegetables grown that year, as well as individual awards for their beets, cucumbers, cabbages, onions, cauliflowers, tomatoes, and rhubarb. And their produce, which Clark Shipman peddled door-to-door in little towns from Lewistown to Utica, continued to win prizes over the next decade.

By the dawn of the twentieth century, the farm produce, livestock, and handiwork of students from Fort Shaw Government Indian Boarding School in the Sun River Valley could be seen at fair exhibits throughout Montana. Their lacework and beading, their moccasins and leather shoes, as well as their finely crafted furniture, drew the praise of visitors, many of whom would otherwise have remained unaware of the skill and craftsmanship of their Native American neighbors.

The nearest Indian neighbors of our *Frontier House* families were the Crow people, whose reservation had, up until 1882, encompassed most of the Boulder River Valley. Understandably, over the next two decades there was relatively little contact between the area's earliest homesteaders and the people they had displaced. However, in 1904 families living in the Boulder Valley—and all across Montana—were invited to visit Crow Agency for the first annual Crow Fair, a celebration devised by a government Indian agent and patterned after county fairs in Montana and across the country. That first Crow Fair offered prizes for the best produce, handicrafts, and native foods. Though envisioned by the government as one more means of encouraging the reservation population to take up non-Indian ways, the Crow Fair would, over the next century, evolve into a means of reviving tribal rituals, games, and customs while celebrating the survival of a people—and a heritage—too strong to be destroyed.

Early the next morning a sober atmosphere took over in the valley. Each household was nervous about the arrival of the *Frontier House* consultants, aware that their entire efforts over the last five months were about to be judged. Bernie, Sue, and Rawhide had been joined by Linda and Ursula, project historians, who have spent many years studying the lives of pioneers, particularly in the West. Their job wasn't simply to look back on how well our families had done over the spring and summer; their primary focus was on whether the families were well enough prepared to survive a winter—the acid test for all homesteaders.

Each of our consultants would now make individual assessments based upon their specific areas of expertise. Bernie was examining the buildings, exploring how soundly they had been constructed with a particular eye for the way winter storms could penetrate. Every inch of daubing (the cement-type filler between each log) and floorboarding was checked for holes. Roofs were scrutinized by ladder. Rawhide was studying the animals to determine how they would fare in the worst of the weather. After the dry months of the fly-infested summer, all the milk cows were looking emaciated. Did each family have enough provisions set aside for months without access to fresh pasture? Susan was assessing the quantity and quality of foods set by to sustain the families through what could be a long spell of harsh weather. She was specifically interested in the types of nutrition available, keen to see a balance of foods including valuable vitamin sources. Linda and Ursula were examining how closely the families' activities and winter preparations had mirrored those of successful homesteaders in 1883.

During this last exploration a number of curiosities came to light. Up at Nate and Kristen's a set of contact lenses, complete with cleaning fluids, was found. From her very first introduction to period eyewear, Kristen had disliked wearing what she saw as the "ugly glasses" in the style of the era. Having been allowed to wear contacts for her wedding, she'd kept them and sheepishly confessed to having worn them while in Frontier Valley. Nothing untoward came to light at the Glenns', but the Clune cabin revealed departures from 1883. While examining the beds the families were sleeping on, Linda and Ursula discovered a twentieth-century box-spring mattress under Gordon and Adrienne's quilt. Upstairs, too, modern fly-papers were wedged into the gaps between the logs. Thickly covered in dead insects, they'd clearly been there some time. Neither of these items had been provided in the period-correct goods made available. Quizzed about the bedsprings, Gordon defended his actions: "My biggest thing was day-to-day survival and making the next step. If you had a problem, you figure out how to take care of it. If you need a nail, you find one and straighten it out and use it.... My family became astute at finding stuff and using it." He explained how he and the children had walked to a nearby abandoned homestead some way off. A pile of unwanted goods there had presented opportunities, including a queen-size box-spring mattress. Gordon noted, "Imagine hiking two and a half miles lifting two hundred and fifty pounds with three people over all sorts of obstacles so your wife could have something more comfortable to sleep on. I think that is admirable." Other matters also came to light that raised questions about the total authenticity of the Clunes' experience. A letter to Adrienne had arrived, addressed to her via one of the modern neighbors the Clunes had met during Gordon's "malnutrition" scare. The implication was they were receiving mail from the modern world in other ways than the mail deliveries from the store. (All store mail was vetted to ensure nonperiod items were not allowed in.) Both Gordon and Adrienne strongly denied receiving any modern goods from outside sources. However, materials remaining after the family had left the cabin showed that Aíne and Tracey had been making telephone calls to the outside world during the period of trading with the modern neighbors. Modern fishing tackle had also been found, and at the creek was a large box labeled "Club Del Gourmet." In their evaluation Linda and Ursula praised the Clunes for their many successes on the frontier but were disappointed at the family for stepping outside the time period: "There's no doubt in our minds but that you *could* have been stellar homesteaders. And yet, for reasons beyond our ken, you opted to sabotage your homesteading experience by matching wits with those who'd made the rules by smuggling in goods for your personal comfort and conducting unauthorized trading with neighbors."

Linda and Ursula also found the Clunes' plan for their ongoing survival as homesteaders unsatisfactory. By her own admission, Adrienne was never going to survive the cold of Montana in the worst of a typical winter: "Winter here would be so hard; maybe some women loved it, being out in the country and isolated, but for me personally I am a city slicker and I want to go back to the city. In 1883 I really did have an uncle living in Montana running a store, and if I was here then, I would go and join him." Adrienne and Gordon explained to the consultants that in their plans for facing an 1883 winter, Adrienne, Aíne, Tracey, and Conor planned to leave the cabin to stay in town. This explained why they'd put only small quantities of food aside in their winter larder, as only Gordon and Justin would stay on the homestead throughout the long months ahead. Likewise, there was little hay for their horse as the family also proposed sending Cowboy to town. "There's a lot of artful dodging going on here," said

ABOVE: The growing shadow of winter looms over the valley.

Linda in her reaction to the curious plan. "But in Montana and other hard-to-live places, you don't bend nature's rules." Having visited all the families and made their appraisals, each of our consultants went home to write up their final reckonings.

"Regardless of What I Did the Cold Crept In"
Life in the Crucible of Winter

After the hard, seemingly unceasing work required of them through spring, summer, and fall, many homesteaders looked forward to the quiet of winter as a time when fieldwork was over and they could catch up on such indoor work as sharpening saws and axes, repairing tack, mending clothing, weaving rugs, and sewing curtains. Even so, the first winter storm served as a rude reminder of the harshness of that "quiet season." Winter weather often posed physical dangers and invariably heightened emotional stress by necessitating prolonged periods of confinement in small quarters. Biting winds and freezing temperatures hampered travel and complicated outside work essential to a family's survival. Snow and sleet driven by icy winds invaded all but the stoutest dwellings, and blizzards disoriented anyone caught in the out-of-doors. Winter was, in effect, the crucible in which homesteaders were tested.

By 1883, the year our *Frontier House* families staked their mythical claims in Montana's Boulder Valley, stories of winter hardship abounded, and they, like hundreds of first-year homesteaders before them, would have been aware of the need to prepare themselves well for the season ahead. Memoirs of late-nineteenth- and early twentieth-century homesteaders indicate the importance of gathering sufficient fuel to last the winter through, and families devoted many summer and fall hours to felling standing deadwood, sawing logs into appropriate lengths, and stacking a minimum of six to eight cords against the coming cold. Early settlers also made careful provision for their winter water supply. And they dried and preserved meats, fruits, and vegetables and dug and lined root cellars for food storage—including, in some cases, huge barrels of buttermilk for drinking and making biscuits during the winter months when the cows went dry. One pioneer recalled with pride stocking her root cellar with "wine, malt, spirits, sauerkraut, jerked deer and buffalo tongue, bear bacon, and a thousand other things" each autumn. In addition, savvy settlers rechinked logs, banked the lower portions of their outer walls with mounds of dirt or piles of straw or sod, layered their interior walls with newspaper, and covered the cracks in wooden floors with straw, rugs, and animal skins. Those in blizzard country strung rope between house and barn to avoid getting lost during blinding snow squalls.

Though newcomers did their best to follow the example of their more experienced neighbors, hearing about a frontier winter was one thing, while actually experiencing one was quite another. North Dakota pioneer Lucy Goldthorpe Vandeberg never forgot the "many long, cold days and nights" she spent during her first winter in a homestead shack whose "walls were only single board thickness, covered with tar paper on the outside.... I'd spent money sparingly, because I didn't have much, but I had worked hard all during summer and fall...to winterize the structure.... To help seal out the cold I'd added layers of gunny sacks...on the floor and then the homemade wool rugs." It was all of no account, she recalled years later. "Regardless of what I did the cold crept in through the thin walls...[and] the mournful wail of coyotes searching the tormented land for food did nothing to make the winter any more pleasant."

Blizzards were another winter reality settlers never really understood until they'd experienced their awesome strength and disorienting effects. The Ammons sisters of St. Louis settled in Lyman County, South Dakota, in 1907. That first winter, as the sisters set out from the schoolhouse where Ida Mary taught, en route to their tar-paper shack a half mile distant, they glimpsed a blizzard "coming like white smoke" across the plains. Racing for home, they were barely inside before the storm struck. Years later, Edith Ammons Kohl recalled that "Cowering in that tiny shack where thin building paper took the place of plaster, the wind screaming across the Plains, hurling the snow against that frail protection, was...like drifting in a small boat at sea, tossed and buffeted by the waves, each one threatening to engulf you."

The Ammons sisters survived that first winter and went on to establish themselves securely in the West. Indeed, for them, as for most settlers, the dangers posed by blowing snow and subzero temperatures proved less worrisome than the confinement imposed by such weather. Anna Marie Bergan, a single homesteader who spent her first winter in Dakota Territory in a dugout, was trapped inside for almost a month when the heavy snows piled up drifts against the door. Yet she not only survived her

Caught by an early winter in south-central Montana, this homesteader sets about the chore of sawing and splitting more firewood.

trying ordeal but made the most of her difficult situation by spending those long weeks spinning yarn, knitting, and doing fancy needlework. Anita Brannin Ward was a young bride pregnant with her first child when south-central Montana was hit with the heavy winter snows of 1917. "You couldn't get in or out," she recalled in later years. "Oh, I'll tell you, we had a wonderful time.... [But] I stop and think about those things [now] and it scares the dickens out of me. I don't know how I did it."

Some winters were legendary. The snowstorm that blanketed Dakota Territory in mid-October of 1880 buried both buildings and livestock. Iva Van Loan King was a child then, living in a tar-paper house on her parents' homestead near the Big Sioux River. "Our house was covered [with snow]," King recalled in her later years, "and we could not get out except by a window. A neighbor came and asked Father to bring a shovel and help him find his barn. [The snow had drifted] higher and higher, hard as ice and high as his house...covering his barn and hay stacks completely. They located the barn by stepping [off] the distance from the house and then digging down. They were lucky enough to find

Ben Miles prepares to take two ladies on a winter outing in Boulder Valley, Montana. Such outings were tonic for "cabin fever."

the barn and the stock all safe inside except for about twenty head of hogs.... Many of the [neighboring] homes were without flour, sugar, kerosene, coffee, and other staples, as the storm came before [people] had laid in their winter's supply."

That same winter of 1880–81 was seared in the memory of Sarah Ann Klebsch. She was fourteen years old and living with her parents and four siblings near Huron, Dakota Territory, when the first storm of the season struck. "We had no meat, sugar, coffee, flour, and other staple foods," she recalled. "[We] lived [for] three months on muffins and pancakes made from wheat which we ground on a hand coffee mill. We also had potatoes, rutabagas, and milk and fortunately had plenty of firewood."

The historic winter of 1886–87 struck the plains of Montana and Dakota Territories on November 13, 1886, when it began to snow and didn't let up for a month. January of 1887 set records for low temperatures, and all across the plains livestock froze to death, with Montana losing some 60 percent of its cattle in what became known as the Great Die Up. George Jackson, the son of homesteaders in the Judith Basin, was fifteen years old that spring of 1887 when he took part in the gruesome roundup of the frozen carcasses that littered the range. It was then that he vowed he would never own cattle he could not afford to feed through the winter.

Not all winters were the stuff of legend. For instance, the winters on either side of the Great Die Up were warm and "open," with little snow cover. The winter of 1882–83 was equally mild—and sufficiently open to allow Clark Shipman, with the help of his fifteen-year-old son, Henry, to work through the season, building a twelve-by-sixteen-foot log house for his two daughters, Winnie and Gertie, homesteading schoolteachers newly arrived in the Judith Basin from Vermont. The young Shipman women were able to move into the house in March, when, in any normal year, construction would have been just getting under way. Though open winters made life easier for the homesteader, they could cause some anxiety as well, for the lack of snow invariably meant dry conditions for the crops of summer and fall. Winter, whether mild or fierce, gave homesteaders plenty to fret about.

Yet winter could bring comfort as well as stress, especially to youngsters. Iva Van Loan King looked back with nostalgia at "long winter evenings" in the family homestead by the Big Sioux River. She recalled, "We [would sit]...before the open grate.... Mother and Grandmother each had her knitting and sat in the semi-darkness, their needles keeping up a constant click, click, as they made mufflers, stockings, and mittens for the family." Adults also found ways to beat the winter blues. When cabin fever set in, Hilda Oakland would organize sleigh rides among her North Dakota neighbors, piling the sleigh high with straw and going from house to house to round up others who felt a need to experience the freedom of all outdoors—if only for a few brief hours.

For many homesteaders, the Christmas season provided a welcome midwinter diversion. Those living on claims located near stands of pine or fir or cedar could cut a tree and haul it home to be strung with popcorn and paper chains, topped with a star made of wire and paper, or adorned with small candles to be lit on Christmas Eve. On Christmas morning, children might find a stocking full of oranges and nuts, holiday letters and small gifts from loved ones far distant, and perhaps a mysterious package that might contain a long-wished-for toy, but more often than not held some very practical article of clothing— wool cap and stockings, a new pair of shoes.

Sometimes a community celebration was the holiday highlight. In 1879, Nebraska homesteaders Mattie and Uriah Oblinger and their three little girls joined their neighbors around a Christmas tree at the schoolhouse. "We had a Norway spruce evergreen tree. It looked nice filled with presents for the little ones," Mattie Oblinger wrote her mother back home in Indiana. Her husband, Uriah, had played Santa, "but the little ones most all knew him." In a note added to her mother's letter, the eldest Oblinger daughter, eight-year-old Ella, reported to her "Dear Grandpa and Grandma" that she and her sisters had each received "a new red…calico dress…and a doll and…a string with candy and raisins on it."

For Lucy Goldthorpe, the young school-teacher from Iowa who filed on a claim near Epping in the northwest corner of North Dakota, "the outlook [for the Christmas holidays]

This rare long-exposure photograph shows the Ed Kopac homestead near Okaton, South Dakota, on a cold winter night in 1906. The clothesline stretched from house to outhouse might have provided security on a dash outside during a blizzard.

was mighty bleak"—until Anna Kallak, another single woman homesteading just a couple of miles away, arranged to spend Christmas with her. "Hiring a livery rig, Anna drove over early and suddenly we were planning a gala day," Lucy later observed. "Inviting the two boys that had claims near mine gave the dinner an extra holiday note. In spite of the limited variety of food and the temperature hovering over thirty degrees below zero, the dinner was a great success."

Lucy Goldthorpe, like thousands of other homesteaders, not only survived the hardships of winter on the American frontier but learned each year ways of being better prepared to weather winters to come. And though there would always be days when "the cold crept in" and nights when no one dared venture outside, those whose forethought and preparation enabled them to survive the harsh test of their first winter as homesteaders were, as a rule, well on their way to proving up on the land they hoped to make their own.

With the assessment and Frontier Fair behind them, all of the residents in the valley were suddenly brought up sharp with the realization that the project truly was moving to a close. In five days they would be back in the modern world. Accepting that was somehow much tougher than anyone had bargained for. While everyone had had a different experience, some more difficult than others, it had proved an extraordinary adventure in everyone's life. No matter how passionately people had silently pleaded for the end to come, letting go was going to be painful. Without wood to gather, hay to cut, or any of the hundred jobs that had propelled each family along for the last five months, there was the unfamiliar sensation of having time to kill. These last few days cued everyone to become deeply reflective on the purpose of his or her stay.

Mark had taken great comfort during his time on the frontier in reading the few books that had been provided. Among them was Emerson's *Nature*, which he felt hit right at the heart of what they'd been trying to achieve:

> *In the woods, we return to reason and faith. There I feel that nothing can befall me in life—no disgrace, no calamity...which nature cannot repair. Standing on the bare ground—my head bathed by the blithe air, and uplifted into infinite space—all mean egotism vanishes.... I am the lover of uncontained and immortal beauty. In the wilderness, I find something more dear and connate than in streets or villages. In the tranquil landscape, and especially in the distant line of the horizon, man beholds somewhat as beautiful as his own nature.*

Gordon Clune, too, had drawn from the experience and was intent on changing things when he got home. After five months of hard physical labor, he reflected:

> *I think corporate America misses a lot of things, like what put them on top. What put them up there was the hard work and creativity of their descendants...of pioneers. Corporate America is too busy nowadays working out in*

the gym when they should be using their energy to create something, to do something with their hands. I now realize it's important for the president of the company to get his hands dirty, we need to get on the floor and make things happen.

Changed attitudes began to be expressed by everyone up and down the valley as the time away from the twenty-first century began to trickle away. For Nate and Kristen the experience had most strongly resonated in a reassessment of their modern priorities. Standing alongside the cabin he and Rudy had built, Nate looked at all the improvements his family had achieved in their time on the frontier:

It's amazing how much you can get accomplished. In the modern world we are trying to do so many things—lose ten pounds, master the guitar, read books—we can't really do any of them as fully as we like. One of the things that Kristen and I have taken away from this experience is that we concentrate on being successful in one thing and focus on that alone. Then we can move on, rather than not having the satisfaction of completion when you have four projects that are never finished.

Karen was also eager not to leave behind what she'd taken from the experience:

After this, I will advise my friends and family that they have got to find a way now and then of getting away from the twenty-first century. Even if that

means throwing all the breakers in your house one evening and just spending time with your family to find out who they really are. No Game Boys or videos. When you live in a one-room cabin, there is nowhere to retreat so you can get things on the table. It's so much healthier.

The children were also recognizing new aspects in their family. Aíne Clune had arrived with mixed feelings about the project:

When I arrived, I thought this was going to be like a work camp, and lots of my friends tried to talk me out of coming. My dad did this to try and get the family closer together, but I thought we'd end up getting sick of each other, five months every single day. But now I know that it's not like that. I definitely got a lot closer to my dad, as most of the time he was at work and when he came home, I would not be in a good mood as he'd say I could not go to friends' houses. Now I understand why he wanted to be with us and I feel bad for being mean to him. Now I'm a lot more proud of him for doing this with me.

Her cousin Tracey had probably had the toughest experience out on the frontier; far from her mother and father she'd had lots of moments when she'd really doubted the wisdom of her coming. But she felt she'd been strengthened by the endeavor:

I think I learned a lot out here. I think I have grown up. I have more confidence in who I am. When I get home, I won't let people boss me around anymore. Coming out here gave me a second chance about what I want to be when I grow up and how I want to live my life.

Both Aíne and Tracey said they now felt different about what they'd value in the future. They agreed that no longer would makeup and wearing the latest clothes be so important. Only time would tell if they'd keep their pact to turn their back on consumerism, but their relationship with Frontier Valley had undeniably been turned upside down. Particularly for Tracey:

Last night I stayed up and cried as I thought about leaving here and it's funny; we wanted to leave so badly and it is really sad because we built all this and now it has grown on us.

In an uncanny moment of anticipation winter really did return to Frontier Valley in the last couple of days of the experience. With departure due on Friday, October 5, a heavy snow began to fall just twenty-four hours before. Unlike the earlier few, isolated flakes, a four-inch-thick carpet lay across the land within a few hours. It was a timely reminder that all the efforts the families had gone to weren't for some far-off event that bore no relevance to their encounter. "It could set in for a long stay," said Mark Glenn as he eyed his winter fuel pile that had taken every spare moment to build since arrival. "Not sure I cut enough now." He'd never get the chance to find out.

At 10 A.M. on the morning of October fifth the first of our families began their journey out of Frontier Valley. A brilliant blue-sky morning started a gradual thaw. The Glenns had asked to leave first as they knew every minute spent on their homestead that last day would prove increasingly painful. Karen's jokes about having to comb the mountains to find her were only half in jest; everyone in her family had invested so much in the daily running of their home, it truly tore them apart emotionally to leave. Erinn had built such a bond with the animals, especially her horse Snowball, she could barely look at the corrals as she ventured out of the cabin: "I was trying to become 1883 so badly and I loved it so much that I don't want to leave now. I wish in some ways I had not done it as it makes me so sad to leave." Her ambition in life prior to coming to Montana had been to work as a fashion designer in New York: "Now I want to be a rancher in Montana." Logan was in turmoil, too. The chicken-man bade farewell to his stock and silently headed for the gate. Karen and Mark closed up the cabin and walked out, unable to look back. Mark said, "I am not walking away from a job but a place I love. This isn't a place where I live anymore, but it is the first place I have lived in for years I can call my home. No one can take away from me what I did here." Karen was equally grim, tears streaming down her face as she led her family out of the valley for the last time. "This was our home. Now it's gone."

The Clunes chose to leave by car. Their modern experience couldn't come fast enough. In contrast to the Glenns they were in better spirits, having said good-bye to the project some time back. Only Tracey found the departure really hard that morning, being visibly upset as she looked back on the cabin she'd had such a

TOP: Aine and her dad grew closer.

BOTTOM: Erinn was devastated to leave the animals.

bittersweet relationship with. Despite her prophecy, Adrienne didn't jump for joy when she stepped outside the gate. The last few days had proved complex for her, too, in her assessment of what the experience had meant for her: "Now I have mixed feelings. I want to leave here but I am not keen to encounter the twenty-first century. I think we have changed a lot, and the more I think of what we return to, it feels superficial."

Nate and Kristen were, as ever, levelheaded in their emotions. Saying good-bye to Glo-bug and Rachel, their goats, and Fluff, their dog, was hard, but they took the day in stride. Nate said, "I think we put our fingerprint here. Things change over time, but even just in our memories to know we lived in this cabin and raised sheep here is enough. The folks who come through will see it, we've made our mark."

Walking through the valley after the families had departed was eerie. Each home empty. The animals watching on in silent curiosity. In every corner lay ghostly reminders of the homesteaders: the spoils of a hard spring and summer's work paying quiet tribute to their efforts. What we'd witnessed over five full months of challenging circumstances made it hard to imagine that no one would take any of this endeavor any further. All of the investments made here were suddenly without meaning. The animals were destined for new homes. The cabins would shortly be boarded over. The contents stripped. The rancher who owned the land paced it with us. He planned to fill the root cellars in. Fencing that had caused hands to blister and bleed was facing demolition starting the very next day. The land was to be transformed back to open pasture. Such incredible efforts seemed somehow all for naught. Yet was this any different from the majority of homesteaders who failed? The 60 percent who never managed to gain ownership after losing the battle to survive. Probably not. Hard to imagine the torment those people went through when they walked out on their land after their dreams had been dashed. The pain of the Glenns' departure was probably an echo of many thousands of such broken spirits. Now Frontier Valley, our homeseeker's paradise, would be left for nature to reclaim. But Nate was right, the fingerprints of all our families would forever be left on this land.

12

New Frontiers

Fast-forward one hundred twenty years. It's three months since our families left Frontier Valley and a more unlikely venue for a one-day reunion could not have been found. The place, the Ritz Carlton Hotel in Pasadena, California. In the oak-lined bar Karen Glenn is trying her first martini, while the Clunes admire the fine artwork that hangs throughout the hotel. A limousine arrives from the airport with the Brookses. The last time everyone was together they were engaged in essential duties like cleaning out the chicken coop and washing down at the creek. This time they're cocooned in luxury. Everyone is nervous; they're here to meet the press as special guests in the PBS press tour that sees scores of journalists descend to preview new series that are about to air.

The first striking impression of seeing them all is just how well they look. Everyone has maintained their trim figures since leaving the frontier. "I have suits I still cannot fit back into," remarks Gordon Clune. "I like this weight." Adrienne in a cutoff T-shirt that reveals a midriff is a curious contrast to the image of her in a corset and swathed in layers of clothing. Karen Glenn has remodeled her hair; it's an elegant style that prompts a double take after the carefree style of her homestead days. Her husband Mark looks ten years younger, clearly more rested after his intense regime on the frontier. "My chiropractor is still working on a shoulder injury I may have picked up out there. It was easy to overdo it," said Mark. Nate, Kristen, even Rudy Brooks are back, and each is curious to discover how everyone has re-evaluated their experience. The children bring new attitudes. They are clearly more confident since our first meeting and—intriguingly—look comfortable in this sumptuous environment, quickly jumping back into their old casual relationships. Some things haven't changed. The Clunes and the Glenns, even three months later, were maintaining a distance from one another, choosing to sit at separate tables during dinner.

Despite their apparent confidence in facing the press the next day, a different attitude emerged after spending more time with all the families. The adults were sending off a similar but largely unspoken feeling—a sense of being unsettled in their modern lives. For everyone, adjusting to life in the twenty-first century was proving to be a challenge. Tracey Clune, who at one time had keenly looked forward to a return to her modern-day life, was conveying her feelings most openly. "I want to go back to life in 1883. I want to go back to Montana. Life in 2001 is boring. Where's the fun in going to the mall every day?" Of all the participants, Tracey had found the adjustment most difficult. Returning to life in California had proved an unsettling experience. She'd found many of her old friends now so very different from her in outlook. She had become estranged from some of her closest associates. She even missed the cow, Blanca, a feeling shared with her cousin Aíne. The same cow that had prompted them both to make protests against hard work in Frontier Valley. "We've tried interesting her in lots of things since she came back, even taking her horseback riding," said her parents, Bill and Cindy. "But she finds it all unsatisfying. Who would have thought it?" Aíne was lost. "There are too many options for us in 2001 so we all end up separating and going our own way. We were all together on the frontier and had the same things to do. Now the only thing my family gets together about is what to do for dinner."

In the most bizarre transition imaginable the Clune family had returned from their compact cabin in Montana to a new life in a mansion overlooking the ocean at Malibu. Having sold their Los Angeles home before going to the frontier, they'd commissioned a new residence to be built for them while they were away. "You could not get anything more extreme in lifestyle. From a 600-square-foot cabin to 6,000 square feet in our new home," observed Adrienne. "That was the old us. Now the new house feels unnecessary." Returning to California—after five months on the frontier—the Clunes had had to wait ten days before their new home was completed. Adrienne recalls, "I walked around on a visit and I thought, 'Why do we need this? It's way too much.' Before I left for the frontier I thought it was important to have space, but when I got back it felt all wrong." On the eve of moving into the new home, Adrienne had wrestled with the decision. Late one night after retiring to bed, she spoke to Gordon about it. "I said to him I was feeling confused about the move and he said he was feeling the same way. We said there and then, 'Let's stop everything and see what we really want.' So we called the next day and said 'Hold everything!' It was because of our Montana experience." The Clunes eventually moved into their new home and after the experience of living in a one-room cabin, they had to reorient their lives. "I was actually lonely for the first couple of nights as the children were sleeping so far away from us. It felt like we were moving further apart. It has been a huge adjustment for me." Aíne agreed with her mom. "I like the new house but it's kind of weird, as when you are in it by yourself there is too much room. I liked being in a smaller place. It's kind of lonely here. Some rooms don't even get used." Hearing the echo of Adrienne feeling lonely—both on the frontier and back in Malibu—was uncanny, but most curious of all were her shopping habits since returning. "When I got back I postponed buying groceries for three weeks for fear of being overwhelmed. Before I knew it my cart had filled with the foods we had on the frontier. I did not want to be running to the store every week so I just got everything we were used to. People thought I was mad, but it works. The kids still like food from the frontier. Peaches are still a big luxury. I make pancakes twice a week. It's like a comfort thing having that food. I don't think I am completely out of my mind!"

Gordon was equally phased, returning to a frantic business life where he found himself on a bewildering series of business trips, leaving home for days on end to jet across America. "It's funny. I had a lot better sense of satisfaction in 1883. My family was in business together, trying to improve our life. This is sad, but in five months in 1883 I got more satisfaction, accomplishment, and appreciation than in my entire career. I get my paycheck [direct-deposited] in the bank today and my kids don't appreciate what it is I do. I have realized that more so since I got back. Yesterday I ended up mowing our lawn with my kids. I got a real sense of satisfaction from it." Although everyone in the family remembered the bad times too—the freezing nights lying damp in their tent and the lack of popular foods—life in 1883 would continue to shape the Clunes. Gordon explained. "I will find myself reflecting on it for years. I do appreciate what we have in the twenty-first century after our experience. We have got a greater standard of living and I have realized how much there is as a common denominator to all people, and I feel that in this century we have so much to give people as a leg up in life. They do not have to go through the tedious burdens of the past."

For the Glenns uncertainty had characterized their return in different ways. After months of marital tension out on the frontier, Mark and Karen knew that they'd have to confront their relationship once home. Today Mark lives in an apartment in Nashville, but regularly returns to see Karen, Erinn, and Logan. "I think that more than anyone else I needed some space to think through what happened out there. It's so easy to fall back into the traps and pitfalls of the twenty-first century. Maybe it was time that we spend some time away from each other," Mark explained. "I need to step back and re-examine my relationship and ask what is happening. The only preconceived notion that we had was that we thought it would bring us closer together. In a very strange way it did, by pulling us apart. Strange, because it brought us together as we started to understand some things about each other that we may have liked or disliked." For now, both Karen and Mark are reviewing their relationship. Karen reflected, "In a way it was to our benefit that we weren't this perfect little couple because there weren't perfect little couples in 1880 either. People stayed together because it made sense to, not because they had this big romantic thing going on. It was a working environment and I think that Mark and I showed that you can be a successful unit and not be head-over-heels agreeing and loving. It is about work. It is not about all these romantic images that we have of the West."

The Clunes, just before leaving the homestead.

Although discord more often characterized the relationship out on the frontier, the Glenns and the Clunes did find harmony in reflecting on the awkward landing both made in their return to the modern day. Karen remarked, "We get lulled into this expectation that this life is normal and how things should be and that we are so smart nowadays. Yes, we have done remarkable things but they are not necessarily the best way. Dishwashers. Instant foods. We live in a world where everything is about saving time and energy, and as a result we get more obese. Erinn and I grieved when we got back because we had nothing physical to do. It's hard to come up with something other than to join a fitness club, which does not have the same sense of productivity. We miss it so. If I let him, Logan would be on the computer twenty-four/seven, but I encourage him now to go out and play. Yesterday he came back muddy and it was great to see he was at least playing outside!"

Mark Glenn finds he simply cannot stay indoors since his return. "I just can't do it. I was deeply affected by life in Montana. To such an extent that when I left that day, I went down on one knee and was a wreck. It was crushing to leave. It's an unnatural life that the twenty-first century offers. The number of choices that we have, you can make more wrong choices than right ones. Your ideals, morals, and principles are all for sale or easily traded. You can validate or justify them with a glib comment. That was the hardest for me to realize and I don't compromise anymore. What happened in Montana was that the experience showed us ourselves, warts and all. What made it hard for me was how many warts I had. I realize now that I may have been denying a lot of things. It allowed us to see ourselves in depth. I returned with an understanding that whatever I had done in the past, I could not let it bother me for the rest of my life. So the homesteader experience was a pretty good mirror. I think what we proved was that modern-day people went back there and could succeed and make a difference and from that learn the value of succeeding." Mark hasn't returned to teaching but is currently working in a friend's business.

Perhaps the most personal growth has been experienced by Nate and Kristen Brooks. Instead of plunging back into their old lifestyle and their routines, in education and social work, they've chosen to become free spirits and enjoy "going where the wind takes us. There's doubt and fear, but there's excitement about what is going to come next. *Frontier House* was reflective of who Kristen and I are and with it we are looking for new opportunities," said Nate. Pausing to take a proper honeymoon on the beaches of Baja after leaving the frontier, Nate and Kristen are now living with best man Alan, who'd joined them in Montana to help complete the cabin. Alan was engaged in the construction of facilities for the 2002 Winter Olympics in Salt Lake City and has convinced Nate and Kristen to work with him. But the homesteading experience has made the newly married couple cautious of immersing themselves in the intensity of modern-day living. Kristen recalls, "The best period I had was coming off the frontier and coming back to modern life. That was the best week of my life. All the good attributes of coming off the frontier were now being applied to modern life. I was healthy, tanned, and trim, and also enjoying showers and food. Now I can feel this world seeping into me. I can almost feel it in my neck and shoulders. I was so relaxed and everyone said, 'You are almost glowing with inner peace.' It felt so nice. Now I can feel the world creeping back into me and I'm saying, 'Noooo!'" As Kristen put it, "Life in the simplicity of 1883 homesteading had allowed us to 'reset our compass.'

The Glenns.

I think my ideas were preset before *Frontier House,* but it gave me the confidence that whatever happens now is okay. There's so much opportunity in the modern world. You can be so much and do so much, but it can be exhausting to pursue every opportunity, whereas on the frontier you had no opportunities, no options, nothing. There was freedom in that. It felt good to not have to pick out which friend to call or what clothes to wear or what to eat. It was easy, yet it was exactly what I hated the most, a lifestyle where there wasn't that much choice. I lived a dull routine, everything that I am not, and yet I kind of liked it. I felt a kind of calmness and it felt nice in some ways. Now I am trying to keep that memory alive and use it to be okay with whatever I'm doing. I think something profound happened out there."

Living "as gypsies" without mortgage payments, a car, or jobs, it will be interesting to see if Nate and Kristen can shape their lives to take advantage of what life has to offer without being drawn back into the rat race. Nate considered how he had seen himself emerge from the experience. "I think in the past I have made some decisions out of fear and doubt and wanting to

Frontier House gave the Brookses a new outlook.

protect myself. Having come through the other side, I want to be more open, be willing to trust in what people say and open myself up to maturity. Some of the reflections I have had have to do with what it means to be a man in our society, how to be a husband. Everyone has an image of what it takes to be a good husband or partner. They think of accountability and responsibility, and I realize that being with my father, the fact that he would show up at sixty-eight to come out and share a crazy experience and pour himself into it, that's what I want to take away. You know that integrity and trust to be able to be vulnerable and open yourself up. So I hope in the end that growth is the biggest impact, instead of looking for jobs or houses or cars or vacations."

Nate's dad, Rudy, even after just six weeks, had soaked up the experience, too. Quietly watching the families gathered together again at Pasadena he reflected warmly on what could have proved a trial in his retirement days. "Ask my wife, Eileen—she'll tell you of my changes. I have slowed everything down. Where I would watch television and listen to the radio a lot, I've cut it by two-thirds. I used to be eager to hear every ball game. No longer. I would describe myself now as laissez-faire in my outlook on life. Out in Montana we did everything at the speed required, and I ask myself now, 'Why hurry?' I could be impatient before. More than just helping Nate, this was a positive experience."

As Gordon pointed out to the press, it was now close to a year since each of our families had first heard of the project, when appeals for *Frontier House* volunteers first aired. Within a comparatively short time, the experience had brought everyone to new horizons. Looking back on their original applications is intriguing, early hopes matched with their situation today. Summarizing his aims for his family's participation, Gordon had written, "I would like to know if we would actually prefer to live a simpler life than the fast-paced life that we lead now. It would be interesting to compare the contentment of the simpler life to the contentment of the fast life." Karen Glenn's hope had been twofold: to take away "lots of remember-whens," but most important, "the chance to separate from what we perceive as a 'normal' all-American life and be given the chance to live as a family." In some ways the encounter brought the Glenns closer, but it also raised big questions in Karen and Mark's relationship. Nate and Kristen had wished for "confidence that comes from doing, overcoming, and achieving." From the past it seemed that everyone had drawn lessons for the future.

One last question remained to be answered: Would our homesteaders have made it through the harshness of a winter in Montana? After returning home each family received their verdict in a report from the *Frontier House* consultants. Linda, Ursula, Susan, Bernie, and Rawhide had written up their assessments and had pulled no punches. Regarding Nate and Kristen, concerns were outlined that, despite their hard work, their garden had been too small, the water flume would have frozen in the heart of winter, their elevated chicken coop would have exposed their livestock to freezing conditions, an outhouse open to the world would have been intolerable in icy weather, their stored food reserves were on the low side, the cabin needed work for winterizing, and they had not cut sufficient wood reserves. But strong praise was forthcoming from everyone in their many achievements, especially as they had plowed the hardest land and had to build a cabin from scratch. Taking into account their superb fitness and the ingenuity demonstrated throughout the summer to deal with every situation, our consultants were unanimous and optimistic. "Overall, we feel that your homesteading venture was carried out in the spirit and within the restrictions of 1883, and with the exception of the concerns raised above, you would very likely be able to survive your first winter. Youth and good health would serve you well through the coming season, and provided the stork didn't visit in the spring, you should emerge from your cabin ready to get on with the business of proving up. Well done!"

Succeeding was an important factor for the Glenns, who admitted that they had been partly motivated in their energies by the competition that had clearly fueled everyone at different times. Karen explained. "We were the family that represented the South and we were all competitive enough to want our side to come out looking good." High praise was forthcoming from each of the consultants in the authenticity of their experience. "Historically, we did not find one instance in which you strayed from the confines of 1883 living," wrote Linda and Ursula. "Your willing suspension of disbelief allowed you to live almost as if you *were* 1883 homesteaders, not just a 2001 family determined to succeed in a sociological experiment." Although Susan was concerned that insufficient vegetables had been put aside in their food stores and Bernie still felt that, despite Mark's gigantic wood stack, more wood might have been required to outlast the worst of the weather, everyone felt the Glenns stood a fighting chance of seeing it through winter. Particular praise was meted out to Erinn who, Rawhide reckoned, had done an incredible job with the animals, making him proud of having been her coach.

Despite their many months of hard work, the Clunes failed to impress the consultants. Their stamina and courage to endure the experience was congratulated, but many factors drew fire from the consultants. Although Adrienne's homemade foods received well-deserved recognition, their food reserves were called into question with concerns over a lack of vitamin C; a shortfall of warm clothing and blankets drew criticism; the cabin was structurally unprepared for winter; wood supplies were estimated to be woefully inadequate; homemade snowshoes were deemed useless; and a plan to sell off their animals was seen as naive. All in all, the report made hard reading for the Clunes, with a unanimous judgment that they would have had trouble making it as homesteaders. In particular the consultants were unimpressed with the idea that the family would separate for winter, sending Adrienne and the children to work in town, leaving Gordon and Justin to stay in the cabin. In response to the report, Gordon said, "I feel our plan was based on what

we experienced in the summer when we had snow-storms, and we felt the plan of splitting up the family was the most advisable; it put us less at risk. I feel that it was right even if your historians disagree. All Justin and I would have had to worry about was keeping warm. We would have made it—there is no question." But Linda and Ursula summed up the mood of all the consultants. "Consider how the one consultant who's not yet spoken might weigh in. Winter would have no patience with why you did this or why you failed to do that. Winter would be totally impartial, sending sleet and snow and freezing winds through the cracks you never got around to chinking and up through the floors you chose not to insulate and cover. Winter wouldn't let up, even after Gordon and Justin realized they'd never thought to learn how to make bread or prepare and cook a chicken before sending Adrienne off to Butte for the season. Winter wouldn't postpone or cut short a ferocious blizzard just because the only wood left was unsawed logs buried under three feet of hard-packed snow or just because there was no food or water left in the house and no guide rope to help Justin find the root cellar to bring in more canned goods and meat or locate the stream so he could chop through the ice to the water underneath. Winter wouldn't take pity when the first steps you took in those innovative but fragile snow-shoes broke the threads and sent you knee-deep into the cold stuff. And over in Butte, winter wouldn't have let up any earlier as Adrienne and the girls had discovered right away that female shopkeepers were unacceptable. For as thousands of other less than well prepared Montana homesteaders came to find out, winter snows on the prepared and unprepared alike, freezes the workers as well as the shirkers, and pauses not once to listen to complaints or excuses or cries of 'it's not fair,' but simply continues to winnow out those who are not well suited to frontier living."

A week after the families departed Frontier Valley, one other factor emerged that sent a shiver through the small community who had watched over the home-steaders throughout their stay. Early one morning a carcass of a deer lay badly mutilated on the path between the Glenns and the Clunes. Tracks that lay along-side the remains prompted the arrival of wildlife experts. What emerged was a shock even to the long-term residents of the valley: the tracks and a visual sight-ing some days after strongly suggested that a large grizzly bear and two cubs were also living in Frontier Valley. The thought that youngsters had spent five months in the same vicinity is chilling and prompts questions about what we would have done if we had detected the danger during the project. Only last summer a grizzly killed an adult who'd strayed into its path not many miles from our valley. We'd been lucky right to the very end.

No one can predict what would have happened had our homesteaders stayed on for another six months. "Now, *that* would show a different story. My parents made it through forty winters out here, but it wasn't out of choice. They had nowhere else to go," explained one of our elderly visitors to the Frontier Fair. In a world that's often determined by how much we can achieve in one day, it's hard to grasp that an entire lifetime of endeavor could have, comparatively, produced so little. But it was the values of the "simple" time that came to haunt our participants. On one of his last days in Frontier Valley, Mark Glenn was moved to tears in this recognition:

> *I believe the object of this project was to see how modern people could adapt themselves to an 1883 mentality. To have a glimpse of what it took to start a new life. I think it was a noble objective, but I now think that the frontier was the last really noble time, the last time Americans were across the board genuine. After that we became slanted, tainted, a bit full of ourselves. This was an appropriate time to pick just to see the last glimpse of innocence before we started that machine rolling toward the great American dream. I think we are a nasty, jealous society. But every once in a while we get an opportunity to prove ourselves and the three families here got a chance to prove that we still have qualities where we can work hard when things are up against us. We can still accomplish things. My judgment of society has been tempered because of what's been accomplished here. We can go out with our heads held high.*